"YOU JUST
NEED TO
LOSE WEIGHT"

"YOU JUST NEED TO LOSE WEIGHT"

AND 19 OTHER MYTHS ABOUT FAT PEOPLE

AUBREY GORDON

BEACON PRESS, BOSTON

BEACON PRESS
Boston, Massachusetts
www.beacon.org

Beacon Press books
are published under the auspices of
the Unitarian Universalist Association of Congregations.

26 25 24 23   8 7 6 5 4 3 2 1

This book is printed on acid-free paper that meets the uncoated paper
ANSI/NISO specifications for permanence as revised in 1992.

Text design and composition by Kim Arney

Library of Congress Cataloging-in-Publication
Data is available for this title.
ISBN: 978-0-8070-0647-4
E-book: 978-0-8070-0648-1; Audiobook: 978-0-8070-0681-8

For Rita and Henry

CONTENTS

Introduction ix

How to Use This Book. xiii

A List of Terms xvii

PART ONE: "BEING FAT IS A CHOICE"

MYTH 1 "Being fat is a choice. If fat people don't like how
they're treated, they should just lose weight." 2

MYTH 2 "Any fat person can become thin if they try
hard enough. It's just a matter of 'calories in,
calories out.'". 13

MYTH 3 "Parents are responsible for their child's weight.
Only bad parents let their children get fat.". 25

MYTH 4 "Thin people should help fat people lose weight.". . . . 32

MYTH 5 "Weight loss is the result of healthy choices
and should be celebrated.". 37

PART TWO: "BUT WHAT ABOUT YOUR HEALTH?"

MYTH 6 "Obesity is the leading cause of death in
the United States.". 44

MYTH 7 "The BMI is an objective measure of size
and health." 52

MYTH 8   "Doctors are unbiased judges of fat people's health.
Fat people don't like going to the doctor's office
because they don't like hearing the truth." 63

MYTH 9   "Fat people are emotionally damaged and cope
by 'eating their feelings.'" 73

PART THREE: "FAT ACCEPTANCE GLORIFIES OBESITY"

MYTH 10   "Accepting fat people 'glorifies obesity.'". 82

MYTH 11   "Body positivity is about feeling better about
yourself, as long as you're happy and healthy." 88

MYTH 12   "We're in the middle of an obesity epidemic.". 98

MYTH 13   "Fat people don't experience discrimination." 109

MYTH 14   "I don't like gaining weight, but I don't treat
fat people differently.". 117

PART FOUR: "FAT PEOPLE SHOULD . . ."

MYTH 15   "Fat people shouldn't call themselves fat." 128

MYTH 16   "People who have never been fat have
'internalized fatphobia.'". 137

MYTH 17   "No one is attracted to fat people. Anyone
who is has a 'fat fetish.'" 145

MYTH 18   "Fat people should pay for a second
airplane seat." 152

MYTH 19   "Skinny shaming is just as bad as fat shaming." 158

MYTH 20   "Anti-fatness is the last socially acceptable form
of discrimination.". 166

Acknowledgments 175
Notes 177

INTRODUCTION

As is the case for many fat people, myths about my body have followed me for nearly all my life, rattling behind me, loud as a string of tin cans. Since grade school, I have been taught that some bodies are meant to be seen, and that mine isn't one of them. I've worn plus sizes since adolescence. I've worn the larger end of plus sizes, size 26 and up, since college. In that time, my politics around fatness have been increasingly clearly articulated to my friends, family, colleagues, and acquaintances. They know that I am fat, and that I have long since stopped trying to make myself thin. Some have worked to better understand and respect my experience as a fat person. Despite all that wind at my back, even in my closest relationships, I am followed closely by a series of nagging myths about what it means to have a body like mine. Even those who have known me for years still wonder aloud about my health and mortality. Some wince or correct me when I refer to my own body as fat. And holidays with family still include open complaining from thin members who sat next to a fat person on a plane.

Even after years of researching, writing about, and trying to understand anti-fatness, I continue to be caught off guard by their comments. They're rarely a surprise, but I still sometimes find myself straining to explain why what they just said was profoundly misguided and hurtful. And I know I'm not alone. Fat friends regularly reach out to troubleshoot moments of anti-fatness in their closest relationships. Many of us are followed nearly everywhere by anti-fat myths about fat people. And most of us do our best to muddle through those conversations, but we're also aware that's just what we're doing: muddling through.

Still, myths about fatness and fat people abound. *Only bad parents let their children get fat. Any fat person can become thin if they try hard enough. Fatness is the leading cause of death in the United States. Anti-fatness is the last socially acceptable form of discrimination.* These myths persist not because they are factual nor because they help us better understand people who are fatter than us. Instead, they allow us to confirm what we already think we know about fatness and fat people. Cultural conversations prompt us to regard thinness as a major life accomplishment; these myths lend credence to that belief. Many of these myths center around treating fat people as failed thin people, implying that thin people are superior to fat people. These myths aren't just incorrect or outdated perceptions: they're tools of power and dominance.

Like many current and past community organizers, I struggle with the strategy behind myth busting. Debunking myths starts with *repeating those myths*. Doing so can seem like uncritically accepting an opponent's premise. Depending on the myth in question, it can also mean quietly assenting to debating the humanity of the community being discussed. And political researchers have long known that facts don't change our positions on social issues—human stories do. Most of us don't make up our minds on key social issues because we've reviewed all available research, looked at crosstabs, written executive summaries for ourselves. We make decisions about when and whether to support social issues based on their human impact, as it's presented to us. Those of us who aren't directly, personally impacted by those social issues are much less fact-driven than we like to think. Why, then, give these myths more airtime?

On the other hand, these myths continue to persist, despite the deep harm they cause and the erroneous and oppressive beliefs they're built upon. Every day, fat people are pushed to defend our health, our desirability, our bodies, our place in the movements we built. Even if the premises of those myths are flawed, they continue to restrict and confine the spaces that fat people are allowed to occupy. As a former community organizer, I know that when many of us don't feel like we've got the facts we need in conversations about oppression, we can clam up. We avoid conversations about oppression and marginalization that don't directly impact us, and not feeling well versed in a topic certainly doesn't help us take those essential conversations head-on. If you feel ill-equipped in tackling regressive conversations about fatness and fat people, research and resources can help provide a touchstone. In the pages ahead, I hope you'll find a place both to anchor and spur your own thinking. I hope, too, that you'll use the recommendations herein to find or continue your way to more fat perspectives on these topics. Myth busting can be a fraught strategy, but it is ultimately one that widens the path for more of us to take action against anti-fatness.

It's a complicated time for our public discourse around fatness, fat people, and weight loss. Increasingly, the rhetoric of dieting and weight loss is seen as falling out of favor. Even one of the most enduring diets in the United States, Weight Watchers, has changed its name to WW, and reoriented its marketing toward more holistic "wellness" branding. Weight-loss methods aren't marketed as diets but as "lifestyle changes," "detoxes," "cleanses," and "cognitive behavioral therapy." That shifting language allows the weight-loss industry to cloak its same old diets in the languages of holistic wellness and self-care. We may talk about diets differently today, but social mandates to become thin are as strong as ever. Alongside that shift in the diet industry is a growing popular interest in critical conversations about fatness. Recent years seem to have brought a new wave of thin people thinking more broadly about their own body politics and, more precisely, about their role in ending anti-fatness. And that influx of new attention is prompting vital conversations about the goals and strategies of fat activist movements. What are fat people's visions for harm reduction, justice, and liberation? What strategies will most effectively get us there? Can differing or conflicting strategies coexist? Under what circumstances? Do thin people have a role to play in ending anti-fatness? What should their role be—or not be? As I write this in early 2022, a range of answers to each of those questions is being advanced by fat activists every day. These conversations are at once endemic and vital to any movement for social justice. They collectively drive us toward clearer visions of a more just world and more focused strategies to deliver us to those visions. And against that increasingly complex backdrop, fat people are still navigating anti-fatness on a daily basis. We are still besieged with incessant and unsolicited instruction about our perceived health, our clothing, our love lives, and more.

What lies ahead is an offering for anyone, fat or thin, struggling to interrupt moments of anti-fatness in their daily lives. It's a compilation of research and thinking on some pernicious and persistent myths that perpetuate anti-fatness, disregard fat people's humanity, and pathologize our bodies. It's an invitation to revisit the anti-fat biases nearly all of us carry with us and to reground our ideas about fatness in personal experience, data, and the fundamental dignity of fat people. As with any resource or offering, take what's useful here, and leave what's not. Put this to use as you see fit. But however you use this book, let it propel your advocacy for fat people beyond what you find comfortable or easy. Let it drive you toward confronting anti-fatness more regularly and confidently.

Whatever you do next, let it be more meaningful to fat people, more effective in dismantling anti-fatness, and sustained enough to make a lasting impact.

HOW TO
USE THIS BOOK

This volume exists as an introductory guide to deeper thinking about immensely popular anti-fat myths, offering springboards into interrogating anti-fatness. It draws on a mix of quantitative academic research and qualitative, personal, and cultural sources. And it's designed to point you toward more and deeper conversations about fatness, fat people, and systemic anti-fatness. It should be read in concert with other works by fat people about fatness and anti-fatness. Some of those works are referenced and cited throughout this volume.

The scope of this book is narrow, aiming squarely at responding to profound and common anti-fat myths. This shouldn't be considered a movement vision document, charting a path forward to justice or liberation. Nor should it be considered an encapsulation of where most or all fat people stand on a given issue or topic. Like any community, fat people are far from monolithic. Getting a range of fat perspectives will require reading many more works by many more fat people. Many more works by many more fat people need to be published too. This should not be the only book you read by a fat person about fatness and anti-fatness. Read Sonya Renee Taylor's *The Body Is Not an Apology*, Da'Shaun Harrison's *Belly of the Beast*, Charlotte Cooper's *Fat Activism*, Roxane Gay's *Hunger*, Caleb Luna's *Revenge Body*, Kiese Laymon's *Heavy*, Nicole Byer's *#VeryFat #VeryBrave*, Esther Rothblum and Sondra Solovay's *The Fat Studies Reader*, Rachel Wiley's *Fat Girl Finishing School*, and more. Whether you're new to thinking critically about anti-fatness or a longstanding fat activist, be sure to locate this book, accurately, as just one of many fat perspectives available to you. Writers who aren't fat have made substantial contributions here too. Sabrina Strings's *Fearing the Black Body: The Racial Origins of Fat Phobia* is an indispensable history linking anti-Black racism to anti-fatness. J. Eric Oliver's *Fat Politics* analyzes the emergence in the 1990s and 2000s of the United States' so-called obesity epidemic. Each of these works offer vital analysis of the mechanics and history of anti-fatness. And each will deepen your thinking about anti-fatness and your clarity in countering anti-fatness.

This book is organized by the myths it aims to tackle. As such, it can be read straight through, cover to cover, or it can be read in pieces. It can also be used as a reference volume, a quick resource when you find yourself stymied by common anti-fat myths.

REFLECTION QUESTIONS

In some sections, you'll find reflection questions. These are designed to help in unpacking some of your own anti-fatness. Anti-fatness is ubiquitous, endemic in the United States—and that means that, even without intending to, many of us replicate and uphold anti-fatness. Because anti-fatness is so popular and so unquestioned, we carry it forward without questioning or even examining it. These questions are gentle provocations intended to expose some of the roots of your anti-fatness to you. Consider these questions as beginnings, not endings.

Note, too, that these questions are designed to be taken on alone, or with a small group of peers who consent to reflecting on anti-fatness with you. Reflecting on our biases requires getting uncomfortably honest with ourselves and examining thoughts about fatness and fat people that are directly harmful to those who are fatter than us. Discussions about anti-fatness can also prove challenging for people with eating disorders or body dysmorphic disorder, for whom conversations about fatness and anti-fatness can be triggering. For those reasons, be thoughtful about when and whether you invite others into your own reflection. Should you decide to engage others in your reflections, do so only with their enthusiastic and unreserved consent.

If you feel the urge to pull others into that reflection, think critically about who you want to involve, and why. If you're inclined to do that reflecting with people who are fatter than you: Why do you think that is? Why do you need those who are fatter than you to hear your harshest thoughts about them? What outcomes, if any, are changed by doing that work with others instead of alone? Do other participants benefit? Or will entering that reflection space require them to hear insults to their own bodies or hear their most anti-fat fears given voice and credence? Should you decide to involve others in that reflection, be sure to ask for their consent, and be prepared to graciously accept if they decline.

OPPORTUNITIES FOR ACTION

In other sections, you'll find a list of opportunities for action. These are chances for you to engage in some harm reduction in anti-fatness, both interrupting your own role in anti-fatness and stemming the seemingly unending tide of anti-fatness aimed at fat people. These lists are far from exhaustive and focus on addressing unambiguously anti-fat attitudes, actions, and approaches.

The best way to engage with these opportunities for action is to *do something.* Too often, we read or hear about critical issues of social justice, decry their injustice, and then fail to take meaningful action to *stop* that injustice. We stop short because those issues can seem overwhelming, next steps feel unclear, or the path forward is simply exhausting, more work than we're prepared to take on. Remember that awareness can lay a foundation for change, but learning more about anti-fatness does not, in itself, change the conditions that fat people deal with every day. In order to change things, we've got to be willing to stretch out of our comfort zones, speak up about things we haven't spoken up about before, and think more expansively about our own power and influence.

Sometimes, too, our power may not be clear to us. Each of us may forget the influence that we have over those we know and love.

We may also forget that we've developed a sharp skill set for shifting the thinking and actions of those closest to us. Those working or learning in schools may not realize they can request more accessible seating options for fat and disabled students and faculty. Those in workplaces with human resources departments can advocate for the end of anti-fat "workplace wellness" programs, or workplace "biggest loser" weight-loss competitions. Health-care providers and administrators can make sure that medical equipment like blood pressure cuffs and exam tables are built for fat bodies, and start difficult, vital conversations about tackling anti-fat bias in health care. And nearly all of us can do more to interrupt vicious anti-fatness when it rears its head in public. None of these actions in and of themselves will end anti-fatness, but they can help stem the tide of anti-fatness that fat people contend with every day. Take these opportunities for action as footholds, options for next steps in your work to support fat people, but don't stop there.

FURTHER RESOURCES AND CITATIONS

Each chapter includes citations for primary research sources. Those serve not only as bibliographies but as resource lists. Should you want to deepen your learning on a particular topic, consider those sources for further reading. They are by no means exhaustive, but they can offer a starting point. Note also that academic and medical research cited may include anti-fat language, premises, and frameworks, as many institutional perspectives on fatness do. Engage with these sources critically, and take care in reading them.

A LIST OF TERMS

Talking about fatness and thinness means navigating choppy waters. Even attempting to pin down *what thinness is* and *what fatness is* can prove challenging. In some ways, the terms are solid: fatness and thinness reflect externally observable characteristics that lead to concrete differences in interpersonal, cultural, and institutional experiences. In other ways, they are liquid: *fatness* and *thinness* are deeply subjective, defined differently by different people, in different households, and in different cultural contexts. What is considered "fat" or "thin" in one nation or neighborhood may vary greatly in the next. And in some ways, these terms become vapor, too ethereal to grab onto. Many of us maintain different definitions for what we consider fatness in ourselves and what we're willing to name as fatness in those around us but still reveal anti-fat biases even to those who fall short of our expressed definitions of fat. Thinness, too, can be tough to wrap our arms around: it is a concrete state of being that allows for more unfettered access to clothing, health care, public spaces, and social acceptance. But those who receive that access still may not consider themselves thin, reserving thinness as some kind of out-of-reach ideal, defined by its unattainability. Still, those same people need to be able to locate themselves within a conversation about the social and political realities of moving through the world as fat and thin people. And still, we need to have an anchored conversation about how anti-fatness operates, who pays its biggest prices, and how our experiences relate to those of others.

What follows is a list of terms to anchor the analysis you'll read in the pages ahead. The definitions here reflect only how these terms are used in this book, which may differ from other fat people's defi-nitions of these terms and concepts. As such, these shouldn't be regarded as definitive definitions but as part of an operating guide to terms as they're used in the chapters that follow.

FAT is a neutral descriptor for predominantly plus-size people. While fat is frequently used to insult people of all sizes, many fat people—those of us undeniably, indubitably fat by any mea-sure—reclaim the term as an objective adjective to describe our bodies, like *tall* or *short*. It is used, accordingly, in a matter-of-fact way throughout the pages ahead. Fat stands in contrast to an endless parade of euphemisms—*fluffy, curvy, big guy, big girl, zaftig, big-boned, husky, voluptuous, thick, heavyset, pleasantly plump, chubby, cuddly, more to love, overweight, obese*—all of which just serve as a reminder of how terrified so many thin people are to see fat bodies, name them, have them.

Fat hasn't become a bad word because fatness is somehow inherently undesirable but because of what we attach to it. We take "fat" to mean unlovable, unwanted, unattractive, unintel-ligent, unhealthy. But fatness itself is simply one aspect of our bodies—and a very small part of who each of us is. It deserves to be described as a simple fact, bearing little relevance to our worth or worthiness but a great deal of relevance to how we're treated by individuals and institutions.

Body size, like so many aspects of human experience and identity, exists on spectra and scatterplots. As such, there are no hard and fast rules for who qualifies as "fat enough to be fat." When I look for my fat people—the community I call home—I look for people who are united by experiences of widespread exclusion. I don't just look for people who've been called fat, as all of us have, but folks who are shut out of having their basic needs met because of the simple fact of their size. Not just people who struggle to find clothing they like but people who struggle to find clothing *at all*. Not just people who feel uncomfortable on buses or airplanes but people who are publicly ridiculed for daring to board public transit at all. For my fat people, our size isn't just an internal worry, it's an inescapable external reality. We aren't held captive by our own perceptions but by others' beliefs that we are immoral, unlovable, irredeemable. All of us have felt the sting of the rejection of our bodies—either at our own hand or another's. But not all of us have been repeatedly, materially harmed by the universality of that rejection. That's an experience shared by those of us who are unquestionably, undeniably fat. But that's one of many, many approaches to defining fatness. There are nearly as many definitions of fat as there are people in the world.

OBESE AND OVERWEIGHT are terms that have been most popularized by their use in the body mass index (BMI). While both terms existed before the mid- to late-twentieth century rise in use of the BMI, our current understandings of both exist within the BMI's medicalized context. *Obese* and *overweight* reflect BMI weight classifications popularly believed to present added health risks not shouldered by thinner people. And because the BMI was developed exclusively for the bodies of white, Western European men, our current concepts of the health risks of fatness are directly tied to age-old racist constructs of health and size. The United States is also home to a culture of deep ableism and healthism—one that looks to individual health status as a referendum on work ethic and character. Thinner people are seen as working hard to achieve their thinness, therefore as dedicated and tenacious. Fatter people are seen, consequently, as failing to put in the effort needed to become thin, or healthy and virtuous. We are defined as categorically unhealthy, and therefore as categorically irresponsible.

These are terms that are also reductive and judgmental by their very definitions. The term "obese" is derived from the Latin *obesus*, meaning "having eaten oneself fat," inherently blaming fat people for our bodies. A growing number of fat activists consider the term to be a slur, and many avoid it altogether. The term "overweight" implies that there is an objectively, externally determined correct weight for every body. Both terms are derived from a medical model that considers fat bodies as deviations in need of correction. Both are also defined terms used frequently within medical and academic research. Both terms are used sparingly throughout this book, but neither are fully absent.

SMALL FAT AND VERY FAT are used here to refer to different sizes of fat people. Different levels of fatness invite different experiences. People who wear smaller plus sizes (say, a US size 18) may frequently be on the receiving end of unsolicited diet and weight-loss advice. But people who wear extended plus sizes (a size 34, for example) may face open street harassment, hear jeers from passing cars, or find health care inaccessible to them because providers hold profound biases and medical equipment, like MRIs and exam tables, aren't built for their bodies. Naming these gradations of experiences is essential to pinpointing the differing faces of anti-fatness and to identifying the relative privileges and blunted edges of anti-fatness that smaller fat people may receive by virtue of their proximity to thinness. Throughout this book, I use "smaller fat people" to refer to those who wear plus sizes on the smaller end of the plus-size spectrum (for example, a US women's size 24 and under) and "larger fat people" to refer to those who wear larger plus sizes or extended plus sizes (for example, a US women's size 26 and larger). There are vast differences of experience within those categories, so consider their use to be broad guideposts for how anti-fatness can impact fat people at different sizes.

THIN AND NON-FAT describe those whose bodies are thinner than fat people's, and who receive social, cultural, and institutional privileges on the basis of that thinness and proximity to thinness. Those same people may describe themselves as "feeling fat" or may not describe their own bodies as thin. But the privileges we receive are based more on how others perceive us than how we perceive ourselves. Because fatness is often defined relative to thinness, thinness itself often goes unnamed, treated as a default not worth commenting on. But tackling biased myths against fat people requires naming thinness too, so that we can identify the ways in which these myths allow some thin and small fat people to evade and perpetuate anti-fatness by aligning themselves with thinness instead.

ANTI-FATNESS is an umbrella term used here to describe the attitudes, behaviors, and social systems that specifically marginalize, exclude, underserve, and oppress fat bodies. They refer both to individual bigotry as well as institutional policies designed to marginalize fat people. *Anti-fatness* and *anti-fat bias* are also sometimes referred to as *fatphobia*, *fatmisia*, *sizeism*, *weight stigma*, or *fattism*.

While "fatphobia" has become a popular term to describe anti-fat beliefs and behaviors, mental health advocates and Mad Pride activists alike have been clear: oppressive behaviors aren't the same as phobias. Phobias are real mental illnesses, and conflating phobias with bigoted beliefs and behaviors invites further stigma and relies on ableist language. For more on these troubling dynamics, I strongly recommend Denarii Monroe's excellent piece for *Everyday Feminism*, "3 Reasons to Find a Better Term Than '-Phobia' to Describe Oppression."[1] Accordingly, throughout this book, I'll be using the terms *anti-fatness* and *anti-fat bias* in place of "fatphobia."

DIET CULTURE is a system of beliefs and practices that elevates thin bodies above all others, often interpreting thinness as a sign of both health and virtue. It mandates weight loss as a way of increasing social status, strengthening character, and accessing social privilege. Diet culture disproportionately benefits people whose bodies are naturally predisposed to be thin and people with the wealth and privilege to pay the high prices of customized diet foods, personal trainers, weight-loss surgery, and more.

Even as "wellness" gains popularity as a way to talk about weight loss, it bears a striking resemblance to diet culture. While many interventions are being made into diet culture, many oppose diets on the grounds that they fail to deliver weight loss, often implicitly and explicitly reinforcing anti-fatness in the process. Uprooting diet culture is essential to ending anti-fatness, but that won't end anti-fatness on its own. Indeed, diet culture can be countered in ways that continue to lift up thin people and advocate for weight loss. As such, anti-diet projects and those aimed at diet culture are rightly met with skepticism from many fat people, who are clear that ending diet culture alone won't save us. In order to deliver a changed world for fat people, the work to end diet culture must be driven by a broader commitment to ending anti-fatness and supporting justice and liberation for fat people.

STRAIGHT-SIZE CLOTHING refers to clothing sizes that can be purchased from nearly any clothing retailer. US straight sizes, usually sizes 00 to 14, are available at almost every store in a given shopping mall. Straight size is a way of referring to people with relative size privilege, instead of using value-laden terms such as "normal" or "regular" or inaccurate terms like "average" (in the US, the average size *is* plus size).

PLUS-SIZE CLOTHING cannot be reliably purchased in department stores or mainstream clothing retailers. It must be purchased from either a limited plus-size section or a specialty plus-size retailer, such as Torrid or Lane Bryant. In the US, this generally refers to women's sizes 16 to 28.

EXTENDED PLUS-SIZE CLOTHING cannot be reliably purchased from mainstream retailers *or* from most plus-size retailers. In the US, women's extended plus sizes are usually size 30 and up. Even basic essentials such as raincoats and sweatshirts are often unavailable in extended plus sizes. When extended plus-size clothing is available, it is almost exclusively available for purchase at exorbitant prices and only online. In some cases, extended plus-size clothing requires custom sizing or construction. Even retailers that proudly describe themselves as "size inclusive" often don't offer extended plus sizes.

PART ONE

"BEING FAT IS A CHOICE"

"BEING FAT IS A CHOICE. IF FAT PEOPLE DON'T LIKE HOW THEY'RE TREATED, THEY SHOULD JUST LOSE WEIGHT."

In 2016, *Us Weekly* published a story about plus-size model Rosie Mercado.[1] It wasn't about her career in modeling or about her professional accomplishments. It was about her weight loss.

Mercado's story as told by *Us Weekly* has a familiar arc. It paints a bleak before picture of her life as a fatter person, from challenges with the built environment ("I couldn't fit in certain cars") to self-esteem issues ("I felt that I wasn't worthy of love") to stories of public humiliation. In school, her classmates "would say things like 'There goes that fat bitch,' or 'Why doesn't she just lose weight?'"[2] In adulthood, those experiences of public humiliation continued. When Mercado boarded a flight to New York, a flight attendant loudly announced that she wouldn't fit in an airplane seat, which the magazine says she took as "a wake-up call—one that changed her life forever."[3] This is where the article reveals the prestige, asserting the model turned that degradation into weight-loss motivation, losing 240 pounds. Mercado is careful to state how much effort she puts into weight loss. "My first 100 pounds I did by myself by running, walking and Zumba. [. . .] I walk 15,000 steps every single day."[4] In this story, and so many others like it, weight loss is presented as the result of a series of choices that can only be made by people with strong and admirable character: those with tenacity, determination, and a dogged work ethic.

Stories like Mercado's are frequently lifted up in popular media, offered ostensibly as inspiration for the rest of us, presuming that nearly every reader longs or intends to lose weight. Those human-interest weight-loss stories are often accompanied by advertisements for specific methods of weight loss. From fad diets to "lifestyle changes," juice cleanses to intermittent fasting, surgery to Cool Sculpting, all bill themselves as choices that we are free to make, and if we choose wisely, thinness will be delivered to us. Nearly everywhere we go, we are reminded that our bodies are a choice, and that our choices are being judged. Chain restaurants offer "healthy options," and snack-food marketing refers to low-calorie options as "guilt free," both of which serve as coded ways to tell us which foods will or won't supposedly make us fat. Diets may be eschewed but only in favor of "lifestyle choices." We are told that our choices are our own, and our bodies are reflections of the rightness of those choices. If we are thin, we will be presumed to have made good choices. If we are fat, we must have chosen poorly. Our bodies are believed to be meritocracies, direct reflections of the work we're willing to put in. We are expected to judge ourselves on what we're told are the objective measures of our bodies, and we are reminded that others will judge us based on our bodies too.

The belief that anyone can and should lose weight is widely held. After twenty years of the "obesity epidemic," those human-interest stories and marketing campaigns for weight loss have been accompanied by public policy interventions designed to reduce population-level rates of fatness. In other words, our cultural attitudes stigmatizing fatness have been fortified, lent legitimacy by mainstream "anti-obesity" campaigns that aim to reduce the number of fat people. (As of 2022, no nation or jurisdiction has done so, revealing this strategy to be at once profoundly anti-fat, punitive, and ineffective.) Most adult Americans have become accustomed to never-ending headlines about the "obesity epidemic" and evening news stories that feature footage of fat people filmed from the neck down. We watch hours of news that show fat people as faceless threats, disembodied torsos made up only of the fat rolls that are expected to define us. And when those news programs take a commercial break, advertisements tell us about the many miracle weight-loss cures that are supposedly available to us. Fat people are reduced to our bodies, our bodies are recast as burdens, and then we're offered up a thousand ways to make those burdensome bodies disappear. In that context, for fat people, weight loss is less a suggestion than a mandate. All of us can lose weight, but in an "obesity epidemic," fat people *must* lose weight.

Whatever our size, many of us have been trained to see it as a choice and to see fatness as an irresponsible and immoral one. It is an overtly biased belief in its own commitment to assigning value to differing body types and its insistence on blaming fat people for what it contends are our burdensome bodies. Moreover, research shows that belief—the belief that fat people can and should become thin—is a predictor of individual anti-fat bias. Questions about the controllability of weight are used in most academic tools to assess anti-fat bias, including the Fat Phobia Scale[5] and the Attitudes Toward Obese Persons Scale.[6] But how is such a commonly held belief, held as an objective truth, an indicator of bias?

Nearly every cultural message about fatness and weight loss insists that anyone can choose to lose weight, and many of us deeply believe that to be true. In truth, some fat people *do* choose fat bodies; some do not. But this cultural insistence that fatness is a choice isn't about the veracity of that claim: it's about minimizing fat people's experiences, dismissing our needs, and perpetuating anti-fat bias. And in its determination to do so, it steamrolls over copious evidence that challenges the belief that thinness is a choice that's always available to fat people.

Medical researchers who specialize in fatness are clear that fat people are fat for a wide range of reasons, but public perceptions still lag behind.[7] In 2016, the *New York Times* published a report with the headline "Americans Blame Obesity on Willpower, Despite Evidence It's Genetic."[8] Indeed, our cultural beliefs about weight loss and weight gain are miles apart from what research shows and what some fat people have long maintained: that our body size isn't solely, or even primarily, the result of choices. Many health conditions lead to the accumulation of fat that is resistant to traditional methods of weight loss. Lipedema causes fat to accumulate and swell in one's legs, buttocks, and upper arms and that fat does not respond to traditional dietary or exercise interventions for weight loss. The condition's cause is unknown, and there is currently no cure.[9] While this under-discussed health condition may seem niche, researchers estimate that it impacts up to 10 percent of those assigned female at birth.[10] Polycystic ovary syndrome (PCOS) is an endocrine disorder impacting androgen production and is also resistant to traditional weight-loss methods.[11] According to the Centers for Disease Control and Prevention, PCOS affects 6 to 12 percent of Americans assigned female at birth—as many as five million people.[12] Even type 2 diabetes, commonly thought of as a result of weight gain can instead be a cause of it: treatments like insulin[13] and sulfonylureas can lead to weight gain, as can many others.[14] According to the American Diabetes Association, 11 percent of Americans had type 1 or type 2 diabetes in 2019.[15] These health conditions have high levels of prevalence, and all of them complicate our brutally oversimplified understanding of weight gain and loss. As fat people have long known, our assumptions about the ease of weight loss are not only judgmental, they're inaccurate and stigmatizing, reducing chronic health conditions and disabilities to character flaws revealed by the "choice" of having a fat body.

Research shows, too, that we are surrounded by images and messages about fatness and fat people that foment anti-fat bias in many of us. In 2011, researchers from the University of Connecticut's Rudd Center for Food Policy and Obesity studied over four hundred images of fat people alongside stories in major news outlets about fatness and the "obesity epidemic" and found nearly three-fourths of the images showed fat people in "a negative and stigmatizing way." While thin people were depicted as individuals, whole people with faces, lives, and expertise to offer, fat people were "more likely to be portrayed as headless, without clothing (e.g., bare stomach), eating and drinking, and portrayed from unflattering side or rear views."[16] Their research also found that fat people were "far less likely to be portrayed as experts, advocates, journalists, or professionals compared to thinner individuals."[17] In a 2013 study analyzing 371 videos of news coverage related to fatness and fat people, a commanding majority of images reinforced biased attitudes toward fat people, showing us as inactive, eating foods commonly considered to be "unhealthy," and wearing ill-fitting clothing.[18]

Media images of fat people are also deeply racialized. A 2012 study in *Social Science & Medicine* looked at news coverage of fat people in *Time* and *Newsweek* from 1984 to 2009, including images and written descriptions of fat people. In that span of twenty-five years, fat elders of all races were "starkly underrepresented," an omission that quietly reinforces the idea that fat people don't survive to old age and fat deaths are a fait accompli. Troublingly, researchers also found that the two magazines increasingly depicted Black people, Indigenous people, and People of Color as fat. "Even with increasing representation of non-whites over time, news magazines still underrepresented African Americans and Latinos."[19] These issues of media representation become even more troubling when examining the behaviors they prompt. A randomized controlled trial in the *Journal of Health Communication* found that when viewed by individuals, "negative, stereotypical" images of fat people, like those used widely in news media, increased not only those individuals' anti-fat bias but their personal dislike of fat people. When the images were analyzed on the basis of race and gender, Black women were met with substantially higher ratings for personal dislike and social distance.[20] These widely used images not only increased anti-fat attitudes, they stoked misogynist and racist attitudes too. And these images aren't just a problem for news media: in a 2019 randomized controlled trial, images in public health "anti-obesity" campaigns produced not only more negative feelings toward fat people but "more desired social distance" from us.[21] In a series of 2019 studies, most participants believed fat people were "less evolved and human" than thin people and tended to support overtly discriminatory policies targeting fat people.[22] For most of us, given this profound and pervasive bias, anti-fatness is the rule, not the exception. For those who believe fatness is a choice, its solution is clear: simply choose to be thin. But when fat people do attempt to choose thinness, through dietary changes and exercise, it paradoxically increases the likelihood that we'll gain back more than we lost. A well-known 2016 study of former contestants on *The Biggest Loser* found that their precipitous weight loss permanently suppressed their metabolisms, making weight loss and maintenance extraordinarily difficult as time went on.[23] A 2013 research review found, in 75 percent of its studies, engaging in dieting behavior or the pursuit of weight loss was a predictor of future weight gain.[24] Even when we try to become thin, many fat people stay fat or get fatter. A 2015 cohort study found that the probability of very fat people (those with body mass indexes that the journal describes as "morbidly obese") reaching their BMI-recommended weight were extremely small: 1 in 1,290 for very fat men and 1 in 677 for very fat women.[25] Diet and exercise-based weight-loss interventions extremely rarely produce significant weight loss in very fat people. According to the National Institutes of Health, very fat women—like me—have a 0.8 percent chance of becoming thin in our lifetimes.[26] If thinness, like fatness, is a choice, it is an overwhelmingly unsuccessful one.

The monolithic belief that fatness is a failure, and that failure to become thin is the result of individual choices, is clearly inaccurate. But some fat people *do* choose their fatness. Some fat people identify as gainers, whom writer Bruce Owens Grimm calls "fat on purpose." Gainers are often pushed to the margins by anti-fatness and body positivity alike because of our cultural certainty that fatness is a choice, and the wrong choice. Grimm describes his experience as a gay man and a gainer as one fundamentally shaped by shame: "It's what kept me in the closet. It's what made me afraid to be fat, made me keep those secrets from the people closest to me. It's part of what has made me feel that I don't fit in the world, a world that doesn't necessarily want to make room for queer people or fat people, so a

queer fat person is sometimes too much for some people."[27] Grimm
asked fellow gainers what they wanted the rest of the world to better understand about them. Their requests were painful reminders
of the assumptions made about fat people in general, and gainers in
particular. Said one, "Gaining isn't about self-destruction or self-
sabotage." Said another, "The majority of us have real jobs, other
interests, aren't lazy, have dreams, desires, etc., however we just want
to do so in larger bodies."[28] These simple facts eluded those around
them, leading to isolating and dehumanizing assumptions. Regardless of how our bodies came to be, fat people are widely subjected to
biased actions and bigoted attitudes. Scholar and writer Caleb Luna,
too, identifies as someone who chooses fatness. "As queers, we saw
the failures in the 'born this way' argument decades ago. It doesn't
need to not be our fault for it to be okay to exist. I choose queerness
every day. I choose fatness every day. And those are both legitimate
and desirable choices that improve my life."[29]

Proclaiming that a marginalized identity, body, or experience is
a "choice" is far from power neutral. In a society that stigmatizes
fatness, saying that fatness is a choice implies that choosing fatness
is the wrong choice. It echoes a long history of pushing marginalized communities aside by insisting that the source of their difference wasn't immutable; it was not just a choice but a choice made
to get attention, a kind of histrionic demand for care. It's a tactic
that was targeted at queer people throughout the twentieth century,
when the perceived choice to be queer was used to brush off any
and all requests made by queer people, from ending anti-LGBTQ
discrimination to ending the US government's years-long silence
on the AIDS epidemic in the 1980s. If HIV/AIDS was the result of
a deviant choice, then it was an issue of personal responsibility and,
therefore, not cause for care or support from institutions like the
Centers for Disease Control and Prevention. By the 1990s, the idea
that "being gay is a choice" fueled a renewed moral panic in which
straight people believed that queer people couldn't be trusted to
spend time with children, either as teachers or parents, lest we try to

sexually assault children or "recruit" them to make the same choice we're believed to have made. And in the 2000s, the idea that sexual orientation was a choice was also used to legitimate ex-gay conversion therapy. Today, the belief that gender identity is a choice is used to marginalize and oppress transgender and nonbinary people, often violently. Believing that transgender identities are willful choices paves the way for wave after wave of anti-trans legislation across the United States. If children can choose to be trans, cisgender people (people who aren't transgender) can choose to exclude them from bathrooms, health care, and sports teams. If adults can choose to be trans, governments can choose to permit anti-trans discrimination. And if being trans or nonbinary is a choice, then none of us need examine our own learned transphobia.

If a marginalized identity or experience can be established to be a choice, then solving the problems that marginalized individuals face falls to those individuals themselves rather than a broader collective. If marginalized people are choosing to deviate from the norm, the thinking goes, then any negative experience they face is a natural consequence of their poor decision-making. And the aggressors who create those negative experiences don't have to reflect on their own complicity and accountability. The trauma of and accountability for oppression always run in one direction: toward marginalized communities. When we assume marginalized identities and experiences are a "choice," we aren't doing so out of concern for the people living those experiences. We do so instead to set people with relative power and privilege at ease with their own biases. And it works. Those biases start to seem like natural consequences of others' deviant choices, not our own callousness to their needs and experiences.

Whether being fat is a choice for an individual or not, they do not deserve discrimination, harassment, or unkind treatment because of the size of their bodies. None of us should have to change our appearance in order to "earn" basic respect and dignity. In a world of before and after pictures, we are reduced to "befores." "Befores" don't try hard enough. "Befores" don't want it badly enough. It's up to the "afters" to remind them what their lives are missing. The answer for every cruel comment and every moment of harsh treatment, it seems, is to become an "after." Fat people can only attain social worthiness by becoming thin, which we are told is a simple matter of individual: *just lose weight*.

Just lose weight falls from the mouths of people who haven't been fat with a cutting simplicity. My life as a fat person, I am told, will be all stick and no carrot. I will continue to face indignities, insults, material harms until my body becomes what it has never been: thin. The reward for thinness is so modest and yet so important. Only thinness, I am told, earns doctors who will listen to you. Thinness secures a loving response to a difficult moment. Thinness ensures that a plane ticket affords a guaranteed seat. Thinness wins indifference from strangers, an end to the shouts that follow fat bodies, the reliable echoes of our footfall. All those carrots, dangling from that one simple, distancing phrase: *just lose weight*.

Just, as if it were both possible and likely to quickly shrink to one-third my size. *Just*, as if I and so many other fat people hadn't spent years, decades in pursuit of a thinness that never came. *Just*, quietly erasing the Herculean efforts so many of us have lent to attempting to change our bodies. *Just*, as if 50, 100, or 200 pounds would be as quick to lose as the freshman 15. *Just*, a lifetime of trying to escape stigma reduced to a simple, tossed-off command.

Just lose weight is deeply dismissive, incuriously judgmental. It assumes that fat people have neither considered nor attempted weight loss and, more than that, that thin experts need to teach us about the wrongness of our bodies and how to make them right. For the person commanding that fat people *just lose weight*, it reveals what they have either forgotten or refused to learn about what it means to live in a fat body, under constant pressure to become thin immediately. Even if weight loss were as simple as *just*, those who tell fat people to *just lose weight* have rarely done the simple arithmetic of what it would take to diet one's way to thinness. If dietary interventions worked as they claimed to (they don't), safe weight loss moves at a glacial pace.

For example, in order to reach a BMI-mandated "healthy weight" for my 5'10" frame, I would need to lose 220 pounds. Most health-care providers recommend losing no more than one to two pounds per week. As such, I would need to diet steadily for three years. Three years of perfect weight loss. No plateaus, no slipups, none of what so many diets refer to as "moments of weakness." No work meetings or family gatherings with unapproved foods. No temporary sickness or long-term illness. Three years to transform my body into one I've never, ever had. Three years to stop strangers' stares at restaurants, their surreptitious photographs at swimming pools, their open laughter in gyms. Three years until I would be worth defending. Three years until I would be worth hearing out.

As a fat person, *just lose weight* reveals so much to me about the people who insist on my weight loss. When someone tells me to *just lose weight*, it teaches me that I can never expect their advocacy on behalf of fat people. The best I can hope for is their indifference. They will choose the comfort of bias over the work of ending anti-fatness, even if that anti-fatness hurts them too.

Just lose weight is a kind of self-absolution, a way for people who aren't fat to ignore fat people's needs and leave their own complicity uninterrogated. Whether it means to or not, *just lose weight* defends and preserves anti-fat bias, thrusting the responsibility for anti-fatness back onto fat people. *Just lose weight* is a way to throw up one's hands at grappling with the complexity, difficulty, and hard truth of anti-fatness, including their own. It shuts out the harsh social realities created by their dismissiveness—realities that fat people are left to shoulder alone. And whether intentionally or unintentionally, *just lose weight* tells fat people that we will only be worth hearing out once we do something that's all but impossible: become thin.

REFLECTION QUESTIONS

+ What is your personal experience in attempting to change your weight? How have those attempts turned out? Does your personal experience influence your attitudes toward people who are fatter than you? How?

+ In the United States, anti-fatness is the rule, not the exception. Where have you been taught anti-fat bias?

+ What would it look like to embrace fat people *without* knowing the histories of our bodies or expecting an explanation for them? How would your behavior or treatment of those fatter than you change?

"ANY FAT PERSON CAN BECOME THIN IF THEY TRY HARD ENOUGH. IT'S JUST A MATTER OF 'CALORIES IN, CALORIES OUT.'"

Note: This chapter includes calorie counts and discussion of specific weight-loss methods.

Have you ever tried losing weight? It's not that hard."

I was nineteen, attending my first college party. I was acutely aware of my fatness, my queerness, my then-profound social anxiety, differences that felt like they stuck out like a sore thumb among my peers. I hadn't wanted to go to the party (I've never loved parties), but it felt like an important experience. I spoke sternly to myself, insisting that the party was important to some nebulous college experience, that I'd thank myself later. So I went. My first conversation was with this stranger, a man whose opening salvo was to ask me to account for my body. How had I gotten so fat, he wondered aloud, and why wasn't I thin?

"You should try—it's really not that complicated. It's not like diets are rocket science. It's just calories in, calories out."

I assured him that I'd lost weight in the past but had ultimately regained more weight after my diet. He responded with a lengthy lecture about calories, fat, and carbohydrates. "Just look at the science. It's pretty clear." I stumbled through more clumsy responses, reaching for an acceptable explanation for why I was so inexcusably fat. He wanted me to account for my size, and it had never occurred to me that I didn't owe a detailed history of my body to anyone who asked. Friends, family, acquaintances, and strangers alike expected answers about why I was so fat. I learned that being fat meant providing explanations of my size to thin people who would then explain to me why I was wrong and how I could look more like them. This stranger at the party was no different. Like so many before him, no explanation of my body satisfied him. He only relented when I reassured him, three times, that I was still trying to lose weight. When his interrogation ended, he left to find a cigarette and another beer. I left the party.

Even at such a young age, I had become accustomed to cold, incurious responses like his, nearly always delivered by people thinner than me. All of them presumed that my body was a failure, universally undesired because it was inherently undesirable. They assumed that my body was inferior to theirs, and they inferred that was because my character and work ethic were inferior too. And they insisted that, as thin people, they were experts on weight loss—even if they'd always been thin. Even if they'd never lost as much weight as the one, two, or three hundred pounds they expected fatter people to shed as soon as possible. If they were some of the rare few that had sustained major weight loss, they were more likely to be relentless, insistent, inescapable. *I did it. Why can't you?*

Most of us have been told that weight loss is a direct reflection of our effort: if we try hard enough, we'll lose weight. But the science of weight loss paints a much more complicated picture.

One of the most important components of any weight-loss attempt, we're told, is willpower. Yet the science around diet and willpower doesn't bear that out. Much of what we think of as insufficient willpower in dieting is a biological response to food restriction. Hormones like ghrelin and leptin are powerful regulators of our health and satiety. Ghrelin, the so-called hunger hormone, creates a powerful drive to consume the nutrients our bodies need to survive. A

2011 study of fat adults found that those who lost weight had higher levels of ghrelin for at least one year after weight loss. Rather than a lack of willpower, dieters had gone through a physiological change that increased their biological drive to eat.[1] Leptin, nicknamed the "satiety hormone," tells us when to stop eating. Higher body weights have been linked to leptin resistance, a condition in which patients have high levels of leptin circulating, but their bodies don't respond to it.[2] It seems that leptin plays a role in weight regulation and that leptin is produced by fat cells, but researchers do not know precisely how leptin works, nor why some patients are leptin resistant and others aren't.[3] Ghrelin and leptin are just two of fifteen hormones that are believed to help shape our appetites. Dopamine, serotonin, and insulin have all been shown to influence hunger, satiety, and desire for food.[4] Research indicates that our endocrine systems, not our willpower, are significant mechanisms that determine, in part, when and whether we feel the drive to eat. Our bodies have also been shown to drop their energy usage by about two hundred calories per day when we restrict calorie intake.[5] According to researchers, our body weights are "tightly regulated by hormonal, metabolic, and neural factors," factors that "appear to defend an individual's highest sustained body weight."[6] That is, regardless of our willpower, when we lose weight, our bodies seem geared toward returning us to our highest weight.

Exercise is frequently pointed to as a key factor in weight loss. But research has long since debunked the myth that exercise is a primary driver of weight loss. A 2001 research review on exercise studies found that in the short term (sixteen weeks or less), exercise led to three times more weight loss than in the long term (twenty-six weeks or more). While that may sound like a ringing endorsement of short-term exercise programs for weight loss, the raw numbers are significantly less impressive. Intensive short-term exercise programs of under four months yielded a loss of 0.18 kilograms, or 0.4 pounds. Longer term programs led to a weight loss of one-third that—0.06 kilograms, or 0.14 pounds.[7] That echoed a 1999 research review, which found similarly underwhelming results.[8] A later review in the *Cochrane Database of Systemic Reviews* looked at 43 studies in which

3,476 participants with "overweight" and "obese" BMIs participated in exercise programs lasting between three and twelve months. The review's narrative trumpeted the success of exercise as an intervention for weight loss, but even fat participants who took on high intensity workouts for up to a year found only modest weight loss (1.5 kilograms, or 3.3 pounds).[9] For me, as a 340-pound person, those 3.3 pounds would represent a less than 1 percent reduction in my body weight—a far cry from making me thin. Exercise can, however, reduce risk factors for heart disease, support cognition, and provide a wide range of other health benefits. Physical movement can offer a lot—it just doesn't lead to significant weight loss. And exercise isn't accessible to everyone: Many are too busy working multiple jobs or raising children to fit in an exercise regime. Others may live in inaccessible neighborhoods that make outdoor activity difficult, with a lack of sidewalks, parks, and disability accessible infrastructure. For still others, exercise may bring with it painful memories of being bullied or feeling judged in gym class or by loved ones who pushed them into weight loss. Exercise is fraught territory for many of us, and promoting exercise without accounting for whom it might be inaccessible is simply exclusionary.

Some say that weight loss is a simple matter of finding the right diet for you—the one that works, that you can sustain. But time and time again, research shows that diets and "lifestyle changes" don't result in lasting weight loss. As Harvard University's Robert H. Shmerling put it, "You can't pick the right diet if none of them work."[10] Shmerling was referencing a 2020 research review published in the *British Medical Journal*, which represents one of the largest research reviews yet of popular weight-loss diets, digging into 121 randomized trials that included 21,942 participants with "overweight" or "obese" BMIs.[11] Researchers looked into fourteen popular diets: Atkins, South Beach, the Zone, the Biggest Loser, DASH, Jenny Craig, the Mediterranean diet, Portfolio, Slimming World, Volumetrics, Weight Watchers, the Ornish diet, and the Rosemary Conley diet. Low-carbohydrate and low-fat diets had similar results, each leading to a weight loss of about 10 pounds (or 4.5 kilograms) in fat people—and that weight loss diminished after a year in every diet studied. Essentially, multiple diets provided short-term weight loss, but all stopped working by the twelve-month mark. Additionally, "the benefits for cardiovascular risk factors of all interventions, except the Mediterranean diet, essentially disappeared."[12] Thirteen years earlier, UCLA researchers published similar results in a thirty-one-study research review in *American Psychologist*, finding that "you can initially lose 5 to 10 percent of your weight on any number of diets, but then the weight comes back."[13] Indeed, research has shown short-term weight loss leads to long-term weight gain. A clinical trial with 854 subjects found that, after weight loss, only a sliver of study participants maintained a lower weight. "More than half (53.7%) of the participants in the study gained weight within the first twelve months, only one in four (24.5%) successfully avoided weight gain over three years, and less than one in twenty (4.6%) lost and maintained weight successfully."[14] And longitudinal studies of twins have found that a greater number of attempts at intentional weight loss "predicted accelerated weight gain" and that frequent attempts "render dieters prone to future weight gain."[15] Whether we call it a diet, a detox, a cleanse, or a lifestyle change, intentional weight loss frequently produces long-term weight gain.

Popular weight-loss interventions largely fall into three camps: low-carbohydrate, low-fat, and low-calorie diets. A closer look at all three provides similarly lackluster results. Not only do low-carbohydrate and low-fat diets both produce underwhelming weight loss, each also presents unique possible health risks. Low-carbohydrate diets like Atkins, keto, paleo, and South Beach have seen a surge in popularity over the last twenty years. But a 2019 study linked carb-restricted diets to significant increases in mortality, including a 51 percent increase in mortality from coronary heart disease.[16] While mortality rates can be difficult to determine definitively, this study had some advantages. First, it combined its research with a meta-analysis of existing studies. Second, it used a large, existing, nationally representative data set of 24,825 participants. And third, instead of attempting to *predict* mortality, researchers looked at *actual* mortality. The results seemed to indicate that low-carbohydrate diets were far from risk-free. As one of the study's authors told one reporter:

> Low-carbohydrate diets might be useful in the short-term to lose weight, lower blood pressure and improve blood glucose control, but our study suggests that in the long-term they are linked with an increased risk of death from any cause, and deaths due to cardiovascular disease, cerebrovascular disease, and cancer. [. . .] The findings suggest that low-carbohydrate diets are unsafe and should not be recommended.[17]

Low-fat diets, like Weight Watchers and Ornish, saw their peak of popularity in the 1980s and 1990s. Those diets can be misleading, says researcher Dierdre Tobias, "because a food's fat content doesn't do a lot to determine if it's healthy or not."[18] As with any diet, hyperfocus on restriction of calories and macronutrients can lead us away from a wider range of foods with a wider range of nutrients. The most extensive studies into low-fat diets find only minor weight loss, and no impact on other health risks, like colon cancer,[19] breast cancer,[20] or cardiovascular disease.[21] Fat and carbohydrates are themselves nutrients, and each is essential—carbohydrates are key for brain function, and fat is essential for metabolic processes. For those without specific health conditions and disabilities to manage, neither of these diets leads to significant, sustained weight loss, and neither is free of health risks.

But perhaps the most deceptive diet approach is a low-calorie diet focused on "calories in, calories out." It sounds so simple: Take in less than you burn. Eat less, exercise more. But countless people count calories every day, and only a sliver of us lose weight in the long term. So why do we keep repeating it?

"Calories in, calories out" dates back to a 1959 paper published in the *American Journal of Clinical Nutrition*.[22] Its author, Max Wishnofsky, laid out an analysis of existing literature on weight loss and concluded that each pound lost or gained had a "caloric equivalent" of 3,500 calories. Years later, an influential medical textbook, *Modern Nutrition in Health and Disease*, echoed Wishnofsky's work, writing that losing one pound would require "an energy deficit of approximately 3,500 kcal."[23] That concept—that each pound lost was a matter of simple arithmetic, cutting 3,500 calories from one's diet—was repeated widely in medical literature and popular media alike. Researchers' understanding of metabolism and the human body's composition has progressed significantly since 1958, and many of the assumptions that led to Wishnofsky's rule have since been disproven. He also drew from the evidence available at the time—short-term studies with small sample sizes. But the body of evidence surrounding weight and weight loss has grown by leaps and bounds since then. By today's standards, Wishnofsky's evidence wouldn't be considered strong. Plus, researchers have since found a wide range of influences on our ability to lose weight, from hormonal influences to genetic markers—none of which are captured in such a simple equation. In 2015, a paper in the *Journal of the Academy of Nutrition and Dietetics* compiled all of the ways in which Wishnofsky's work fell short, became outdated, or was inaccurate. Its authors concluded that his rule is easy to use but "lacks a contemporary scientific foundation and leads to a large error in weight-loss prediction, even over the short term."[24] They further argued that newer models of weight-loss prediction couldn't yet be established as definitive, and that even the best population-level models won't capture individual biological differences. Models like these, then, cannot be used to predict any individual's weight loss or gain.

Over sixty years of new evidence shows that, at the population or individual levels, we certainly cannot claim that weight loss is as simple as "calories in, calories out." Despite clear, consistent evidence that our body weights are a result of much more complex processes than just calorie-counting, we continue to center calorie restriction in weight loss and public health. We mandate calorie labeling on menus, despite evidence that they increase awareness of calorie counts, but don't change the number of calories we order in restaurants.[25] We rely on nutrition labels on packaged food as guidance, presuming that 2,000 calories per day is the correct amount for our health and for maintaining weight. Most of us don't know that the US Food and Drug Administration (FDA) designed nutrition labels primarily as popular education tools. Their 2,000-calorie recommended daily allowance didn't come from nutritional or medical best practices. It didn't have any scientific basis at all. Instead, the FDA based its recommendation on Americans' self-reported calorie intakes, which ranged primarily between 1,600 and 3,000 calories per day.[26] They initially proposed a recommendation of 2,350 calories per day but, amid fears that it would encourage overeating, rounded down to an easier-to-use number of 2,000 calories per day.[27]

Calorie counts and labels, it seems, have always been shaped by social anxieties about fatness. And while those labels do reflect the number of calories in a particular food, they don't reflect their caloric availability: the number of calories our bodies can actually metabolize from those foods. University of Cambridge researcher Giles Yeo asserts that understanding caloric availability is central to understanding the science of weight and metabolism. "Caloric availability is the amount of calories that can actually be extracted during the process of digestion and metabolism, as opposed to the number of calories that are locked up in the food."[28] That is, while a food may have one hundred calories in it, our bodies may be able to digest only a portion of those. Accordingly, Yeo argues, every calorie count on every nutrition label and restaurant menu is, at worst, false and, at best, misleading.

Ultimately, there's a lot we don't yet know for certain. We don't know precisely why some people are fat and others are thin. We don't know why weight loss is so limited in the short term, or why the vast majority of those who lose weight cannot maintain that weight loss for more than a year or two. The worlds of nutrition and weight loss are full of unanswered questions. Nearly all available weight-loss interventions are ineffective for most people, most of the time. But each drives toward a proudly exclusionary vision of a world without fat people. And each presumes that fat bodies are broken and must be fixed.

Often, that impulse to "fix" fat bodies is referred to using a particularly pernicious euphemism: "getting healthy." "Losing weight" conjures the uphill battle and low success rates of outdated diets. For those of us with mothers who dieted, "losing weight" calls up their endless, futile struggles at once to change their bodies and make peace with them. "Getting healthy" is aspirational, optimistic, laudable. It seems to eschew size, instead prioritizing health, but quietly, implicitly links the two. Referring to weight loss as "getting healthy" reveals so much about our assumptions and values around health, size, chronic illness, and disability.

For years, "getting healthy" has paved the way for conflating fatness with ill health, assuming that anything that delivers thinness is healthy and anything healthy will lead to thinness. But paradoxically, many of us pursue weight-loss methods that put our health at risk. Crash diets and low-calorie diets of less than 1,200 calories per day can cause loss of muscle mass.[29] Popular appetite-suppressant lollipops and teas have a laxative effect that can lead to dehydration and, if used for more than two weeks, can cause dependence on laxatives.[30] Immensely popular low-carbohydrate diets like Atkins and keto can lead to weight loss in the short term but may lead to an increase in all-cause mortality when followed in the long term.[31] Even when we make seemingly less risky decisions to pursue weight loss, some health indicators may worsen. Weight loss brings a greater risk of gallstones, loss of muscle mass, liver dysfunction, digestive issues, and hair loss.[32] Weight loss is also associated with weight cycling, or repeated loss and gain of weight. Those fluctuations can be caused by repeated attempts to lose weight, sometimes described as "yo-yo dieting." Whatever its cause, a research review of twenty-three studies with over 440,000 participants linked weight cycling to an increased risk of cardiovascular disease, hypertension, and mortality from all causes.[33] Some research indicates that dramatic weight loss may permanently suppress one's metabolism.[34] And according to Australia's National Eating Disorders Collaboration, attempting intentional weight loss by restricting one's diet "is one of the strongest predictors for the development of an eating disorder."[35]

But, of course, none of that eases the cultural pressure for fat people to lose weight because that pressure was never born of support for fat people or our health. Too often, the stigma fat people face is thinly veiled by a purported "concern for our health," a kind of well-intended bullying that ends up compounding the harms we face. But that "concern for our health" isn't rooted in any hard-and-fast knowledge of our health. Overwhelmingly, those who offer unsolicited weight loss and health advice haven't read our medical charts, participated in our health care, or learned the intimate details of our health history. They do not know the state of our health markers, nor will they ask after our blood pressure or mental health. Their concern is prompted solely by our appearance. To be fat, they believe, means to be unhealthy. And to be unhealthy shirks some perceived moral responsibility to deliver the *appearance* of health to those around us. In that way, purported concern for the health of fat folks is deeply rooted in healthism, or the belief that those we perceive as healthy are morally superior to those we perceive as unhealthy.

Healthism is itself a facet of ableism, the web of beliefs, behaviors, and institutional practices that marginalize disabled people. Our cultural perceptions of health and beauty have long been rooted in the rejection of disabled people. For example, in the late nineteenth and twentieth centuries, municipalities across the United States passed so-called "ugly laws," banning the public appearance of disabled people. According to Canada's Eugenics Archive, "ugly laws were concerned with more than appearance, prohibiting both the activity of street begging and the appearance in public of 'certain persons.'"[36] Many of these local ordinances referred to disabled and disfigured people as "disgusting objects," presumed to be "disease-ridden." In so doing, these laws tied "ugliness" to poverty, disability, and a perceived threat to wealthy and nondisabled people. They subsequently weaponized "ugliness," newly enshrined in public policy, against disfigured and disabled people, banning their appearance in public. Healthism and ableism have long sought to ascribe meaning to others' perceptions of our health.

For fat people, the biggest barrier to health may be pervasive anti-fatness. Many of us face bias, misdiagnosis, and poor treatment at the hands of our health-care providers (discussed in more depth in the chapter of this book on that topic, "Myth 8"). Additionally, providers frequently lack appropriate equipment for treating and diagnosing fat people. Exam tables that don't support fat people directly limit our access to care. A lack of appropriate equipment can also lead to inaccurate readings and diagnoses. For example, a blood pressure cuff that fits too tightly can lead to inaccurate results. From bias in our providers to exclusionary equipment, health-care systems seem to reject us at every turn. That discriminatory treatment can lead fat people to postpone care or avoid it altogether, wishing to avoid yet another encounter with a health-care provider who brings us little support and plenty of shame.

If so many are, as they claim, "just concerned about fat people's health," the best way to express that concern is to address the overwhelming stigma facing fat people in doctor's offices. After all, while some of us may be sick, stigma from health-care providers often prevents us from accessing the care we need, which only makes us sicker. Until providers' biases are effectively addressed, the privilege of reliable, respectful health care will, paradoxically, be reserved for those already seen to be healthy. Supporting fat people means providing us with appropriate preventive care that doesn't stigmatize us, and that respectfully delivers accurate diagnoses and effective treatments. And it means addressing anti-fat bias beyond medical institutions and health-care providers too. The solution to fat people's perceived health problems isn't more shame—it's less discrimination.

That, too, doesn't influence those who instruct fat people to lose weight "for our health." That's because the cultural mandate for fat people to lose weight isn't about health—it's about power and privilege. The logic goes like this: fat people have failed to effectively perform health for the thin people around us. Thin people have succeeded where those fat people have failed, their perceived health evident in their thinness. Thinness is always the result of hard work in pursuit of health, so thin people must be experts in both weight loss and health. Consequently, fat people are positioned as inept and irresponsible keepers of our own bodies, and we must be corrected and saved by the thin experts around us. After all, we must be ignorant of anything related to our own health, often willfully or self-servingly so. How could we know anything about health? Just look at us.

REFLECTION QUESTIONS

+ Does this information change your understanding of dieting and weight loss? If so, how?
+ Does this change your understanding of fat people? If so, how? Are there outdated or inaccurate ideas about fatness, fat people, and weight loss that you need to abandon? If so, what are they? What can you do to uproot those beliefs and any behaviors they foster?

"PARENTS ARE RESPONSIBLE FOR THEIR CHILD'S WEIGHT. ONLY BAD PARENTS LET THEIR CHILDREN GET FAT."

Note: This chapter includes discussion of childhood abuse and neglect.

In 2021, an English family-court judge removed two West Sussex teenagers from their home. Speaking in court about her decision, she said, "Everyone agrees that this is a very sad and unusual case, of a loving family, where the parents meet many of the basic needs of the children[. . . .] The case was such an unusual one because the children had clearly had some very good parenting, as they were polite, bright, and engaging."[1] Why remove such remarkable children from a loving home? Because their parents failed to make their fat children thin.

This case may seem extreme, but it's not uncommon. In 2011, an eight-year-old in Ohio was removed from his mother's care after a year of social services pressing her to make her fat son lose weight. She made changes, but none made him thin. So the child was taken from his home and placed in the state's foster care system.[2] The very next week, authorities in the United Kingdom removed a five-year-old from her parents' care because she was considered too fat.[3] That same year, the *Journal of the American Medical Association*

(*JAMA*) published a commentary paper in which the authors, Harvard University researchers Lindsey Murtagh and David Ludwig, argued that the state should remove children from their homes in cases of "life-threatening obesity,"[4] lending intellectual credibility to an extreme intervention in fat kids' lives. Social services in the UK separated fat children from their parents at a startling rate. According to *The Guardian*, seventy-four fat children were removed from their homes in England, Wales, and Scotland between 2009 and 2014.[5] In all of these cases, fat children were seen as evidence of an abject failure of parenting. Each presumed that parents were responsible for their children's size and that their children's size was, in itself, proof of neglect.

The belief that parents are responsible for the size of their kids' bodies is a pervasive one, reflected in policy and practices alike. It shows up in the common practice of issuing BMI (body mass index) report cards in US public schools. The Centers for Disease Control and Prevention have been careful not to "make a recommendation for or against BMI measurement programs in schools."[6] Still, half of US states have statewide programs to monitor student BMIs. Many also issue BMI report cards, for which children are weighed in school and have their BMIs calculated. The results are mailed to parents along with weight-loss and maintenance recommendations. As of 2022, 40 percent of American kids live in states with BMI report card programs.[7] A 2020 randomized controlled trial of over 28,000 students found that BMI report cards have no effect on children's weight. The study, published in *JAMA Pediatrics*, did find that the report cards negatively impacted kids' relationships to their own bodies.[8] Students who were weighed at school experienced a marked decrease in satisfaction with their own weight, and their peers were more likely to engage in discussions about weight and dieting. Students also engaged in "concerning weight control behaviors" for the first year of weight monitoring at school. Sending BMI report cards changed their family life too. Students who considered themselves fat reported that pressure to diet from their families increased over two years of report cards. And case studies suggest that school-based

BMI monitoring increases weight-related bullying, which itself can lead to disordered eating.[9] Under pressure to make their children thin, parents put their fat kids on diets, beginning as early as elementary school. A 2004 paper in *Paediatrics & Child Health* stated plainly that "[t]here is no evidence that commercial weight-loss programs are safe or effective for children or teenagers."[10] In the years since, those findings haven't changed. In childhood or adulthood, whether we call them "cleanses" or "lifestyle changes," dietary adjustments for weight loss don't produce long-term weight loss in most cases. Beyond being ineffective, childhood weight-loss interventions can leave young dieters with lifelong impacts on their physical and mental health. Researchers have known for more than twenty years that, in the short term, dieting can lead to nutritional deficiencies, growth deceleration, and disordered eating. According to *Paediatrics & Child Health*, "Teenage dieting is the usual antecedent to anorexia and bulimia nervosa. In prospective studies, dieting has been associated with a fivefold to 18-fold increased risk of developing an eating disorder." Researchers note that short-term dieting can, paradoxically, lead to long-term weight gain.[11]

Fat camps are offered up as a solution to the perceived failed parenting of fat kids. They often take on extreme methods to make child and teen campers lose weight, including calorie restriction to near or below starvation levels, and mandatory workouts for hours at a time. Nevertheless, fat camps, sometimes called "weight management camps" or "wellness retreats," remain a popular option for parents who can afford them in the United States. In the United Kingdom, fat camps are increasingly a priority of the National Health Service (NHS). In 2016, NHS Health Scotland issued a report recommending treatment of fat kids at state-funded fat camps.[12] And by 2021, NHS England launched fifteen clinics for kids' weight loss,[13] which the *Daily Mail* termed "fat camps."[14] Fat-camp directors cite high success rates, producing sometimes dramatic weight loss in short periods of time. Many campers lose weight during the camp itself, but research shows that many regain weight after camp. As one clinical psychologist told the *Washington Post* in 1980, "The problem is, what happens when the kid leaves the camp?"[15] As it turns out, 90 percent of campers regain weight within ten months of leaving.[16] After fat camp, most campers' bodies remain unchanged, and they are left only with a sense of the profound wrongness of their own bodies. When dieting and "lifestyle changes" fail, as they so frequently do, some parents opt for weight-loss surgery for their kids. Centers like Children's National Hospital provide gastric sleeves and gastric bypass to children and adolescents. That hospital doesn't list age limits on its pediatric weight-loss surgeries. Eligible kids and teens, they say, have had BMIs in the "obese" category for at least three years and "understand the lifelong dietary commitment required after the surgery."[17] A 2013 case study discussed weight-loss surgery on the youngest patient to date: a two-and-a-half-year-old.[18] England's NHS began considering providing weight-loss surgery to adolescents, issuing an internal memo on the topic in 2017.[19]

Each of these increasingly extreme options are built on the assumption that parents can and should control their children's food, movement, size, and appearance. But in recent decades, research has shown that the logic of "personal responsibility" falls flat when it comes to body size and weight loss. First, most weight-loss interventions fail, and some seasoned researchers have concluded that long-term dieting and lifestyle changes are "impossible."[20] Second, researchers have pinpointed dozens of genetic markers that influence weight and identified fifty-nine different subtypes of fatness, noting the science behind weight is immensely complicated and weight-loss interventions frequently fall short.[21] Third, in recent decades, public health researchers have established that much of our individual health is determined not by our behaviors but by social determinants. A 2019 study, for example, found that "[r]acial inequality in poverty, unemployment, and homeownership were associated with higher obesity rates" and health outcomes for Black people, Indigenous people, and People of Color were inextricably linked to experiences of racism and inequity.[22] And fourth, fat adults have long given voice to the lifelong pain caused by knowing that our parents are monitoring our bodies, that our bodies are never thin enough to earn their approval, and that, in their eyes, our size is a marker of their failure.

Threatening parenthood is a common cudgel used to control and further stigmatize communities deemed socially undesirable. In the early twentieth century, the American eugenics movement forcibly sterilized people who were disabled or mentally ill, immigrants, and more, all under the banner of "improving" humanity.[23] While state-run eugenics boards in the US closed down by the 1970s and 1980s, the practice of forcible sterilization continued. Between 1973 and 1976, the US Indian Health Service sterilized 3,406 American Indians without their consent.[24] A 1977 United Nations report found that 24 percent of American Indians assigned female at birth had been forcibly sterilized.[25] Most recently, an audit in California revealed that the state had forcibly sterilized 144 people in prisons between 2006 and 2010 alone. California has since launched a program to compensate survivors,[26] offering them approximately $25,000 each.[27] Targeting parental rights is a tactic to marginalize and threaten trans communities too. In 2022, Texas attorney general Ken Paxton released an opinion asserting that providing gender-affirming health care, like puberty blockers, hormones, and surgery, constituted child abuse.[28] The very next day, Governor Greg Abbott called on Texans to report trans youth who appear to be receiving transition-related care and instructed the state's Department of Family and Protective Services to investigate these reports.[29] State child protective services are infamously rife with racist practices and devastatingly disparate outcomes. A 2021 report in *Proceedings of the National Academy of Sciences* found that Black children were at highest risk for investigation by Child Protective Services (CPS) and that Black children, Indigenous children, and children of color experienced "extreme rates of later-stage CPS interventions."[30] According to *Time*, "More than 200,000 children of color are in government custody in our foster system."[31] Taken together, these interventions place immense pressure on families. Not only must these parents figure out how to raise children, a job that is difficult enough in its own right, they must do the difficult and unjust work of navigating oppressive systems and pervasive discrimination. All just to keep children and parents united. The impacts of parent-child separation are profound and well-documented in peer-reviewed psychological and medical literature. From 1974 to 1989, Romania was ruled by dictator Nicolae Ceausescu, who thought that increasing the country's birthrate would stoke its economy. He outlawed contraception and abortion in Romania, eventually levying a "celibacy tax" on families that didn't have more than four children.[32] But with a depressed economy, many parents couldn't afford to raise all of their children. As a result, the country opened state-run orphanages, which provided one of the largest data sets to date on the effects of parent-child separation. Researchers found that the trauma of parental separation fundamentally altered the children's brains, leading to less gray and white matter, both of which are central to brain function.[33] Indeed, many of the children had less intensive brain activity than peers who were never separated from parents.[34]

Of course, not every child who undergoes parent-child separation is institutionalized; many enter into foster care and other non-institutional settings. There, too, research consistently illustrates profound, heartbreaking, lifelong results of parent-child separation. An Australian report on Indigenous children removed from their homes found that in adulthood, their risk of alcoholism, gambling addiction, and arrest all nearly doubled compared to peers who stayed with their families of origin.[35] Similarly, research on children whose parents move away for work found that those children developed "more symptoms of anxiety and depression."[36] A 2007 paper found that children placed in foster care are also more likely to have lower earnings in adulthood,[37] suggesting a link between home removal and long-term economic insecurity. And like any major childhood trauma, losing parents "is strongly correlated with increased risk of suicide attempts, drug addiction, depression, chronic obstructive pulmonary disease, heart disease, and liver disease."[38] Paradoxically, when fat children are removed from their homes "for their health," their health markers are likely to worsen. That includes conditions like heart disease and hypertension, which are frequently attributed to body size and presumed poor health habits in fat people, rather than traumatic events.

Ultimately, the ineffectiveness of these measures reveals that our political interventions around the parenting of fat children isn't about their health, dignity, or wellbeing. If it were, we wouldn't issue BMI report cards that lead not to weight loss but worsened body image. We wouldn't pressure parents to send their kids to fat camps, which are not proven to work in the long term. And we certainly wouldn't remove children from loving homes when we know that the effects of parental separation are catastrophic and lifelong.

Blaming parents for their children's weight isn't based in any observable scientific truth, nor does it remedy anything. It only leads to stigma, isolation, and fractured family systems, inviting more pain into the lives of fat kids. It is a reflection of a society that rejects fatness at every turn, making it an issue of personal responsibility so that it can reject fat people once again. And it is a reflection of a society that projects adult anxieties about a purported "obesity epidemic" onto children, then expects children to resolve those anxieties for us. In the process, we make children into political footballs, and we sacrifice their physical health, mental health, self-esteem, relationships, and dignity in the process.

"THIN PEOPLE SHOULD HELP FAT PEOPLE LOSE WEIGHT."

For me, growing up fat meant that weight-loss encouragement and advice followed me everywhere, sticking to me stubbornly as a shadow I can't shake. Stretching back to childhood, thin people regularly offered unsolicited diet advice. In grade school, trusted adults suggested buying a smaller children's size than the one I wore. The too-small clothing, they hypothesized, would inspire me to restrict my food, shrink, and wither. In its way, it worked: even the suggestion made me feel small.

In adulthood, the ceaseless advice continued. Supervisors at work would ask about my plans to lose weight, suggesting that advancement would follow if I did. Even dates offered up suggestions of diets, workouts, and incentives to lose weight. For me, pressure to lose weight from thin loved ones hurt more than even the harshest jibes from strangers or the cruelest internet trolls. It's easy to disregard strangers: we know one another for only moments at a time. Few things sting like rejection from those we love most, or conditional love offered with the insistence that they *just want to help*. "I love you" doesn't ring so true when it's followed by "I just want to fix you."

For many fat people, our bodies seem to invite constant, unsolicited, proud, and hurtful weight-loss "advice." Whatever the intentions behind them, "advice" and "encouragement" to lose weight send a series of clear messages: I'm watching your size. I'm monitoring what you eat. I disapprove of how you look. I pity your size, so I won't tell you directly. But above all: I think your body is a problem, and you've failed to solve it. It's a logic that assumes that thin people are experts in weight loss, whether or not they've lost the amount of weight that fat people are expected to lose. And it's a logic that presumes that nearly all thinness is a sign of expertise in weight loss, rather than simply being a different body type. In this logic, thinness is always a hard-fought victory, and only the noblesse oblige of thin people can rescue fat people from our own bodies. People who have been thin for the duration of their lives have little instructive feedback to offer fat people, many of whom have years' worth of experience in both navigating anti-fatness and pursuing weight loss alike. Functionally, lifelong thin people lack the life experience to offer meaningful input. And regardless of our current or past size, unsolicited weight-loss advice still presumes that fat bodies are a problem to be solved, and that fat people *must* be unhappy, desperate for rescue from such universally reviled bodies.

Regardless of the intent behind it, thin people "helping" fat people lose weight is often experienced by fat people as anti-fatness. A 2005 study looked at fat people's experiences with weight stigma, pulling its research subjects from a weight-loss program.[1] Subjects were disproportionately white, not living with a partner, and un-employed or self-employed. Those participants filled out question-naires to report their experiences with anti-fatness. The results were striking: experiences of anti-fatness were all but universal. The most common source of stigma for subjects was their families, with a stag-gering 98 percent reporting that family members make disparaging remarks toward them; 86 percent said their loved ones were embar-rassed by their size. When loved ones tell us whether and how to eat, move, and look, the message to fat people is clear: even those closest to us can be ashamed of our size, even if we're not.

And those messages—that fat people somehow owe our loved ones thinness—are *everywhere*. Others inform us of how many calories or grams of carbohydrates are in our meals and snacks, reminding us that they're taking note and making judgments about each of our foods. *You know, there's a lot of calories in that* reveals a plethora of messages in its underpinnings: *You must not know anything about calories. I noticed that you are fat, which means you must not know how to lose weight. If you knew how to lose weight, you wouldn't be fat, I wouldn't have to see your fat body, and I wouldn't have to bring this to your attention.* They may assume that we wish to lose weight urgently, offering up that "keto is super easy. I lost ten pounds!" In so saying, they don't realize the assumptions they're making: that the fat person they're talking to must want to lose weight, that what led to weight loss for them must be a universal experience, that they do not perceive a meaningful difference between a weight loss of ten pounds and a weight loss of two hundred or more, and that the fat person they're talking to has the resources, ability, and desire to lose weight following the specific (and often costly) method they themselves prefer. All of these reveal that fat bodies are being monitored, that we're expected to deliver thinness to those around us, and that if we don't, we'll be met with heightened scrutiny, disapproval, and even rejection.

While offering weight-loss advice cloaks itself in good intentions, it is fundamentally an act that asserts a thin person's superiority over fat people. Unsolicited weight-loss advice is a kind of zealotry, a seemingly religious fervor in those who practice it. Who else can save such ignorant fat people?

If this sounds reminiscent of the racist logic used by white missionaries colonizing Black and Brown Indigenous cultures, it should: anti-fatness often echoes its racist roots. In Sabrina Strings's landmark work *Fearing the Black Body: The Racial Origins of Fat Phobia*, the sociologist maps out the anti-Black history of anti-fatness.[2] Strings shows that white supremacy produces standards of health and beauty that align with whiteness and thinness, and that alignment is far from accidental. In establishing the transatlantic slave trade, white Europeans looked to Black people's bodies for any perceived evidence that would reinforce their own worldview: that white people were superior and Black people were inferior. During and after the American Civil War, racist science boomed, asserting a litany of pseudoscientific, intellectualized justifications for racism and enslavement, allowing white people to prove to ourselves, once again, that our supremacy was innate, earned, and somehow right. That boom time in racist science also left us with the body mass index, a measurement derived solely from the heights and weights of white men conscripts in the nineteenth century and never tested or meaningfully adjusted for anyone else. Nevertheless, the BMI has been enshrined to the point of being inescapable in US health-care systems, claiming to measure the health of Black people, Indigenous people, and People of Color against the yard stick of white men's bodies. Into the twentieth and twenty-first centuries, racist associations and policies persisted, reasserted time and time again by public policy, public health programs, the diet industry, medical institutions, and more. Our contemporary attitudes toward fatness and fat people aren't exceptions to this history of anti-Blackness but products of them. And those attitudes shape our behaviors and cultural expectations—including the expectation that we ought to encourage fat people to "correct" our bodies and become thin.

Ultimately, unsolicited weight-loss "help" and "encouragement" are neither. Instead, they convey a series of alarming biases, harmful judgments, and threats of rejection. For many fat people, these are more likely to lead to shame and isolation than to weight loss. No matter how well-intended, weight-loss "advice" causes more harm than good.

OPPORTUNITIES FOR ACTION

✦ *Interrupt unsolicited health and weight-loss advice when you see it.* If you feel unsteady doing so, practice ahead of time. Some options to consider:
  • "Please don't talk about weight loss without consent."
  • "This topic is hard for a lot of people, so I try not to talk about it."
  • "I don't really want to hear everything you're doing to avoid looking like me."
  • "This isn't an appropriate topic for the workplace" (or family time, a holiday gathering, etc.).
  • "What's wrong with being fat?"
  • "I support you, but I don't need to hear about your diet."
  • "I don't participate in food shaming."
  • "No more diet talk." (Repeat as necessary.)
  • Change the subject.
  • Walk away.
✦ *When discussing health and weight loss, center fat people as experts with lived experience.* After all, fat people face the greatest pressure to lose weight, and many of us have a lifetime of experience in weight-loss attempts and in navigating health systems built to exclude us.

"WEIGHT LOSS IS THE RESULT OF HEALTHY CHOICES AND SHOULD BE CELEBRATED."

n 2020, Adele posted a photograph of herself on her Instagram account. The caption addressed her birthday and the still-new COVID-19 pandemic. "Thank you for the birthday love. [. . .] I'd like to thank all of our first responders and essential workers who are keeping us safe while risking their lives! You are truly our angels."[1] The accompanying photograph showed the singer in a fitted black minidress, standing with a series of elaborate beige flower arrangements, noticeably thinner than she ever had been before.

Adele didn't address the change in her size, but the comment section did. In the absence of a narrative about the singer's changed body, fans flooded her account with congratulations for what they termed "getting healthy." "Now more than ever, being healthy and strong is of the utmost importance. Congrats and happy birthday," wrote one user. "You look fabulous! I KNOW that was a LOT of hard work! Congratulations on all your success!!" wrote another. Of course, none of the commenters "knew" for sure that Adele's weight loss was the result of "hard work" or even that it was desired. The only person who could provide a narrative of her body was Adele herself, and at that point, she'd done no such thing. In the coming weeks, Adele would address her weight loss, acknowledging that it was intentional, unattainable for most, and a result of struggling with her own mental health. Her narrative was cautionary, far from the full-throated endorsement of weight loss many assume is behind what are often billed as "weight-loss journeys" and "weight-loss transformations." Indeed, the wave of popular and media reactions to Adele's changing body revealed nothing about the singer and everything about our collective assumptions about weight loss. In the absence of any firsthand information at all, Instagram followers and reporters alike constructed a narrative of their own. In their collective imagination, no matter what Adele herself said, her weight loss was intentional, it was the product of hard work, and her newfound thinness was desired. It was worthy of congratulations. Thinness always is.

Still, before long, the singer began to prompt and accept comments on her weight loss. In a November 2020 appearance on *Saturday Night Live*, she addressed her changing size. "I know I look really, really different since you last saw me. But actually because of all the COVID restrictions and the travel bans, I had to travel light and bring only half of me. This is the half that I chose."[2] The studio audience erupted into cheers and applause; Adele smiled warmly. The monologue recast her weight loss as desired and intentional, a far cry from her previous cautious, couched, and sometimes uncomfortable remarks on her changed body. Article after article about Adele's rumored diet, the extremely restrictive Sirtfood Diet, flooded entertainment and wellness media alike, trumpeting the "dramatic results!" of the one-thousand-calorie per day diet. Over time, that inundation of media coverage and weight-loss compliments overtook her own narrative of her own body. The transformation of her weight-loss narrative was complete, returning to its rightful role validating thinness, however it is attained.

Bubba Smith's weight-loss story ended differently. Smith was a career football player and a star. He'd been the number one overall draft pick in the NFL's 1967 draft. Over the course of his career, he led the Baltimore Colts to a 1970 Super Bowl win, played in two Pro Bowls, and earned a spot in the College Football Hall of Fame. After retiring from football, Smith pursued acting, playing Moses

Hightower in nearly every *Police Academy* movie. By all accounts, Smith's life was a remarkable one, finding success in two extremely competitive fields. That remarkable life was cut short in 2011, when Smith's caretaker found him dead in his home. He was just sixty-six years old.[3] The Los Angeles County Coroner later ruled that Smith's death was the result of an overdose of diet pills.[4] Smith had taken phentermine, a prescription diet drug whose popularity peaked as half of the 1990s purported weight-loss "miracle drug," fen-phen.

Fen-phen, a combination of phentermine and fenfluramine, was pulled from shelves in 1997, after being found to cause fatal heart issues. Phentermine, however, remains on the market today as Adipex, still prescribed for weight loss. The coroner found that the late football player had heart disease and high blood pressure, health conditions popularly attributed to fatness. Smith, it appears, did what many others had done before: he sought a medical method to lose weight. With hypertension and heart disease, his heart may have been extra susceptible to a drug linked to heart failure. Instead of leading Smith to thinness, pursuing weight loss caused his death. Smith's story calls the pursuit of thinness into question, illustrating that weight loss is far from a risk-free venture.

But Smith's death received little media attention and even less analysis. His story flew in the face of countless assumptions about fatness and weight loss. Weight-loss conversations did, and do, center the experiences of thin white women. Smith, a Black man and retired athlete, had no place in those conversations. Sports media only occasionally covered stories about body image, and when it did, it largely focused on the stories of thin women. And Smith's was an uncomfortable story because it failed to do the one thing we expect of weight-loss narratives: illustrate the inherent superiority of thinness.

In our cultural conversations about weight loss, we expect that our assumptions about thinness will be upheld, reinforced, and celebrated. Weight-loss stories can only be told if they valorize the pursuit of thinness and uphold the presumed superiority of thin people. Weight loss, we are told, is always desired because thinness is always desirable. Becoming thin is worth any cost, because fatness is understood to be inherently inferior to thinness, considered less desirable in both social and medical settings. Thinness is presumed to be the result of hard work, and fatness consequently must be the result of a lack of effort, a failure of tenacity, work ethic, and character. In a society that values a Protestant work ethic and a commitment to restrictive views of professionalism rooted in white supremacy culture, our beliefs about the work involved in thinness and fatness carry a moral overlay and call for social intervention. Fat people's perceived failure must be punished; thin people's perceived success must be celebrated.

When we publicly celebrate weight loss, we uphold all those messages. We presume that weight loss is always desired because people who are seen as "achieving" thinness are viewed as inherently superior to those who don't. In short, thin people are superior to fat people. Conventional wisdom about responding to weight loss upholds those messages. When faced with a friend who we perceive as having lost weight, many of us readily compliment that weight loss. In that moment, we assume that the person we're complimenting wanted to be thinner, worked for that thinness, and desires public accolades for their success in conforming to a thin standard of beauty. We also reveal our own beliefs: that thinness is an accomplishment, that it is the product of hard work, and that it is our job to promote and celebrate it. Conversely, when faced with a friend who we perceive as having gained weight, conventional wisdom dictates that the kindest thing to do is to remain silent. The assumptions underpinning that guidance are steeped in judgments too. We assume and reinforce that weight gain is universally undesirable, that fatness is a failure, and that it's unkind to draw attention to the wretchedness of fat bodies. It is a clear, direct social message: thinness is universally superior to fatness, and thin people are superior to fat people. Thinness and fatness, we tell ourselves, are a direct result of one's character. In this way, we offer ourselves absolution for judging others solely on the basis of their appearance.

Those assumptions echo a long historical pattern, rooted in ableism and racism, of looking to someone's body as a reflection of their character. Those who most align with a restrictive, thin, white standard of health and beauty are seen as harder workers, more virtuous, and more socially desirable. Those who fall short of those standards of health and beauty—including fat people, disabled people, Black people, Indigenous people, and People of Color—are seen as lazier and less socially desirable than thinner, whiter, nondisabled people. As fat scholar Da'Shaun Harrison has argued, health is defined around a thin, white standard, leading to health-care systems that exclude fat Black people, often violently. When we presume that weight loss ought to be celebrated, we reinforce the same ideas that lead to that violent exclusion. The practice of celebrating weight loss not only upholds the supremacy of thinness and thin people, it also upholds restrictive ideas about health and beauty that reify racism, ableism, and other systems of oppression.

Still, many of us know (or are) people in active pursuit of weight loss, and some of those people may still expect social reinforcement. So we assume that any weight loss we observe is desired, healthy, and affirming for the person losing weight. But often, we make that assumption based solely on their changed appearance. We do not consider the many causes of weight loss. We don't remember troubling weight loss is sometimes prompted by grief from a breakup, divorce, or death. We don't think about weight loss caused by cancer or chemotherapy. We don't consider that the person in front of us might be going through a medical crisis, their weight loss a sign of abrupt and troubling change rather than hard-fought victory. And we don't consider that weight loss is sometimes linked to declining mental health or a new wave of disordered eating. In our eagerness to compliment what we assume is desired weight loss, many of us end up congratulating restrictive eating disorders, grief, and trauma in the process, revealing that we are in a constant state of surveillance, monitoring and assessing the bodies of those around us. We keep our disappointment and displeasure quiet, revealing our disapproval of fatness only in our celebration of thinness.

Ultimately, weight-loss compliments don't function without a hierarchy of bodies. Thinness is only worth celebrating if it is an accomplishment, and thinness is only an accomplishment if fatness is a failure. Instead of seeing bodies as *bodies*, we rank and congratulate those we perceive as superior. Many of us claim that "all bodies are good bodies," that no one should be judged based on their appearance alone, and that restrictive beauty and health standards cause more harm than good. If we truly believe those things, we'll need to stop judging those around us on the basis of their size—even when we think that judgment is a compliment.

REFLECTION QUESTIONS

+ Do you compliment others' weight loss? If so, when? Why or why not?
+ When those around you compliment weight loss or imply that thinness is superior to fatness, how do you respond? Does your response uphold the idea that thinness is superior, or does it interrupt that idea? Does your response defend the dignity and humanity of fat people?

OPPORTUNITIES FOR ACTION

+ *Remove unsolicited weight-loss compliments from your repertoire.* Remember that unsolicited comments on others' bodies, good or bad, invite unwanted attention. Instead, practice size-neutral affirmations like "You *always* look great to me!"
+ *Interrupt unsolicited weight-loss advice when you see it happen around you.* Remember that that "advice" is also a clear way to reject and other fat people. Those comments can also trigger relapses of eating disorders and body dysmorphic disorder. For some, unsolicited weight-loss advice and weight-loss compliments are a nuisance. For others, they can hurt in lasting ways. But either way, their message is clear: each of us owes thinness to those around us, and our bodies will be monitored, judged, and assessed until we do.

PART TWO

"BUT WHAT ABOUT YOUR HEALTH?"

"OBESITY IS THE LEADING CAUSE OF DEATH IN THE UNITED STATES."

O*besity kills four hundred thousand Americans each year.*
This number has become ubiquitous, an uncontested and un-contestable statement of fact. It's what philosopher Bruno Latour calls a "scientific black box"—a statement so successfully dissemi-nated that it is no longer considered debatable.[1] It has spent years in newspaper ledes and news broadcasts, on fact sheets and in elected officials' speeches. It is a number that's repeated regularly, with a great deal of certainty and often without citation. It doesn't need to be proven; it *feels* true, and we've heard it so many times in the last twenty years that it must be. Our culture of certainty around fatness as a cause of death wouldn't lead you to question this number, the number of people who die each year, simply from being fat. And that certainty wouldn't lead you to believe that this number was hotly contested among epidemiologists and researchers. But behind this monolithic, seemingly incontrovertible number is one of the strangest, most remarkable stories of scientific debate in the field of fatness research.

Determining causes of mortality at a population level has long been a challenging statistical venture. Determining a *specific* cause of mortality only adds to the challenge—particularly when that cause of mortality isn't a cause at all but a *risk factor for a cause of mortality.*

And the process of arriving at a specific number requires those making the calculation to make a seemingly endless series of subjective, murky judgment calls. In the case of deaths related to fatness, one could tally all of the deaths due to complications of diseases we popularly associate with fatness, like heart disease, type 2 diabetes and hypertension. But even then, those health conditions also affect thin people. So, one might filter this sample even further, sorting out people with "normal" or "underweight" BMIs, leaving only those with "overweight" and "obese" BMIs. But even still, those remaining fat people may have had family histories of the health conditions that contributed to their deaths. Or those remaining fat people could have other health issues or life experiences that complicated their condition: living in poverty, dealing with addiction, handling the stress of living with racism, and facing discrimination in health care can all complicate diagnosis, treatment, and mortality. How could one know that those same deaths wouldn't have occurred had those same people been thin? While these may seem like granular questions, they can mean the addition or subtraction of thousands, even tens of thousands of lives, from this now-ubiquitous statistic. And even the rudimentary questions laid out here are more sophisticated than the methodology that led to the claim that being fat kills four hundred thousand Americans each year.

In 2004, the *Journal of the American Medical Association* (*JAMA*) published "Actual Causes of Death in the United States, 2000," the study that first trumpeted that some four hundred thousand Americans died each year simply from being fat. The study, led by Ali Mokdad, James Marks, Donna Stroup, and Julie Gerberding, seemed to change the public conversation about fatness and fat people dramatically. The findings captured the public's attention and found their way into countless headlines, speeches, and news stories. But among researchers, the findings were controversial.

The first source of controversy for this watershed study was its methodology. Researchers drew from studies from the years 1951, 1970, 1979, 1983, and 1985. This study, published in 2004, drew on data sources ranging from nineteen to fifty-three years old.[2] In those pivotal fifty years, the United States had changed dramatically, from our built environment to our food systems, the types of jobs Americans worked to the way we got to work. During that same time, the thresholds for "overweight" and "obese" BMIs shifted repeatedly too, lowering the bar for Americans to be medically considered fat. But this 2004 mortality estimate didn't account for any of that. Instead, it extrapolated that data to *make estimates* based on the size of the US population. While it is extraordinarily difficult to determine causes of death for a proxy health measure (like fatness), the 2004 study didn't attempt even that. As with the BMI before it, Mokdad et al. made a brutal calculation from simple arithmetic. And for years to come, that broad brush was used to paint fat people as a threat to Americans' health and very lives.

The second reason for controversy: the study's politics. As it stands, public health research and interventions operate in a landscape of forced scarcity. That is, federal and state governments offer significantly fewer resources than are needed to get to the bottom of what they see as the most pressing public health priorities, leading to high competition for resources. For years, tobacco-related deaths had topped the list of leading causes of death in the United States. Anti-tobacco advocates and public health officials worried that being rivaled by fat-related deaths would threaten both the revenue streams and the political clout needed to power their work. As a result, anti-tobacco advocates fired back in the media. Comparing the estimate to more established models for mortality, Stanton A. Glantz, director of UC San Francisco's Center for Tobacco Control Research and Education, estimated that the study inflated fat-related deaths fourfold and that the number was likely closer to one hundred thousand deaths per year. "The kind of policies one would develop for something that is killing about as many people as tobacco or a quarter as many people as tobacco are very different," Glantz told the *New York Times*. The number, he said, constituted "a very, very fundamental mistake that was made in the paper, which they have done nothing to address. This is not some esoteric detail over which there is huge uncertainty."[3]

The third and more troubling source of controversy was its accuracy. The findings of Mokdad and colleagues departed dramatically from existing estimates of fat-related mortality. Just five years earlier, in 1999, another researcher using overlapping data sets had published an estimate of 280,000 deaths attributable to fatness—fully 30 percent lower than Mokdad's 2004 findings.[4] Like the 2004 study, David Allison's 1999 study failed to illustrate a causal relationship between body weight and death. And Allison reportedly had ties to pharmaceutical companies studying weight-loss drugs—drugs whose approval and sales might presumably benefit from fatness being labeled the nation's leading cause of death.[5]

Both studies' methodology to determine a simple correlation was suspect too. Allison wrote that his 1999 study made the foundational assumption that "all excess mortality in obese people is due to obesity."[6] From the study itself was this:

> Also, our calculations assume that all (controlling for age, sex, and smoking) excess mortality in obese people is due to obesity. However, it is not definitively established that if currently obese persons were to lose weight or were to never become obese, they would not still have a higher mortality rate.[7]

That is, if more fat people than thin people died in a given year, the 1999 study would consider those "excess" deaths, and consequently assume that differences in the mortality rates between thin people and fat people were attributable to fatness. Thin people can die of all manner of things, but in the logic used by these studies, any fat person who passed away when a thin counterpart didn't would have died *because of their fatness*. How could two studies be taken seriously when both were built on such faulty, stigmatizing assumptions? And how could both studies, using such similar data sets, come up with such radically different numbers?

The 2004 study's numbers were so out of step that members of Congress took note—a rare turn for disputed research. Congressman Henry Waxman asked the US General Accounting Office to launch an investigation.[8] The Centers for Disease Control and Prevention (CDC) launched an internal investigation into the study,[9] which found that the results were inaccurate and that some researchers with the CDC had raised concerns about the study's methodology before its publication. Ultimately, the CDC published an erratum in *JAMA*, lowering its estimate of annual fat-related deaths to 365,000.[10] Still, other researchers questioned even the lowered number.

Katherine Flegal, a researcher with the CDC, published her own findings the following year, in 2005. Flegal's methodology represented a sharp departure from Mokdad's. Rather than extrapolating population-level trends from decades-old studies, Flegal drew from the National Health and Nutrition Examination Survey (NHANES), a decades-long, nationwide longitudinal study that provided a larger data set with more unified detail. Like Mokdad's projections, Flegal's also made estimates based on existing data sets—an inevitability in projecting population-level causes of death for a proxy measure like body weight. But Flegal's results departed dramatically, finding a "modestly increased risk of mortality" for those with BMIs in the "obese" category and found "a slight reduction in mortality" for those in the "overweight" category, as compared to the "normal weight" category. Ultimately, Flegal found that "for overweight and obesity combined (BMI ≥ 25), our estimate was 25,814 excess deaths [. . .] in 2000." By contrast, deaths related to "underweight" BMIs were estimated at 33,746.[11] The paper also found that the risk of fatness-related death appeared to be decreasing over time.[12] Just one month after its publication, the CDC accepted Flegal's findings as a more reliable estimate of mortality in fat people.[13]

Katherine Flegal was a researcher doing what researchers do: attempting to replicate findings from other studies and driving her field closer to the truth in the process. She anticipated that her colleagues would receive these new findings the way they so reliably did: as new information to incorporate into their work. Instead, she was met with a reaction that was decidedly unusual and surprisingly personal. It wasn't until 2021 that Flegal told her story in a paper for the journal *Progress in Cardiovascular Diseases*. On the very day of her study's publication in 2005, Flegal discovered that Walter Willett, a professor at the Harvard T. H. Chan School of Public Health, had already begun speaking to members of the press about her research. He told the *Los Angeles Times* that "the papers are really naïve, deeply flawed and seriously misleading."[14] Just a week later, another public health professor from Harvard "took the unusual step of pre-empting a planned presentation by someone else to take the stage and deliver a critique of our just-published article."[15] In the weeks ahead, Flegal was met with countless unusually confrontational responses from faculty and students from the university, including a webcast symposium for the press, hosted by the Harvard T. H. Chan School, ostensibly designed to discredit Flegal's findings in the media.[16] Advocates joined in the pile on, too. Anti-obesity organizations circulated talking points designed to downplay and discredit Flegal's findings, one of which was boldly titled "Damage Control for the Flegal Article."[17]

The internet joined in too. Anonymous edits to Wikipedia falsely claimed that Flegal's work had been "discredited" and were "fatally flawed." A postdoctoral student at Harvard later published a blog post, alleging that Flegal's research had been retracted and that she had been demoted. Neither was true, and after being confronted by Flegal, the student apologized and deleted the erroneous blog post. Still, the student wouldn't reveal where he had heard such wrongheaded rumors. Bizarre, false gossip like this followed her for years, frequently published without citation or substantiation. In a field centered around dispassionate observation, Katherine Flegal found herself in the midst of an uncharacteristically personal, decidedly subjective backlash.

Flegal was measured when she finally told this story. She came to recognize these as "partisan attacks masquerading as scientific concerns." At the time, though, she expected this research to be regarded like any other, measured on its merits, critiqued objectively. But this study was regarded wholly differently. She explained:

> I had not expected an aggressive campaign that included insults, errors, misinformation, behind-the-scenes gossip and maneuvers, social media posts and even complaints to my employer[. . .]. It seemed that some felt that our work should be judged not on its merits but rather on whether its findings supported the goals and objectives of the interlocutors.

Those goals and objectives could have sprung from any number of sources: genuine concern, anti-fat bias, the desire to fund a program or study, or something else altogether. But whatever their source, those existing goals drowned out both Flegal's findings and a crucial opportunity for a more nuanced conversation about fatness and health.

With a topic of study as thorny as risk factors for death, it's currently very difficult to determine how many fat people's deaths are attributable to our size. But it's almost certain to be fewer than 280,000 or 400,000 deaths per year, because those numbers, by researchers' own admission, assume that every fat death that isn't accounted for by other predictors like age or smoking status is instead a *direct result of fatness*. It is absurd to claim that all excess deaths of fat people are the result of being fat, just as it would be to claim all swimmers die of drowning, all birthing people die in childbirth, or all people who wore jeans at their time of death were killed by their Levi's. Each of these mortality estimates is just that—an estimate, based on existing available data sets. Few control for family histories of conditions they readily attribute to body weight, like type 2 diabetes or heart disease. None account for the widespread and widely documented substandard health care received by fat people, which can lead to postponement of care, misdiagnosis of crucial health conditions, and denial of care altogether in some cases. (For more on fat patients' experience of health care, see *Doctors are unbiased judges of fat people's health*.) And none account for the harmful effects of dieting, weight cycling, or disordered eating. In short, most of these mortality estimates fail to analyze even the most basic risk factors for specific health conditions, choosing instead to attribute every instance of those health conditions to body weight alone.

Even among those who consider having a BMI in the "obese" category to be a disease unto itself, fatness is only then considered a disease because it presents an increased risk for chronic health conditions like type 2 diabetes, hypertension, and heart disease. That is, what makes "obesity" a disease is its proximity to other, more established diseases. Diseases with proven courses of treatment. Diseases that can themselves cause a person's death. Diseases whose researchers could benefit from an increase in direct funding for treatment, prevention and care, without funding being siphoned off to study a risk factor rather than the disease itself. And diseases whose researchers could greatly benefit from study of the relationship between body size and health in more nuanced, precise terms.

As it stands, researchers disagree on the relationship between mortality and high BMI. But the bizarre, inflated assertion that 360,000 Americans die so-called obesity-related deaths each year has long since been debunked. After all, fat people die of more than one cause—and no one dies from simply being fat.

"THE BMI IS AN OBJECTIVE MEASURE OF SIZE AND HEALTH."

L ike most of us, I was taught to accept the BMI as a simple truth. It was, I had been told, a direct measure of size and health. But for something as universally relied upon as the BMI[1], its history is much less solid—and scientific—than one might think. And medicine's overreliance on the BMI may be actively harming the health of many of us—particularly fat people, Black people, Indigenous people, and People of Color.

The body mass index was invented nearly two hundred years ago. Its creator, Adolphe Quetelet, was an academic flourishing at the beginning of a wave of academic specialization; his studies included astronomy, mathematics, statistics, and sociology.[2] Quetelet was not a physician, nor did he study medicine. Instead, he was a polymath. Following the Enlightenment and the Belgian Revolution, he wanted to create a name for his home country as a thought leader around the world. As an avid relationship builder, he built intellectual and scientific peer networks that spanned Europe but originated in Belgium. A respected astronomer, Quetelet founded the Brussels Observatory, where he served for decades as its director.

Quetelet's biggest project was developing a framework for what he called Social Physics. He wanted to measure, quantify, and study the human social world the way physicists studied the material world. Quetelet sought to catalog the world as it was, find its averages, then lift those averages up as ideals. He expressed a desire to quantify and measure everything from suicide rates to acts of courage. In so doing, he believed he'd find a hidden framework for understanding people as social animals. He looked for laws of human behavior that mimicked the laws of physics. And in finding those laws of human behavior and analyzing our actions, he hoped to identify the characteristics of *l'homme moyen*, or "the average man." To Quetelet, "average" represented a social ideal, a kind of glorious normalcy and conformity to which to aspire.

Quetelet worked in Western Europe during the early nineteenth century—a boom time for racist science—so that idealized norm was a white one.[3] He is credited with cofounding the school of positivist criminology, "which asserted the dangerousness of the criminal to be the only measure of the extent to which he was punishable."[4] That positivist school laid the groundwork for criminologists like Cesare Lombroso, who believed that Black people, Indigenous people, and People of Color were a separate species.[5] *Homo criminalis*, Lombroso argued, were "savages" by birth, identified by physical characteristics that he claimed linked them to primates. For Lombroso, anyone who wasn't white comprised some kind of subspecies, congenitally driven to commit crimes. In addition to paving the way for Lombroso's work, Quetelet is also credited with founding the field of anthropometry,[6] which itself included the racist pseudoscience of phrenology.[7]

Quetelet believed that the mathematical mean of a population was its ideal. But since gathering population-level data would've required significant time and resources, his analysis was largely restricted to data gathered through government entities. But the state didn't keep records of acts of courage, suicide attempts, or other phenomena that Quetelet wanted to study. The state kept only vital records (birth, death, and marriage certificates), compiled crime data, and gathered some information on military conscripts' weight and height. So that's where he began.

Quetelet's desire to identify and quantify the ideal, average man resulted in the invention of what later became the body mass index, a record of what Quetelet believed to be the average—therefore, ideal—ratio of weight to height. Called Quetelet's Index, the measurements became a way of quantifying the weight-to-height ratio of *l'homme moyen*. The formula was derived from data gathered solely from male French and Scottish participants. The index was devised exclusively by, for, and about white Western European men. Quetelet's methodology ensured that if there was to be a universal, idealized average, it would be white, and it would be male.

Quetelet's contemporaries weren't sold on social physics—not because it was fundamentally exclusionary to anyone who wasn't white but because it questioned their own sense of agency. If there were these laws of human nature, what then would become of man's free will? His work was frequently debated among academics of Quetelet's generation and the next, some of whom were great admirers of it. Among his fans: Sir Francis Galton, a proponent of social Darwinism, a leader in scientific racism, and a godfather of the eugenics movement that gathered like a storm in the late nineteenth and early twentieth centuries. According to Canada's Eugenics Archive, "It was Galton who, while building upon Quetelet's notion of the 'average man' (a product of measurement and statistics), effected an important twist: instead of positing the normal as healthy and desirable, Galton equated the normal with the mediocre. Within this tradition the normal state is to be transcended, improved upon, and overcome."[8]

By the turn of the next century, Quetelet's influence was felt throughout the eugenics movement, where it operated as a scientific justification for the systemic, state-run sterilization of disabled people, autistic people, immigrants, poor people, Black people, Indigenous people, and People of Color. Quetelet's influence in eugenics traced back to *l'homme moyen*, the "average man" concept adopted by Galton. This concept rapidly gained popularity, particularly in the United States. Thirty-three states operated state eugenics boards, charged with determining which of their neighbors would be forcibly sterilized. California's program led the nation in sterilizations, offering inspiration to Nazi eugenics programs.[9]

While Quetelet's work was used to justify scientific racism for decades to come, he was clear about one aspect of the BMI: it was never intended as a measure of individual body fat, build, or health.[10] To its inventor, the BMI was a way of measuring populations, not individuals, designed for the purposes of statistics, not individual health. But within a few short decades, that's exactly how it was used.

Weight wasn't considered a primary indicator of health until the late nineteenth century, when US life insurance companies began to compile tables of ideal weights to determine what to charge prospective policyholders.[11] Like Quetelet's Index, however, those actuarial tables were deeply flawed, representing only those with the resources and legal ability to purchase life insurance. Weight and height were largely self-reported, and often inaccurately. And what constituted an insurable weight varied from one company to the next, as did their methods of determining weight. Some included "frame size"—small, medium, or large. Others did not. Many didn't factor in age. And tables were designed for life insurance customers, but only those wealthy enough to purchase it. On top of all that, insurers were staffed by actuaries and sales agents, not medical doctors. But despite insurers' lack of medical expertise and inconsistent measures, physicians began to use their rating tables as a means of evaluating patients' weight and health.[12]

By the 1970s, medical science was on the hunt for a more effective measure of weight. Ancel Keys, a renowned researcher on the effects of starvation, heart health, and more, took on the challenge. He led a team of researchers in a study of 7,500 men from five different countries to find the most effective of medicine's existing measures of body fat, easy and inexpensive enough for regular office visits.

As in Quetelet's work, the subjects in Keys's study were drawn from predominantly white nations—the United States, Finland, and Italy—along with Japan and South Africa, though the study notes that findings in South Africa "could not be suggested to be a representative sample of [Black] men in Cape Province let alone [Black] men in general."[13] Most of its findings, the study explains, apply to "all but the [Black] men." That is, the findings weren't representative of, or applicable to, the very South African men included in the study. Like Quetelet's Index, whiteness took center stage in the research. But unlike Quetelet, Keys and his colleagues set out to test which diagnostic tool was the best existing measure of body fat. Keys's team looked at three imperfect measures to measure body fat: water displacement, skin calipers, and the body mass index. In the landmark study, Keys and his coauthors hedged their findings significantly. "Again the body mass index [. . .] proves to be, if not fully satisfactory, at least as good as any other relative weight index as an indicator of relative obesity."[14] The BMI emerged as the least objectionable about three imprecise measures. Its claim to fame? Accurately diagnosing "obesity" about 50 percent of the time. As recently as 2011, that number held fast, as the *Journal of Obstetrics and Gynecology* found that the BMI detected less than 50 percent of "obesity" cases in Black, white, and Hispanic women.[15]

In his study, Keys renamed Quetelet's Index the "body mass index." And with that, a statistician's largely forgotten index entered the world of individual health care—despite the fact that its inventor had designed the index for population-level statistical analysis, not as a diagnostic tool for physicians.

Keys's work ushered in a decades-long era of repeatedly changing the definitions of "overweight" and "obese." In the early 1980s, the National Institutes of Health (NIH) convened a conference on the health implications of obesity that focused on the creation of medical categories for fat bodies. Those categories weren't defined by increased health risks or the likely onset of specific health outcomes. Instead, they were defined by a percentage of the population at the time. For example, the conference defined "overweight" people as those in the 85th percentile of the population by weight, and "severe overweight" as those in the 95th percentile.[16] "Obesity" and "severe obesity," by contrast, were measured not by BMI but using calipers for a skin fold test. But neither "overweight" nor "obesity" were defined based on specific health concerns. Rather, they were defined by being *fatter than everyone else*. These new categories didn't articulate an existing health risk; they created a new category altogether. Nevertheless, the NIH adopted the new categories. And with that, this perennially imperfect measurement was relatively quickly enshrined in US public policy.[17]

Just ten years later, in 1995, the World Health Organization (WHO) adopted the BMI as an international standard for measuring patients' weight. They did so by convening the International Obesity Task Force, largely made up of directors of medical weight-loss clinics—stakeholders who stood to profit from expanding the pool of people who were expected to seek medical treatments for their weight. Researchers recommended to the task force that the existing standards for a "normal" BMI were too restrictive, and that the range of acceptable BMIs should be expanded. In other words, researchers believed that a larger range of body weights could be medically considered healthy. The task force overrode that recommendation. Instead of expanding the parameters for its definition of a "healthy weight," the task force restricted them. And they extended the BMI—previously used primarily for adults—to use with children.[18]

Later, the *British Medical Journal* reported that the lion's share of the budget for this change in definitions of who was "overweight" or "obese" was furnished by Abbott and Roche, both of whom had weight-loss drugs stuck in the FDA's then notoriously restrictive approval process for weight-loss drugs.[19] From the *British Medical Journal*'s coverage:

> On the question of what was motivating sponsors to be involved, Tim Gill, a representative of the task force and executive officer of the Australasian Society for the Study of Obesity, said that although the task force focused mainly on prevention rather than treatment, drug companies benefited anyway from raised public awareness, as they needed to sell products to only a tiny proportion of people defined as diseased to achieve a good market.[20]

In 1998, the NIH once again changed their definitions of "over-weight" and "obese," this time to align with the new guidance from WHO. In so doing, they substantially lowered the threshold to be medically considered fat. CNN wrote that "Millions of Americans became 'fat' Wednesday—even if they didn't gain a pound" —as the federal government adopted a controversial method for determining who is considered overweight."[21] Within two short years, new weight-loss drugs from Abbott and Roche had been approved for sale in the United States. And with newly expansive definitions of who could be considered by medical institutions to be too fat, their pool of potential patients—and customers—had increased dramatically.

The adoption of these new standards for thinness grew the customer base for weight-loss industries. And it also paved the way for a new public health panic: the "Obesity Epidemic."

By the turn of the millennium, the BMI's simple arithmetic had become a *de rigeur* part of doctor visits. Charts depicting startling spikes in our overall fatness took Americans by storm, all the while failing to acknowledge the frequent changes in definition that, in large part, contributed to those spikes. At best, this failure in reporting is misleading. At worst, it stokes resentment of bodies that have already borne the blame for so much and fuels medical mistreatment of fat patients.[22, 23]

Since then, the cultural conversations about fatness, health, and respect reflect that significant failure in reporting. Views haven't progressed, although the science has started to. In 2015, researchers at Harvard University and the University of Sheffield released a study identifying six different types of obesity,[24] each of which had their own etiology and types of treatment. By the next year, researchers at Massachusetts General Hospital had observed fifty-nine different types.[25] With so many types of fatness—and more still being identified—what could the brutally oversimplified arithmetic of the BMI meaningfully contribute to our understanding and treatment of fat patients? As clinical psychiatry professor Sylvia R. Karasu put it, "Despite all the progress we have made in science since Quetelet's nineteenth-century index, we are still far from being able to measure our body's fat conveniently and accurately in a physician's office."[26]

But more than that, science and history alike have repeatedly demonstrated that a measure built by and for white people is even less accurate for—and may even lead to the misdiagnosis and mistreatment—of People of Color. According to studies published by the Endocrine Society, the BMI overestimates fatness and health risks for Black people.[27] Meanwhile, according to the WHO, the BMI underestimates health risks for Asian communities, which may contribute to underdiagnosis of certain conditions.[28] On a global scale, declaring obesity to be first a "global epidemic" has created profit streams for weight loss and pharmaceutical companies around the world. Now, instead of competing for individual customers, those companies can compete for insurance coverage and state contracts. As with any global issue, news coverage of the "obesity epidemic" includes coverage of where the purported epidemic is at its worst. The nations with the highest rates of BMI-defined obesity are those for which the BMI was never designed: Indigenous island nations like Nauru, the Cook Islands, Palau, Tonga, Tuvalu, the Marshall Islands, Samoa, and the Federated States of Micronesia.[29]

And, despite the purported universality of the BMI, it papers over significant sex-based differences in the relationship between body fat and the BMI.[31] That is, because so much of the research behind the BMI was conducted on those assigned male at birth, those assigned female may be at greater health risk if their diagnosis hinges on a measurement never designed for them. The BMI proves a significant barrier to essential health care for trans and nonbinary people, regardless of their assigned sex. Doctors frequently mandate a lower BMI from trans patients[31] before providing lifesaving,[32] gender-affirming health care.

Beyond that, the BMI has contributed to a common misconception in our popular imagination: it's just a matter of time until people with "overweight" and "obese" BMIs become chronically ill, disabled, or otherwise fall to ill health. But despite our collective certainty, the scientific research into the population-level health of fat people is far from clear-cut. Indeed, researchers have found a wide range of health measures and predictors in which people whose BMIs are "overweight" and "obese" fare *better* than their "healthy weight" counterparts. Researchers have labeled this collective phenomenon "the obesity paradox," so named for the conflict between research findings and popular expectations about fat people's health. One research review of forty studies with participants totaling over 250,000 found "significantly lower risks for total mortality and cardiovascular mortality in overweight patients. These mortality risks were not increased in obese patients compared with normal-weight subjects."[33] The "paradox," then, is that someone can be both fat *and* not at increased risk of mortality or other selected health conditions.

The so-called obesity paradox has been upheld time and time again. In a 2019 study tracking 6.8 million patients in the Korean National Health Insurance Service, being underweight and having diabetes were associated with an increased risk of Parkinson's disease, but being fat wasn't.[34] In a 2020 paper discussing the ethics of clinical weight-loss recommendations, it was noted that the much-touted benefits of weight loss were the benefits of increased exercise and dietary changes—even if no weight was lost. "Systematic reviews and meta-analyses show how health benefits via lifestyle changes can prevent and treat diabetes and heart disease *irrespective of weight loss*."[35] A Brazilian national analysis of patients with type 2 diabetes found "no significant correlation" between an individual's BMI and their blood sugar levels. They did, however, find correlations with lower educational levels and with diets low in whole grains. (The researchers noted that whole grains require time to cook, time many low-income people don't have.)[36] Results like these suggest that economic justice—not weight loss—could be a key component of the management of type 2 diabetes.

Even when a perceived link between a person's BMI and their health risks seems solid in the popular imagination, research often

paints a more complicated picture. A 2020 research paper complicated the much-touted link between BMI and COVID-19, finding that fat Black people and fat People of Color in the UK were
1.75 to 2.56 times more likely to test positive for COVID-19 than
their white counterparts.[37] (Thin Black people and thin People of
Color showed no disparity in test results.) Because most of these
studies don't take social dynamics into account, like income level,
discrimination, and other social determinants of health, they point
to biological causes for what may well be social problems. Findings
like these—and popular perception of them—provide an unsettling
echo of the BMI's racist history. Instead of further examining these
sized and racialized disparities, most of us hear *high BMI* and *health
risk* and intuitively, often uncritically, believe it to be true. But even
scratching the surface of the experiences of fat Black, Indigenous
and People of Color quickly complicates the simple arithmetic of
those judgments.

Researchers and media alike have written a great deal about the
so-called obesity paradox, often without interrogating its premise:
the assumption that fat people *cannot* be in good health. That is,
the phenomenon of healthy fat people is only a paradox if you cannot conceive of fat people being healthy. And, thanks to pervasive,
decades-long conversations about the obesity epidemic, as defined
by the BMI, most of us cannot believe the simple fact that *any fat
person* could have good health outcomes. After all, as the BMI has
taught us, the aberration of fatness *itself* is a transgression of health.
By definition, we believe, fat people simply cannot be healthy. And
structures like the BMI lend false legitimacy to our own faulty, un-
examined assumptions.

Despite its fraught history and proven inaccuracies, the BMI
soldiers on. The science has disproved many common myths about
size, health, and weight loss for years.[38] Yet instead of recognizing
the evolving and increasingly complex science around fatness, people
stick stubbornly to the truisms that allow them to freely marginalize fat people. Like phrenology and positivist criminology before it,

the body mass index is a product of its social context, which proudly held up whiteness as an idealized kind of normalcy. Because of its ubiquity in public policy and global institutions, the BMI remains— even though its biggest champions say it's not an effective measure of fatness, much less overall health.

"DOCTORS ARE UNBIASED JUDGES OF FAT PEOPLE'S HEALTH. FAT PEOPLE DON'T LIKE GOING TO THE DOCTOR'S OFFICE BECAUSE THEY DON'T LIKE HEARING THE TRUTH."

In 2018, Ellen Maud Bennett's obituary made headlines. Bennett had planned for her own passing. She had been diagnosed with cancer, but her diagnosis arrived too late for treatment: it was terminal, and she had only days to live. All that was left for Bennett, then, was to prepare for the end of her life. She selected her own obituary photo ("I look so good for someone almost dead!"). She asked her siblings for some of her favorite foods: lobster from Nova Scotia, shrimp wonton soup from Victoria. And she told her siblings what to include in her obituary. The memorial statement read:

> A final message Ellen wanted to share was about the fat shaming she endured from the medical profession. Over the past few years of feeling unwell she sought out medical intervention and no one offered any support or suggestions beyond weight loss. Ellen's dying wish was that women of size make her death matter by advocating strongly for their health and not accepting that fat is the only relevant health issue.[1]

Ellen Maud Bennett's final wish struck a chord. Fat people and our loved ones alike shared the obituary on social media and recounted our own experiences of the health-care system, many rife with stories of misdiagnosis and mistreatment. Some fat people had fought for years for basic tests and treatments, only to be told to come back when they'd lost weight.[2] Others avoided that fight, postponing care to avoid the shame and condescension so many of us have faced from health-care providers. Regardless of their strategies for dealing with health care, these fat people had clearly learned the same lesson: like the rest of the world, health-care providers simply treat fat people differently.

And they're not alone. Rebecca Hiles was told that her respiratory issues—including bloody coughing fits—were due to her weight. In a 2018 story for *Cosmopolitan*, Hiles shared that it took six years for a doctor to properly diagnose her bloody coughing fits not as a natural outcome of her fatness but as lung cancer. When she was finally diagnosed, she was angry: "When my surgeon told me a diagnosis five years prior could've saved my lung, I remember a feeling of complete and utter rage. Because I remembered the five years I spent looking for some kind of reason why I was always coughing, always sick. Most of all, I remembered being consistently told that the reason I was sick was because I was fat."[3] Patty Nece shared her story of mistreatment with the *New York Times* in 2016. Nece sought care from an orthopedist for her hip pain. According to the *Times*, Nece had lost roughly seventy pounds when she finally saw the doctor. "He came to the door of the exam room, and I started to tell him my symptoms. [. . .] He said: 'Let me cut to the chase. You need to lose weight.'"[4] That doctor diagnosed Nece with "obesity pain." Later, Nece found out she had progressive scoliosis, a condition that isn't caused by being fat but can be caused by consistent physical activity in adulthood.[5] These stories are anecdotal, yes, but they are plentiful.

My own experiences seeking health care have left much to be desired. Doctors have refused to treat me, refused to touch a body from which they recoiled. Health-care providers have taken my blood pressure multiple times, more ready to assume their cuff had malfunctioned than that my own blood pressure wasn't elevated. No, my experiences haven't been good. But they have been nothing like the sometimes catastrophic experiences of patients like Ellen Maud Bennett, Rebecca Hiles, and Patty Nece. In reading stories like theirs, I find myself reeling with grief, overwhelmed with the vertigo of deepened mistrust.

For many fat people, going to the doctor's office can be a cause for dread. Our experiences of health care aren't experiences of getting a hard dose of some objective truth but of a stubborn refusal to address our symptoms, to believe our accounts of our own bodies, or even to treat us at all. A 2014 study published in *Basic and Applied Social Psychology* showed that 53 percent of women say they've been shamed by their doctors: "Regardless of whether the person felt guilt or shame, self-condemnation and the perception that the physician intentionally induced the emotion were associated exclusively with negative outcomes (e.g., ceasing physician visits), whereas negative attributions about one's behavior (rather than the self as a whole) were associated with primarily beneficial outcomes."[6] And while that may seem bleak, a 2012 study found that fat patients actually *overestimate* the respectful treatment we'll get from doctors, and that "few patients underestimated physician respect."[7] In other words, as low as fat patients' expectations of health-care providers are, they may still be too optimistic. A 2019 research review of twenty-one studies addressing medical anti-fatness found ten themes in fat people's health care: "contemptuous, patronizing, and disrespectful treatment, lack of training, ambivalence, attribution of all health issues to excess weight, assumptions about weight gain, barriers to health-care utilization, expectation of differential health-care treatment, low trust and poor communication, avoidance or delay of health services, and 'doctor shopping.'"[8] Simply put, fat patients' experiences of bias in health care aren't the exception; they're the norm.

If those fat patients hold multiple marginalized identities, bias only intensifies. For those of us not thin, not white, not nondisabled, not cisgender, not straight, there is a strong chance we will face bias from our health-care providers. In some cases, that will result in misdiagnosis. And some of those misdiagnoses will result in otherwise preventable deaths. The specific experiences of fat Black people, Indigenous people, and People of Color in health care are deeply under-researched, but the data around the health-care experiences of BIPOC communities broadly are deeply troubling. Disparities in health care mean that Black women are significantly more likely to die from breast cancer.[9] Black patients of all genders are routinely undertreated for pain due to providers' fantastical and explicitly racist beliefs about Black people having "less sensitive nerve endings than whites."[10]

The experiences of fat transgender and nonbinary people also remain underexamined in scholarly research. Many doctors willing to offer transition-related surgery still place BMI limits on the patients they will treat. A 2020 paper published in *Endocrine Practice* found that high BMIs were a substantial barrier to gender confirmation surgeries. Looking at 1,457 patients at the Mount Sinai Center for Transgender Medicine and Surgery, researchers found that 26 percent of patients had BMIs in the "obese" range at their initial consult, and that their weight-loss attempts led to "no statistically significant change in the rate of obesity."[11] Still, trans patients are regularly excluded from what can be lifesaving care on the basis of their weight—a bodily attribute that researchers and health-care providers alike still don't know how to change. And regardless of size, trans patients' experiences of health care in the United States remain bleak. According to the National LGBTQ Task Force and the National Center for Transgender Equality, 19 percent of transgender Americans have been denied care because of their gender identity or presentation, and 28 percent experienced harassment in medical settings.[12]

Perhaps most troublingly, data on the attitudes of health-care providers toward fat patients bear out fat patients' anxiety. For twenty years, studies that set out to examine anti-fat bias in medical settings have confirmed not only that it exists, but that it is incredibly prevalent among health-care providers of all stripes. In 2001, the

International Journal of Obesity published a study that found those anti-fat judgments caused material differences in the outcomes of care received by fatter patients. In office visits with fat patients, many physicians wrote notes "suggesting a belief that those who are overweight must also be unhappy and unstable," including comments like "this woman has a very unhappy life," "suffering underlying depression," and "most likely a drug addict."[13] Of the 122 primary care physicians who participated in the study, 10 percent suggested antidepressants for their fat patients. Fat patients also received shorter visits. The average office visit for a thin patient with a migraine is thirty-one minutes. For a patient with an BMI considered as "obese," that number drops to twenty-two. "Certainly if physicians give additional tests (whether weight-related or not) to heavier patients, they may be giving compromised care—they are doing more tests in a much shorter period of time. [. . .] The pattern of responses seems to reflect that physicians feel more negativity toward heavier patients." The fatter the patient, the more likely the doctor will describe the office visit as "a waste of their time" and the patients as "more annoying." Physicians predicted that if they were to see more fat patients, they would "like their jobs less."

A 2003 study published in *Obesity Research* confirmed that "primary care physicians view obesity as largely a behavioral problem and share our broader society's negative stereotypes about the personal attributes of obese persons." Of the 620 participating physicians, more than half described fat patients as "awkward, unattractive, ugly, and noncompliant." Over one-third called fat patients "weak-willed, sloppy or lazy."[14] Among health professionals who specialize in the study and treatment of fat patients, research findings are similarly bleak. In a 2012 study, researchers used the Implicit Association Test to measure weight bias in 389 researchers, students, and clinicians who said they specialized in obesity. Participants overwhelmingly believed that fat people were "lazy, stupid, and worthless." The study's authors explain that anti-fat bias is so pervasive "that even those most knowledgeable about the condition infer that obese people have blameworthy behavioral characteristics that contribute to their problem (i.e., being lazy). Furthermore, these biases extend to core characteristics of intelligence and personal worth."[15]

Fat people's mistrust of health-care providers can't be easily shrugged off as imagined or the result of a few bad apples. Research consistently shows that, like the rest of the population living in anti-fat communities, health-care providers have learned to perpetuate anti-fatness. But unlike most of us, they're often in positions of extraordinary power. Providers' bias doesn't end with their own perceptions, either—it measurably impacts fat people's care. A 2013 study in the journal *Obesity* found that doctors "build less emotional rapport" with fat patients.[16] And a 2001 study in the *International Journal of Obesity* found that "although physicians prescribed more tests for heavier patients, [they also spent] less time with them, and viewed them significantly more negatively."[17] A 2018 study found that nurses who believed in weight controllability—that is, that people can control their own weight and that fat people are failing to control our own behaviors—also reported greater weight-based discrimination in medical settings, ultimately negatively impacting their care of fatter people.[18] Some researchers even argue that weight stigma is a primary driver of the so-called obesity epidemic,[19] citing a range of studies showing that experiences of discrimination and internalized weight stigma cause weight gain and that health-care providers' bias leads many fat people to postpone health care or avoid it altogether—another driver of poor health outcomes. A 2019 study published in *Women's Reproductive Health* found that patients seeking reproductive health care can have negative experiences "shaped by dominant notions of health, the body, motherhood and fatness."[20] A follow-up commentary in the journal cautioned that "providers need to examine their own biases" lest they allow those biases to influence the quality of care they provide to expecting parents.[21]

Anti-fatness also extends to the field of dietetics. A 2007 study found that dietetics students believed fat patients to be noncompliant, have poorer health, and have lower "diet quality," despite being provided with similar patient profiles for fat and thin patients.[22] (In treatment, the study found, there was no statistically significant difference in motivation, receptiveness, or success in treatment.)

Notably, anti-fat bias has also been shown to shape the care and health outcomes of gay men, even if those gay men aren't fat. In 2019, *Obesity: A Research Journal* published new findings on weight stigma in LGBTQ communities, which already experience high rates of medical discrimination, leading to significant health disparities.[23] Researchers found that LGBTQ people experience similar rates of weight stigma to straight, cisgender people, but that gay men were most likely to internalize that weight stigma. Coming to believe and internalize weight stigma, according to the study, is also "associated with poorer mental [health-related quality of life], lower eating self-efficacy, and increased eating to cope, controlling for demographics and BMI." Gay men were more likely to believe the stigma leveled against fat people was true and correct, and they also experienced an increase in negative health outcomes across the board. The study's authors found that their findings underscore the need among healthcare providers to recognize that some people "may be vulnerable to stigma and unfair treatment because of both their body weight and their sexual identity." This awareness not only could make medical appointments more comfortable and productive but also may help medical professionals understand that stigma puts people "at additional risk for compounding stressors and adverse health outcomes."

For physicians, data show that anti-fat bias often predates completion of their degree. A 2014 study published in the journal *Obesity* found that 67 percent of medical students exhibit overt bias against fat patients, with over half of respondents characterizing fat people as a whole as being "lazy, unmotivated, noncompliant, and unhealthy."[24] Another study in *Obesity* asked medical students about their beliefs about fat people: 16 percent agreed with the statement "I really don't like fat people much," 13.5 percent reported that they "have a hard time taking fat people seriously," and 36.6 percent—over one-third of students surveyed—believed that "fat people tend to be fat pretty much through their own fault."[25] While one would hope that medical

school would decrease such overt bias, some data indicates that going to medical school and other health-care training programs can
increase anti-fat bias in future physicians. A 2015 study published in
Medical Education randomly sampled forty-nine US medical schools
and looked at attitudes of 1,795 medical students enrolled there.
Researchers found that implicit and explicit bias correlated with
students who had less positive contact with fat patients and with
students who had "more exposure to faculty role modelling of discriminatory behaviour or negative comments" about fat patients.
Even seemingly unrelated trainings, like those on how to deal with
"difficult" patients, increased implicit bias. On the whole, the study
found implicit bias decreased but explicit bias increased in medical
school.[26] Medical school provides a wealth of technical knowledge
and skills, but as it stands, addressing anti-fat bias in health care isn't
one of them.

Of course, many health-care providers gravitate toward their
field out of a desire to help others. And often, they do. But like any
of us, health-care providers have their growing edges, filling in the
blanks of others' lived experience with assumptions, often gleaned
from widely held biases. But unlike the rest of us, they are in extraordinary positions of power, interpreting and divining our bodies. And
when those growing edges aren't pushed, their good-hearted desire
to provide care is undermined by their own lack of understanding.
When it comes to fat people, health-care providers, like the rest of
us, are products of a society that values thinness above all else. The
problem isn't that doctors are bad people or that health-care providers are intentionally malicious movie villains, cackling and tying the
rest of us to the train tracks. The problem is that their biases—the
biases so many of us hold—aren't challenged in their training. And
fat people pay the price.

OPPORTUNITIES FOR ACTION FOR PATIENTS

✦ *Talk to your doctor about their weight-loss recommendations.* If your health-care provider prescribes weight loss, regardless of your size, ask follow-up questions to draw out their thinking and encourage reflection. Follow-up questions could include:

- What methods do you recommend for weight loss? What are their success rates?
- Is weight loss the most successful course of treatment here? Are other treatments available? What are their success rates?
- Most attempts to lose weight in the short term lead to weight gain in the long term. What happens if I don't lose weight, or if I regain it?

✦ *Support fat loved ones seeking health care.* If a fat friend or family member expresses anxiety about going to the doctor's office, offer to go with them. You can provide emotional support, and if you're not a fat person, your presence may well change that health-care provider's behavior, blunting the worst of their biases.

OPPORTUNITIES FOR ACTION FOR HEALTH-CARE PROVIDERS

✦ *Assess your own biases.* There are a number of tools for assessing anti-fat bias, including research questionnaires like the Fat Phobia Scale,[27] the Attitudes Toward Obese Persons Scale,[28] Figure Rating Scales,[29] and Harvard University's Project Implicit, a quick web-based assessment of implicit bias.[30]

✦ *Confront bias in yourself and your colleagues.* Regardless of our own biases and beliefs, we can all do more to confront anti-fatness when we see it. If you hear your colleagues talking to or about fat patients in a dismissive or judgmental way, broach the topic with them. While the conversation may

be uncomfortable, many health-care providers are likelier
to take in suggestions from their peers than their patients,
especially if those patients are the target of their biased
beliefs and practices. And remember, the problem here isn't
too many providers taking imperfect action in the face of
anti-fat bias, it's that many don't take *any* action in the face
of anti-fat bias. All you have to do is *anything*.

✦ *Research medical anti-fatness.* Just as you invested time in
learning biased attitudes toward fat people, you can invest
time in uprooting those biases. Find your favorite research database and look for research around anti-fat bias
in medical care, using search terms like "weight stigma in
health care" or "attitudes toward obese patients." Read the
studies cited in this chapter. Seek out books that address the
racialized medicalization of fat people, like Sabrina Strings's
Fearing the Black Body: The Racial Origins of Fat Phobia and
Da'Shaun Harrison's *Belly of the Beast: The Politics of Anti-
Fatness as Anti-Blackness.* And keep an eye on emerging
research into effective interventions in medical anti-fatness.

✦ *Look into best practices for care of fat patients.* You can also find
further reading and resources on addressing anti-fatness in
health care through the Association for Size Diversity and
Health (asdah.org) and the National Association to Advance
Fat Acceptance (naafa.org). Resist the urge to prioritize
guidance from thin people over that of fat people. Remember that the people who can best tell you how to care for fat
patients are your fat patients themselves.

"FAT PEOPLE ARE EMOTIONALLY DAMAGED AND COPE BY 'EATING THEIR FEELINGS.'"

Despite being central to our understanding of fatness and fat people today, "emotional eating" has only recently been popularized as a cultural concept. And both the history and science behind the concept of emotional eating paint a much more complex picture than our often oversimplified cultural understanding of it.

Emotional eating as a framework had a number of champions throughout the twentieth century, few more dedicated than Jean Nidetch. Nidetch was the founder of Weight Watchers, one of the world's largest weight-loss companies, and a celebrity in her own right, dating Hollywood legends like Glenn Ford and Fred Astaire.[1] She spoke openly about her struggles with what she described as emotional eating, most notably to a crowd of sixteen thousand in New York City's Madison Square Garden in 1973. According to the *New York Times*, the event "was like a revival. Bob Hope, Pearl Bailey and Roberta Peters were there, but the star, in a drift of white chiffon, was Mrs. Nidetch, a combination Cinderella and Aimee Semple McPherson with her own evangelical message: Overeating is an emotional problem with an emotional solution."[2] Her own relationship to food was certainly shaped by her emotional life. Nidetch described receiving food as a comfort in early childhood: "I'm sure that whenever I had a fight with the little girl next door, or it was raining and I couldn't go out, or I wasn't invited to a birthday party, my mother gave me a piece of candy to make me feel better."[3] She spoke about eating whole boxes of Mallomars, which she hid in a laundry hamper and consumed in secret.[4] For her, the explanation was simple: she was an emotional eater.

Nidetch told her personal story with the language and frameworks available to her at the time. But since then, new frameworks have emerged, lending new light and shading to what Nidetch termed "emotional eating." Since Nidetch's time, diagnostic criteria have been established for a range of eating disorders. It wasn't until 1980 that eating disorders were added to the Diagnostic and Statistical Manual (DSM), the American Psychiatric Association's guide to identifying and diagnosing mental illnesses. And binge eating disorder, estimated by the National Eating Disorders Association to be one of the most prevalent eating disorders in the United States, wasn't added until 2013.[5] Binge eating disorder is marked by binge episodes of "eating alone because of being embarrassed by how much one is eating" and is usually followed by "marked distress regarding binge eating."[6] According to the DSM, some emotional eating rises to the level of disordered eating. Recognizing that emotional eating can tip into concerning disordered-eating patterns more often than we might think recasts our understanding of stories of weight loss and gain. Suddenly, stories like Nidetch's look less inspirational and more troubling. They become different kinds of problems that call for different kinds of solutions.

Even without patterns of disordered eating, plenty of people eat for reasons beyond hunger: to comfort themselves, to celebrate, to socialize, to pass the time. They are all valid reasons to eat food, and most of us have engaged in most of them. Like thin people, fat people eat for a range of reasons. But unlike thin people, our food choices are monitored, picked apart, looked to as explanations for our bodies. For fat people, food is rarely allowed to be just *food*. Instead, it becomes laden with cultural meaning. Our food choices become battlegrounds, subject to intense judgment from those around us. Through the prism of that judgment, ordering a salad isn't just picking a meal we like, it's a message that we know we're fat, and we're trying our hardest to become thin. Through that same prism, ordering French fries isn't just a matter of picking a side, it's seen as a commitment to "unhealthy behaviors." All of that monitoring and judgment fundamentally shapes how we view fat people and food. Many are constantly scanning for meaning, looking for ways to explain what they already believe: fat people have failed our bodies.

Because of that, conversations about fat people, trauma, eating disorders, and emotional eating can take on high stakes, a kind of referendum on *why we are the way we are*. But regardless of how our bodies came to be, fat people's own narratives of our bodies ought to be respected and centered. Instead, too often, our accounts of our own bodies are steamrolled by dismissive, judgmental, and pathologizing anti-fat rhetoric. Some fat people may see their relationship to food as being shaped by trauma, eating disorders, or other emotional or experiential factors. Others may not. Either way, fat people's narratives of our own bodies should be the ones we hear out, even if they differ from what others might expect.

The idea that fatness is linked to trauma is one that resonates with some fat people, though certainly not all. Research has borne out some connections between trauma and higher body weights. The CDC and Kaiser Permanente's Adverse Childhood Experiences (ACE) study was started by a physician running a weight-loss clinic. In 1985, Vincent Felitti, head of Kaiser Permanente's Department of Preventive Medicine in San Diego, ran the HMO's weight-loss clinic. The clinic used something called supplemented absolute fasting,[7] an extremely low-calorie diet popularized through programs like Optifast, which, at the time, started patients on just 420 calories per day.[8] (A few years later, Oprah Winfrey used Optifast, then wheeled a red wagon full of beef and pork fat onto her talk show to represent the weight she had lost.) Felitti noticed that his weight-loss clinic had a high dropout rate—roughly 50 percent of fat patients left before completing his program. Felitti only recognized the possible link between body weight and trauma when one patient, on significant weight regain, disclosed she had begun binge eating after a coworker had expressed interest in sleeping with her. After further discussion, the patient disclosed "a lengthy incest history with her grandfather."[9] Felitti was unaware of the patient's disturbing past. He hadn't asked any patients about their histories with trauma. Shortly thereafter, taking trauma histories from his patients at the clinic showed that 55 percent had experienced some form of childhood sexual abuse, and others had experienced additional traumas at a young age.[10] And so, one of the largest-scale trauma studies in the United States was born. The ACE study has grown in scope since, though it was initially introduced not as a way to examine or treat trauma but as a way to make a method of extreme weight loss more effective.

The connection between body weight and trauma isn't limited to one's own lifetime either. The burgeoning field of epigenetics looks at the ways in which our genes are imprinted by our environment and life experiences, expressed differently, then passed to future genera- tions. A 2011 peer-reviewed article in *Maturitas* found that "more than 40 genetic variants have been associated with obesity and fat distribution. However, since these variants do not fully explain the heritability of obesity, other forms of variation, such as epigenetic marks must be considered."[11] Notably, epigenetic "imprints" can be caused not only by one's own childhood trauma but by harm done to our ancestors—including limited or altered access to nutrition, as one might experience through internment, imprisonment, colonization, or migration. According to a 2020 paper in *Trends in Endocrinology and Metabolism*, those experiences can be linked to higher body weights and "metabolic dysregulation." Indeed, these epigenetic imprints "can reprogram the epigenome of the germline (sperm and eggs), which transmits the susceptibility for disease to future generations through epigenetic transgenerational inheritance."[12] That is, ancestral expo- sure to famine or other dietary restriction can alter future generations' metabolisms and body sizes. Even when trauma is at play in our body size, it needn't be trauma we personally experienced in our lifetimes— it can be driven by the traumas of those who came before us.

Anti-fatness *itself* can be a trauma that is linked to higher body weights. Researchers have long known that experiences of anti-fat bias and weight stigma can drive what they call "obesogenic processes"—that is, processes that make people fatter.[13] And those experiences of anti-fatness are hardly rare. One study examined the mental health of ninety-three fat people in a weight-loss treatment center, focusing on assessing depression, self-esteem, body image, overall psychiatric symptoms, and mental health related to patients' experiences of weight stigma and internalization of anti-fat beliefs. Overwhelming numbers of participants had experienced anti-fatness: 97.9 percent said they had experienced nasty comments from family, 89.1 percent reported inappropriate comments from doctors, 86 percent said that loved ones were embarrassed to be associated with a fat person, and 78.3 percent reported that others had made negative assumptions about them.[14] Among fat people, experiences of anti-fatness are hardly niche. Even if some fat people do "eat our feelings," those feelings may stem from relentless anti-fatness from the individuals and institutions that surround us. Blaming fat people's coping mechanisms rather than the ceaseless anti-fatness amplified and perpetuated by so many around us is a way of blaming us for our own experiences of marginalization, trauma, and sometimes abuse.

These are powerful ideas: emotions and traumas determining the size and shape of our bodies. But in both cases, these frameworks around "emotional eating" ignore the fact that even in the absence of major trauma or emotional challenges, *fat people still exist*. Some of us may have bodies shaped by trauma, yes, and others don't. Fat people have existed in every corner of our world, in every moment of our history. Like thin people, some of us experience traumas that stay with us for a lifetime; others don't. Like thin people, some of us eat to comfort ourselves; others don't. While all of the studies cited in this chapter offer sound scientific understanding of a correlation, it is only that: a correlation. We simply *do not know* why some people are fat and others are thin. And the closer we get to an answer, the more complex the picture becomes. Pathologizing fatness as an expression of emotional brokenness is another way to marginalize fat people, first presuming that our bodies are cause for blame, then laying that blame squarely at our feet. Fat people are neither created nor defined by trauma, disordered eating, or some vague idea of emotional dysfunction. These ideas only function if we believe that fatness is a failure, a derivation from the natural ideal that is thinness. They only function when we lash together our drives to stigmatize mental illness, fatness, and trauma. And they allow us to do what so many of us are already driven to do: ruthlessly judge fat people, even in the name of compassion.

Looking at a fat person and drawing the conclusion that they have "eaten their feelings" is a judgment of someone else's character or life experience based solely on their appearance. It does not allow fat people to tell the stories of our own bodies. And more than that, it assumes fat people's bodies need explaining and those around us are owed an explanation for our deviant size. At the same time, this framework of "emotional eating" puts no onus on those demanding an explanation for fat bodies—those who are standing in judgment of us. It is straightforwardly judgmental to look at a fat person and invent a story of how our bodies came to be, how they must be a result of our broken brains, broken willpower, broken lives. It is straightforwardly judgmental to presume a fat person has experienced trauma or mental illness, then hold those imagined traumas and mental illnesses against them. We look to fatter people longing to judge them, and we do.

When we pass those judgments under the banner of "emotional eating," we use a broad and imprecise brush, often painting over more complex scientific findings and even unrelated conditions. We apply a scientific framework—utilizing our limited and oversimplified knowledge of some research—to lend legitimacy to the judgments of fat people that we were already going to make. We base our interpretation of fat bodies not in compassion, liberation, or support, but in the expectation that we are owed an explanation for the existence of fat bodies and that that explanation should further illustrate the perceived wretchedness, failure, and brokenness of fat people.

REFLECTION QUESTIONS

+ What does believing that fat people are emotionally damaged allow me to believe about myself and my own body? Do I feel virtuous by comparison? Frightened of becoming fat if I'm not vigilant enough with my own "emotional eating"?

+ What does believing that fat people are emotionally damaged allow me to believe about people who are fatter than me? What existing judgments of fat people does that belief serve?

+ Do I treat fat people differently if I believe they have experienced an eating disorder or major trauma? If so, how? What would it look like to extend compassion to *all* fat people, even those who haven't offered me an explanation for their fat bodies?

PART THREE

"FAT ACCEPTANCE GLORIFIES OBESITY"

"ACCEPTING FAT PEOPLE 'GLORIFIES OBESITY.'"

The year 2019 was a banner one for "glorifying obesity." Pop star Lizzo attended a Lakers game in Los Angeles, as celebrities often do. She wore something more conservative than her usual stage wear: an oversized knee-length black T-shirt dress with short black boots. The back of the dress was less conservative, with a cutout that showed the singer's buttocks in a thong.[1] The outfit showed less skin than what Lizzo wears on stage and in many of her music videos. It also showed less skin than the thin woman sitting next to Lizzo and the Laker Girls dancers on the court.[2] When the stadium's jumbotron camera found the singer, she greeted the audience with some signature twerking, then sat back down. Commenters on the internet had a heyday with what they saw as inappropriately sexualized behavior. The singer was met with an outcry. An army of internet commenters insisted that her actions "glorified obesity." In response, Lizzo said, "I'm the happiest I've ever been. I'm surrounded by love and I just want to spread that love—and also spread these cheeks."[3]

Lizzo wasn't the only fat person accused of glorifying obesity in 2019. That same year, fat influencer Anna O'Brien modeled for Gillette's Venus razors, wearing a two-piece bathing suit and standing in the surf in front of a blue ocean and bluer sky. Commenters swarmed, accusing the brand of glorifying obesity and promoting what they saw as risky health behaviors. The internet backlash was strong enough to warrant a statement from Gillette, defending their casting decision. "Venus is committed to representing beautiful women of all shapes, sizes, and skin types because ALL types of beautiful skin deserve to be shown."[4]

That summer, singer Miley Cyrus released the music video for her song "Mother's Daughter," which was met with controversy. The debate didn't center around Cyrus's latex bodysuit, the video's title cards with statements like "virginity is a social construct," or the video's kink aesthetic. No, the firestorm was prompted by a six-second shot of plus-size model Angelina Duplisea, lounging nude on a chaise, her back to the camera.[5] Like O'Brien and Lizzo, viewers insisted that one short shot of Duplisea rendered the video dangerous, promoting what they saw as an unhealthy ideal. It strains credulity that a six-second shot of one person in a three minute, forty-one second video promotes much of anything. Still, Duplisea appeared on *Good Morning Britain*, where cohost Piers Morgan tore into his guest for what he viewed as promoting and glorifying being fat.

"It's whether we should be celebrating a body image which is medically defined as highly dangerous," said Morgan, before reading out the model's height, weight, and BMI to the viewing audience, calling her "morbidly obese," an antiquated and stigmatizing term that has fallen out of favor even in most medical literature.

"I think if you were really concerned about glorifying obesity, you would take yourself off the air," said Duplisea. "You're fat, too."[6]

Wherever fat people go, accusations of glorifying obesity follow. They show up when fat people post pictures of ourselves at the beach, lounging in bathing suits; when fat people play sports or go to the gym; and when fat people dare to be seen as we are in popular media and ad campaigns. When done by thinner people, many of these activities are congratulated and celebrated—or at least, uncommented on. When fat people do them, we're told we are "glorifying obesity."

As a fat person, I have repeatedly been accused of glorifying obesity, even before my life as a minor public figure. Early on in my life on the internet, I posted a picture of myself in a new bathing suit on

LiveJournal, a new blogging platform. I was eighteen years old and had found a swimsuit I liked—it had a halter with a sweetheart neckline and a short ruched skirt. Compared to my thinner peers' bikinis, my one piece was conservative, bordering on dowdy. But for once, I felt comfortable. I took my photograph in the full-length mirror in my dimly lit bathroom, then posted it to LiveJournal. My account was public, not because of any desire for attention, but because it did not occur to me that a teenager with under a hundred followers would draw detractors. But in the days that followed, faceless commenters descended. One described in detail their revulsion at having to see my thighs and upper arms. Another commented scornfully about how a whale could think she looked cute. But most elevated their complaints to social issues, accusing me of "glorifying obesity."

I was confused. It was confusing. I was a recent high school graduate, writing regularly about my life, my crushes, school, my mental health. The only people who reliably read what I wrote were close friends. How could I be "glorifying" anything? I couldn't figure out where these complaints were coming from. But I did know that I was supposed to feel ashamed. And I did. I knew I was supposed to conceal my body, that any photograph of me would be met with scorn, derision, disgust, and accusations of "glorifying obesity." I knew I was supposed to hide. So I did that too.

Despite the near-constant invocation of "glorifying obesity," there isn't a clear definition of it. Even the most frequent users of the phrase do not define it. The dictionary says glory consists of "praise, honor, or distinction extended by common consent; renown." I would love to see us bestow praise, honor, and distinction on fat people. But photographing a fat person for a razor advertisement isn't an act of praise—it's just *a company hiring a fat model,* just as they'd hired countless thin models before. The objection to "glorifying obesity," then, isn't about bestowing glory on anything. It's about the audacity to treat fat people as if we were thin. Accusations of glorifying obesity aren't about behaviors, some threatening action fat people are taking. Fat people's accusers are not asking us to behave differently, not lodging a complaint about conduct that harms them personally in some way. In the cases of Lizzo, Anna O'Brien, and Angelina Duplisea, they were objecting to fat people receiving media attention without performing a pursuit of weight loss or expressing a deep and abiding shame about their appearances. Simply put, they don't want to look at us. And if they have to, they certainly don't want to see us depicted neutrally, sexually, or joyfully. That is because objections about fat people "glorifying obesity" are entirely rooted in bias and disgust. Those objections are products of deep anti-fat bias, weapons wielded to perpetuate anti-fatness, to literally and figuratively cut fat people down to size. Commenters don't seek to understand fatness or fat people; they do not want to see us. And the accusation that we are glorifying obesity and exacerbating a so-called obesity epidemic means that they aren't judging others based on appearance; they are vanquishing threats to public health. They aren't judgmental, the logic goes; they're fighting the good fight.

Follow-up conversations about "glorifying obesity" often reveal that the accuser is concerned that seeing fat people depicted without stigma will "encourage obesity." As if we all need to be reminded constantly that fatness means unending sorrow, public bullying, and a life of Sisyphean dieting, losing and regaining the same 30 pounds ad infinitum. It's a bizarre belief that borders on superstition: that seeing a picture of a happy fat person bears some deeper agenda, subliminally encouraging others around us to get fatter. It renders fat people Medusas—any thin person who gazes into our eyes might suddenly turn fat. And it renders thin people powerless and afraid in the face of fatness, which they may well be. But that fear is rooted in deep bias and disgust at seeing fat bodies and deep disapproval of fat people daring to show our faces and bodies in public. So "glorifying obesity" becomes a catchall to externalize that fear, prejudice, and revulsion. It becomes a way to admonish fat people for being seen and to rebuke anyone who would defend us. It's a way to express bias and pin it to some perceived bad behavior from fat people rather than where it is most deeply rooted: in patently discriminatory attitudes that advocate for publicly embracing thin people while pushing fat people into the shadows.

Perhaps the strangest part of accusations that fat people seek to "glorify obesity" is their stalwart refusal to acknowledge the ways in which we constantly celebrate thinness. We congratulate weight loss on sight, presuming that it is positive, desired, and inherently superior to weight gain. Tabloids breathlessly extoll the virtues of celebrities who "lose the baby weight" and tell us about formerly fat celebrities that are "totally unrecognizable" in thinness. (Celebrities who gain weight are relegated to the "worst beach bodies" issue, presented as a hall of shame for deviant bodies.) Magazines marketed to men offer countless tips on how to slash body fat percentages. Magazines marketed to women promise dramatic weight loss, often by way of fad crash diets, sometimes accompanied by a formerly fat person holding the waistband of their older, larger pants while a headline exclaims "Half her size! How she did it." In contrast, there are virtually *no stories* of individuals who decided to gain weight, nor are there cultural templates for congratulating weight gain. At every turn, thinness and weight loss are assumed to be positive and are accordingly celebrated. If anything is being glorified in media and our cultural traditions, it certainly isn't fatness.

Conversations about "glorifying obesity" don't advocate a specific outcome. They don't name or reject specific behaviors. They reveal a naked disgust with seeing fat bodies. And they reflect a deep anxiety about what will happen if fat people aren't constantly rejected, publicly humiliated, reminded of our mortality or perceived ill health. Where does that anxiety come from? Who does it serve? And what would happen if fat people were permitted to live our lives without a Greek chorus reminding us that we ought to be ashamed of ourselves and the only bodies we have?

Instead of giving uncritical voice to that discomfort, those concerned with "glorifying obesity" can and should plumb its depths. Examine it. Take it apart so you can see how it works and what in you is so driven to reject fatness and punish fat people. Reach for the contours of your concern. What would concretely change for you if fat people were more readily accepted? Are you concerned that there might be more fat people? Are you uncomfortable when you see fat people? Are you afraid that you might have to see more of us? What would happen if you saw a fat person in public without registering your disapproval? Has anyone offered unsolicited negative comments on your body before, or do you know someone who has experienced unwanted criticisms of their appearance? How did it feel? What did it change in them, or you?

"Glorifying obesity" isn't about fat people's behavior. It's about the biases and anxieties of people who usually aren't fat. Because of that, the work of uprooting the bias behind "glorifying obesity" has to belong solely to them. Familiarize yourself with your own catastrophizing assumptions and exclusionary behaviors. Learn how they show up, and learn to stop them.

OPPORTUNITIES FOR ACTION

+ *If you don't use the phrase "glorifying obesity"*: Interrupt those around you who accuse fat people of "glorifying obesity." If you're uncomfortable having this conversation, practice short rejoinders and follow-up questions. Some options:
  * "What is this person doing that 'glorifies' anything?"
  * "Wow—they're 'glorifying obesity' just by having their picture taken?"
  * "It looks to me like that person is just having a good day—good for them."
  * "I don't think it's bad to accept fat people as they are. It's troubling to me that you do."
  * "Leave her alone. Let her live her life."
+ *If you do use the phrase "glorifying obesity," or draw on similar frameworks*: Stop. Accusations of "glorifying obesity" are ways to reject fat people, to shame us, to punish us for being seen in public, and to caution others against accepting fat people. If you are uncomfortable seeing fat people, work that discomfort out on your own. Don't make fat people carry it for you.

"BODY POSITIVITY IS ABOUT FEELING BETTER ABOUT YOURSELF, AS LONG AS YOU'RE HAPPY AND HEALTHY."

The body positivity movement has become increasingly contested territory in recent years. Online and in person, arguments abound about who the movement is for and what it is intended to accomplish. Is body positivity a clarion call to body confidence, a way of repairing all comers' damaged body image, regardless of their size? Is it a social justice movement, organizing to end body-based oppression? Or has it gone too far, tipping into what comedian Bill Maher calls "fit-shaming"? Like many movements, body positivity's goals are disputed, held in tension by conflicting visions and strategies proposed by constituents, leaders, opponents, and onlookers alike. While the movement's future is debated, looking to its past can lend some clarity to increasingly muddy conversations about its provenance.

Body positivity's deepest roots lie in the fat acceptance movement, which itself is built on a foundation laid by fat Black women in the civil rights and welfare rights movements. Johnnie Tillmon was the first chair of the National Welfare Rights Organization,[1] and she refused to forego any core parts of her identity and life experience: "I'm a woman. I'm a black woman. I'm a poor woman. I'm a fat woman. I'm a middle-aged woman. And I'm on welfare. In this country, if you're any one of those things you count less as a human being. If you're all those things, you don't count at all."[2] Famed civil rights activist Ann Atwater, too, noted the impact of her fatness on how she was perceived and treated as a Black woman on welfare, telling a Duke University historian that her weight was brought up at the welfare office, where she was regularly asked if she was pregnant.[3] Their work for racial, economic, and gender justice made strides toward ending oppression and reaching collective liberation. And, beyond that, refusing to sideline or shy away from their experiences of fatness as Black women and advocates for justice provided frameworks and rhetoric that fat activists use to this day.

The 1960s saw a rise in organizing for fat acceptance, including direct action, movement building, and the founding of key fat advocacy organizations. In 1967, a radio host named Steve Post held a "fat-in" in New York City. Billed as a public protest of anti-fat discrimination, the action drew hundreds of protestors who burned diet books and carried signs reading "Fat Power."[4] The *New York Times* covered the event under the headline "Curves Have Their Day in Park; 500 at a 'Fat-in' Call for Obesity."[5] Protestors weren't insisting that others get fatter—they simply wanted kinder and more just treatment of fat people. Just one year later, Lew Louderback and Bill Fabrey cofounded the National Association to Advance Fat Acceptance (NAAFA). Louderback and Fabrey were both married to fat women, and both roundly rejected the biased and discriminatory treatment they saw leveled at their wives and other fat people.

By the 1970s, one NAAFA chapter splintered off to form the fat collective the Fat Underground. The collective was decidedly radical, founded by two fat Jewish feminists in Los Angeles. Its work took aim at anti-fat discrimination and what it viewed as one of its major drivers: the diet industry. Historian Charlotte Cooper credits the Fat Underground as "the first to theorise fat oppression, a major contribution to the movement."[6] They are also credited with coining a slogan that has stayed with fat and anti-diet movements for years: "A diet is a cure that doesn't work for a disease that doesn't exist."[7] It wasn't until the 1990s that organizations start using the term *body positivity*. Connie Sobczak, an author, and Elizabeth Scott, a licensed clinical social worker, founded an organization called the Body Positive in 1996. Sobczak had personally struggled with an eating disorder, and Scott specialized in treating them.

Within a few short years, corporations and retailers descended on *body positivity*, creating their own definitions of movements that had long existed and leveraging those self-serving definitions to power sales and increase their profits. By the turn of the millennium, the movement's defanging had begun. Dove launched its "Campaign for Real Beauty" in 2004. With it, they released "The Real Truth About Beauty: A Global Report" in which the brand claimed that just 2 percent of women worldwide would describe themselves as beautiful.[8] "Real Beauty" ads ran for more than a decade, featuring women who weren't models, a move that the brand framed as decidedly political but not *too* political. The ads were multiracial and featured women of multiple heights and builds. But they steadfastly excluded gender nonconforming people, trans women, disabled people, and fat people. They did not depict skin puckered by cellulite, punctuated with stretch marks, expansive in its rolling flesh. The rhetoric and aesthetic of "Real Beauty" challenged perceptions of beauty but only to a point. Presumably, as a multinational corporation owned by Unilever, that point was determined more by profits than an altruistic drive toward inclusion. If consumers' negative beliefs about bodies were already identified and primarily targeted at their own bodies, a feel-good ad campaign about self-confidence would presumably bolster the company's bottom line. If those same consumers carried biases that extended beyond their own bodies—biases against fat people, disabled people, or trans people—confronting them would be a thornier affair, one less likely to increase sales. Real beauty included more women than we'd previously thought, according to Dove, but not everyone. And certainly not fatties.

Dove's ads also defined body positivity as a solution to a problem of mindset. In one ad, a police sketch artist drew two portraits of women: one based on the woman's description of herself and one based on the description of a person who'd just met her. The women were mostly white, none appearing to be older than sixty. None had visible disabilities, none were fat, and none strayed from conventionally feminine gender expressions. Their descriptions of themselves emphasized their perceived flaws. ("She's fatter," says one woman, looking at the portrait drawn based on her self-description.) Reliably, the stranger's description was kinder, resulting in more conventionally attractive drawings with kinder expressions on their faces. The ad closes with a title card reading "You are more beautiful than you think," followed by Dove's corporate logo.[9] According to Dove, the women in their advertisement didn't need to change society, they just needed to change their mindsets. And Dove defined its constituency by omission, making it clear who didn't qualify for "real beauty." As media studies professor Ian Bogost wrote in *The Atlantic*, counter to its explicit goals, facets of the Real Beauty campaign "inadvertently imply there is a best body after all."[10]

In the years that followed, other corporations followed suit with ad campaigns that tried to deemphasize the importance of women's physical appearance, while simultaneously selling appearance-related products. Aerie, a women's clothing brand, has cast itself as a leading body positive retailer, launching ad campaigns like #aerieREAL, which featured unretouched photos of its models and celebrity brand ambassadors.[11] It partnered with the National Eating Disorders Association, including providing training for Aerie salespeople on the importance of body positivity. Its branding worked, landing it breathless media coverage from outlets like *Teen Vogue*, with headlines like "Aerie Is Completely Revamping Its Stores to Promote Body Positivity."[12] Aerie did not then, and does not now, carry plus sizes. It used the rhetoric of body positivity and a defanged version of fat acceptance but still wouldn't serve fat customers. In 2020, Halo Top low-calorie ice cream followed suit, launching its "Stop Shoulding Yourself" campaign.

> There are a lot of "shoulds," or pressures, that come with choosing wellness. Whether you reach for a pint or pop, Halo Top is here to take the pressure out of indulging in a sweet treat,

empowering dessert fans to enjoy what they love—not because they should, but because it feels good.[13]

Halo Top is unquestionably a diet food: its label trumpets its low-calorie count in giant print that towers over the name of the brand or its flavor. But using the language of body positivity allows a diet food to rebrand both its corporate image and its product. You aren't eating low-calorie ice cream because of anti-fat pressure to lose weight; you're doing it because you enjoy it. And you aren't just buying ice cream at the store, you're being empowered by it.

These clothing, skin care, and diet food companies were selling products designed to shape people's appearances. And in their ad campaigns, they used a diluted version of body positivity, fully divorced from the movement's roots, to claim that those products would paradoxically liberate consumers from caring about their appearance. These campaigns focused not on exploding the notion of beauty or on dismantling the social expectation for people (largely women) to appear beautiful. After all, if we obliterated the beauty standard, who would buy Dove skin care products or Aerie clothing? No, these campaigns squarely aimed at slightly expanding the standard of beauty, so that more people stay in its pursuit, buying products that promise them "real beauty." Capitalism is not and will not be a source of justice for any of us.

With each new ad campaign came a new wave of people self-identifying as body positive, joining what felt like a new and enticing movement without any shared definition of what precisely that movement aimed to accomplish. There was no shared commitment to ending anti-fatness, to anti-racist politics, to disability justice, nor even to some broad vision of ending oppression. They came for what they had been promised: better body image, more confidence, more happiness, and nothing beyond that. No movement building, no justice, no liberation. The goals of the body positivity movement that they had learned through advertising weren't about that. They weren't even about other people. The only goal was to view one's own body in a positive light. And that could be accomplished by any means that individual saw fit, including reassuring themselves that they're "not fat" or "not that fat," maintaining that they "look healthy," in contrast to fat and disabled people, and insisting on *happiness and health* for the movement they had just discovered and conquered. These expensive, large-scale advertising campaigns reached a wider audience than fat activists ever had before, and the influx of newcomers drowned out the movement's long-standing leaders and constituents alike. In less than a decade, the ownership of body positivity shifted to the hands of thin people, white people, class-privileged people, nondisabled people—most of whom didn't belong to the communities that paved the way for the movement.

Happy and healthy is a relatively new interjection in a movement that has historically fought for fat acceptance and offered so much to those in eating disorder recovery. For fat people and people in recovery alike, *happy and healthy* are slippery targets. In its contemporary iteration, our cultural definition of health depends on thinness. "Get healthy" is used as a euphemistic shorthand for losing weight. Fat people are pressured to change our appearance out of a purported concern for our health, diagnosed solely by looking at us. For the lion's share of its history, body positivity has concerned itself primarily with institutional and structural barriers to fat liberation and recovery from eating disorders—preconditions for fat people and people with eating disorders to attain happiness and health.

For many of us, culturally dominant definitions of *happy* and *healthy* are out of reach. For people with mental illnesses, happiness can be more a battle than a point of arrival. For chronically ill people, health may feel forever out of reach, all stick and no carrot. And for any of us, regardless of ability or mental health, happiness and health are never static states. All of us fall ill, all of us experience emotions beyond some point of arrival called "happiness." And when those things happen—when we get sick, when we get sad—they shouldn't impinge on our perceived right to embrace and care for our own bodies. Ultimately, "as long as you're happy and healthy" just moves the goalposts from a beauty standard to equally finicky and unattainable standards of health and happiness. All of us deserve

peaceful relationships with our own bodies, regardless of whether or
not others perceive us as *happy* or *healthy*.

The expectation that body positive people appear healthy to
those around them is a product of anti-fatness and of an important facet of ableism: *healthism*. Healthism, as coined by sociologist Robert Crawford in 1980, is "the preoccupation with personal
health as a primary—often *the* primary—focus for the definition and
achievement of well-being; a goal which is to be attained primarily
through the modification of life styles."[14] For Crawford, healthism
flattened the health of whole populations from a dynamic and mul-
tifaceted issue with many and varied influences to a simple matter
of personal responsibility. Crawford saw health as inherently political, an outcome not of individual choices but of systems that create
and perpetuate poverty, racism, misogyny, and more. But under
healthism, health was a decidedly individual matter, not a systemic
one, which meant the individual was primarily responsible for their
own health. According to Crawford, "the solution rests within the
individual's determination to resist culture, advertising, institutional
and environmental constraints, disease agents, or, simply, lazy or
poor personal habits."[15]

In the midst of all this body-positive insistence on happiness
and health, nondisabled fat people often give in to healthism. When
health is a prerequisite for our participation in body positivity, we
defend ourselves not by pushing back against the exclusionary approach but by insisting we are the healthiest in order to earn entry
into a movement that once centered us. Often, we defend ourselves
by insisting that societal concerns about our health are rooted in
faulty and broad assumptions. We rattle off our test results and hospital records, citing proudly that we've never had a heart attack,
hypertension, diabetes. We proudly recite our gym schedules and
the contents of our refrigerators. Many fat people live free from
the complications popularly associated with their bodies. Many fat
people don't have diabetes, just as many fat people have loving partners, despite common depictions of us. Although we are not thin,
we proudly report, we are happy and we are healthy. We insist on

our goodness by relying on our health. But what we mean is that we are tired of automatically being seen as sick. We are tired of being heralded as dead men walking, undead specters from someone else's morality tale. Those defensive assertions about our health may not be incorrect, but they are deeply ableist, and they certainly don't reflect every fat person's reality. Some of us contend with chronic illness, mental illness, eating disorders, disabilities, abuse. Some of us have hypertension, diabetes, heart disease. For those fat people, *happy and healthy* is an alienating aspiration, one that drives out of body positivity the very people it ought to readily embrace.

None of this means that body positivity and its descendant, body neutrality, aren't worthy goals. It's hard to have a body, especially in a world that so deeply reviles fatness, rejecting it wherever it appears. All of us deserve to find peace in our own skin. But we cannot claim to be body positive and then promptly begin to gatekeep who can and cannot be part of the movements and frameworks that have brought so much healing to so many. Body positivity that fails to interrogate biases and systems of oppression will replicate them. Thin, white, nondisabled people will continue to proclaim their body positivity while simultaneously excluding disabled people, fat people, Black people, Indigenous people, and People of Color under the banner of *happy and healthy*. Those same thin, white, nondisabled people will continue to proclaim that they "feel fat," using fat people's bodies as props to illustrate their own anxieties and insecurities, without regard to how that impacts the fat people around them. Body positive influencers will continue to peddle expensive wellness remedies that serve as both a signifier of wealth for those who can afford it and a barrier to participation in body positivity for those who can't. And body positivity will continue to demand *happy and healthy* of its constituents, perpetuating healthism and excluding chronically ill and disabled people. Over time, the term *body positivity* will come to mean less and less, becoming more and more diluted until it means nothing at all. In the process, it will also continue to be wielded as a weapon against the very communities that brought it into being.

This crescendo of bias in body positivity has been growing for years. As a fat person, it's exhausting to witness. It's exhausting to see so many fat people pour so much work and energy into a movement that provides so much healing to so many, including thin people, and then watch those same thin people take their healing, claim the movement for their own, and slam the door behind them. It's demoralizing to watch the work of fat people be appropriated and defanged for the comfort and affirmation of the very people it seeks to hold accountable. And it's deflating to watch movements rooted in fat activism be appropriated to bolster the profits of corporations like Dove, Halo Top, and Weight Watchers. A body positivity that allows these cycles to persist will, ultimately, advocate only for those who can weather them, those with the power and privilege to remain unaffected by their harm, unmoved by those who are.

As those waves of exclusionary politics crash upon body positivity again and again, they erode it. The spirit of the radical work that organizers like Johnnie Tillmon and groups like the Fat Underground fought for is washed away. And so, too, are the many marginalized people whose experiences of oppression bar them from *happy and healthy*.

REFLECTION QUESTIONS

+ Do you describe yourself as "body positive"? Why or why not?
+ Where did you first learn your definition of *body positivity*? Was it from someone connected to an organized movement? Was it clearly, concisely defined, or did the term itself conjure its meaning to you?
+ Does your definition of body positivity differ from those around you? Whose definitions does it depart from? How?
+ If you frequent fat activist or body positive spaces, what do you currently do to center the voices of those with more and different marginalized identities than your own? How effective are those tactics? What could you do to more effectively, fully center fat Black people, Indigenous people,

and People of Color; fat disabled people; fat trans people; and fat people with stigmatized chronic health conditions like hypertension and type 2 diabetes?

OPPORTUNITIES FOR ACTION

✦ *Confront and uproot your investment in healthism and ableism.* Assess your bias using tools like Harvard University's Implicit Association Test on disability, available at implicit. harvard.edu. Read the work of disabled writers, particularly those who hold multiple marginalized identities.

✦ *Read up on the histories of fat activism and body positivity.* Charlotte Cooper's *Fat Activism: A Radical Social Movement* and Evette Dionne's "The Fragility of Body Positivity: How a Radical Movement Lost Its Way"[16] are great places to start. For more on Johnnie Tillmon, read her landmark essay, "Welfare Is a Women's Issue"[17] and the long *New York Review of Books* read "Johnnie Tillmon's Battle Against 'The Man.'"[18]

"WE'RE IN THE MIDDLE OF AN OBESITY EPIDEMIC."

At the turn of the millennium, Americans learned that we were, suddenly, in the midst of an "obesity epidemic."

Some researchers and academics trace rising BMIs in the United States back to the 1960s,[1] others to the 1980s.[2] Those rates didn't suddenly spike in the late 1990s—they continued a steady climb that had been underway for years. For years, *Healthy People*, the US Department of Health and Human Services decennial report on national public health goals and priorities, was largely silent on fatness. Instead, its goals centered hunger as a public health issue. For most, including the nation's leading public health authorities, fatness wasn't a medical or public health issue.

But in a few short years, our rhetoric and beliefs around fatness and fat people shifted radically despite there being no sudden spike in fat people. There was a change afoot in medicine: fatness was no longer to be viewed as a matter of appearance but also as a matter of health. Consequently, fatness was redefined first as a disease, then as an epidemic. "The obesity epidemic" dripped from the mouths of reporters, news anchors, and talk show hosts nearly daily, often accompanied by silent b-roll of fat torsos, faceless, more bodies than people. By the mid-2000s, elected and appointed officials promoted *the obesity epidemic* to *the war on obesity*. In less than a decade, fatness had become a disease, an epidemic, then a war. Fat people were cause for concern, fear, and rage, our bodies newly minted threats to public health, to the economy, even to national security. And, yet still, there had been no spike in BMIs, no sudden surge of fat people.

While our bodies hadn't changed—at least, not any faster than previously—the way we categorized fat bodies did. In 1995, the World Health Organization (WHO) adopted the body mass index (BMI) as its primary measure of body size and, simultaneously, established a new global threshold for who would be considered "overweight" and "obese." Despite its own staff's recommendation to *increase* the threshold for who was medically considered too fat, WHO did just the opposite, making the "healthy weight" category even more restrictive, despite data showing that people now deemed "overweight" weren't at greater risk of morbidities or mortality. Additionally, against the recommendation of staff, WHO adopted the BMI as a measure of size and health in children. Despite the fact that children's growth patterns were distinctly different from adults' relatively static heights, children would now be judged on the curve of a body mass index designed for adult white men.

A few short years later, the National Institutes of Health followed suit, lowering the thresholds for whose BMIs would be considered medically "overweight" and "obese." And in so doing, thirty million Americans became instantaneously "overweight" or "obese."[3] Their body sizes hadn't changed, but charts and heat maps of obesity rates would appear to reflect a dramatic shift in the weight of the nation.

In addition to this new promulgation of the body mass index, advocates had also taken up the cause of declaring an "obesity epidemic." In the late 1990s, an unlikely and disparate group of researchers, weight-loss and pharmaceutical companies, and nonprofits all thought more public attention should be paid to rising rates of fatness. Some saw fatness as an emerging public health scourge, one that needed to be tackled head on by policymakers and the public alike. Others thought that our moralizing about fatness obscured the complicated reasons that some people were fat while others were thin. And still others likely saw an opportunity to both expand and corner the market on weight loss.

Perhaps the greatest advocate for drawing public attention to fatness was William Dietz. In 1997, the pediatrician was named director of the CDC's Division of Nutrition and Physical Activity. At the time, Dietz's views on fatness were rare. While most of his peers saw fatness as a result of lifestyle choices, Dietz and a growing number of medical providers and researchers pointed to the multifactorial nature of fatness. Fatness, they argued, wasn't born of individual choices but of environment and genetics. According to University of Chicago political scientist J. Eric Oliver, Dietz believed "obesity was strongly influenced by the environment and was a condition that people passively experienced, something that happened *to them* rather simply the result of their own choices. In other words, obesity was a disease."[4]

Dietz believed the spread of that disease eluded many of his colleagues, who were failing to give fatness the urgent attention it deserved. So, in the spring of 1998, Dietz created heat maps of the United States to illustrate the spread of what he considered the disease of fatness. The deeper red a state appeared, the greater the number of residents with BMIs in the "obese" category. As the maps progressed from year to year, states turned from white to pink, pink to red, red to burgundy. Viewed in quick succession, the maps appeared to illustrate an outbreak of a disease consuming the nation. The maps, both alarming and alluring, represented a major milestone in making the "obesity epidemic" legible to stakeholders and the general population alike. The maps became popular among researchers and academics, quickly and effectively conveying a vision of a nation in peril.

As "obesity" entered the fray as a concern among academics and public health officials, medical organizations and institutions began to follow suit. Just two short years after Dietz's maps were first released, the WHO defined fatness as a disease for the first time. One journal article on historical attitudes toward fatness summarized the WHO's definition. "In 2000, World Health Organization (WHO) defined overweight and obesity as 'the disease in which excess body fat has accumulated to such an extent that health may be adversely affected' and underscored that the practical definition of obesity is based on the level of body mass index (BMI)."[5] By 2002, the Internal Revenue Service had announced that weight-loss treatments were considered tax-deductible, functionally interpreting obesity as a disease in US tax code.[6]

As fatness was redefined as a disease, its spread was publicly reclassified as an "epidemic." In 2001, Surgeon General David Satcher proclaimed that "obesity is reaching epidemic proportions" and that schools were a key battleground in a nascent fight against an "obesity epidemic."[7] His successor, Richard Carmona, made even bolder claims. In 2004, Carmona seemed to elevate fatness to being a threat to national security. "As we look to the future and where childhood obesity will be in 20 years . . . it is every bit as threatening to us as is the terrorist threat we face today. It is the threat from within."[8] First Lady Michelle Obama focused her efforts on what, on the heels of Carmona's comments, had been termed "the war on childhood obesity." She asserted that rising rates of fat people were "one of the greatest threats to America's health and economy."[9]

As the "obesity epidemic" and "war on obesity" took center stage, so too did deeply stigmatizing, scapegoating rhetoric about fat people. We weren't just fat, we were an *epidemic*, combatants in a *war*. We weren't just unhealthy, we were diseased, our very bodies made contagions. And now our bodies, which had borne so much ridicule and rejection, would also bear the blame for poor public health, for an economy entering a Great Recession, and for lacking national security.

By 2008, the idea of an obesity epidemic had gained so much momentum that the Obesity Society recruited a panel of experts to consider whether fatness was just a risk factor for disease or a disease unto itself. The Obesity Society, a professional organization of clinicians, researchers, and science educators, describes itself as "professionals collaborating to overcome obesity." But when the society was asked to answer this scientific question, science took a back seat, in part because the medical field hasn't agreed on a definition of "disease." A 2016 paper on the redefinition of fatness as a disease summarized the Obesity Society's findings:

> What are the characteristics that define a disease? And what is the evidence that obesity possesses those characteristics? The panel found that the scientific approach was inadequate for answering this question "because of a lack of a clear, specific, widely accepted, and scientifically applicable definition of 'disease.'"[10]

Despite the panel not being able to define a "disease," those working in medicine and medical research seemed to show growing support for considering "obesity" (newly redefined) to be a "disease" (as yet undefined). The panel, too, suggested that reframing fatness as a disease could increase public understanding of fatness not as a personal failing but as an illness that could befall someone through little fault of their own. Without frameworks for "disease," the panel looked instead to social indicators. Ultimately, social—not scientific—reasons led to their adoption of fatness as a new disease.

By 2013, the American Medical Association (AMA) followed in the footsteps of the Obesity Society by officially recognizing obesity as a disease. The press pointed to what it seemed to consider promising possible outcomes: greater understanding from physicians for their fat patients and increased insurance coverage for weight-loss programs, drugs, and surgeries. (They largely did not note that the majority of clinical treatments for fatness failed to produce sustained, significant weight loss for a majority of patients.) The AMA's decision to recognize obesity as a disease drew public attention, not only because of its significance but also its apparent controversy within the organization. The organization had asked its Council on Science and Public Health to study the question, which the council had spent a full year doing. Ultimately, the council advised against the reclassification of obesity as a disease "mainly because the measure usually used to define obesity, the body mass index, is simplistic and flawed."[11] While the AMA's decision still stands as of this writing, it remains an open topic of debate among researchers and clinicians alike.

Redefining fatness as a disease did, as predicted, allow health-care providers to bill for weight-loss treatments, including drugs from Abbott and Roche, the pharmaceutical companies that underwrote WHO's work to lower the thresholds for "overweight" and "obese" around the world. Fatness, once seen as a cosmetic concern, had now been redefined as a medical problem. Our existing, ineffective weight-loss strategies were now recast as urgent clinical interventions. Now that being fat was a disease, the prevalence of fatness could be redefined as an *epidemic*.

Leading the charge for that redefinition was an advocacy organization called the American Obesity Association (AOA). Founded in 1995, the AOA describes its work as centering around those "fighting the chronic disease of obesity."[12] In its early years, the organization proved a strong voice for reclassifying fatness as a disease. And at that time, according to J. Eric Oliver, they were primarily funded by weight-loss industry titans, including Weight Watchers, Jenny Craig, SlimFast, and Roche.[13] According to social scientist Michael Gard in *The End of the Obesity Epidemic*, the AOA was also the source of a wide range of unsubstantiated claims about an obesity epidemic. The AOA president claimed that fatness would cause children to have a shorter life expectancy than their parents, despite the fact that life expectancies in the United States rose steadily throughout the 1990s and 2000s.[14] The organization claimed, too, that "medicine has never seen an epidemic of this proportion,"[15] without offering research citations or explanation of such a bold claim. The AOA was determined to inject public conversations about fatness with a sense of urgency and alarm, and their bold, often unsubstantiated claims did just that. These catchy, declarative, and factually shaky statements were soon parroted by officials elected and appointed, reporters, and news anchors before transforming alchemically into simple, incontrovertible *common sense*.

The AOA's work in the 1990s and 2000s focused on establishing public policy that reflected their belief that fatness was a disease. The group claimed credit for policy changes at the IRS, Medicaid, and the Office of the Surgeon General. But despite their best efforts, the federal government's *Healthy People* reports, in which public health goals are set for the decade ahead, didn't foreground fatness as a primary public health issue. But for an organization that considered fatness to be a disease, simple acceptance wouldn't suffice. The AOA lobbied strenuously to establish obesity as a central indicator of the nation's health. Weight loss shouldn't just be a population-level goal, they argued. It should be a central measure of success or failure in public health.

In 2010, for the first time, "obesity" became a central theme in the nation's public health goals for the next ten years, as published in *Healthy People 2020*. Fatness and weight loss were referenced at every level of the report, from goals and strategies to so-called leading health indicators, the top ten measures of the nation's health.[16] In *Healthy People 2030*, published in 2020, fatness once again took center stage, with goals focused on reducing obesity rates in adults and in children alike. Its leading strategy was exercise.[17] (Despite its many broad benefits to physical, mental, and cognitive health, exercise has long since been debunked as a meaningful contributor to weight loss.)[18] Once again, rather than relying on tested strategies and data-driven solutions, public policy recommendations followed popular beliefs about weight loss, themselves rooted in the stereotype that fat people are lazy: *If she'd just move around more . . .*

The dual declarations of the "Obesity Epidemic" and the "War on Obesity" didn't just rely on stereotypes—they reified them, stoking a nascent moral panic in the process. Media coverage of fatness ballooned from thirty-three national news stories in 1994 to a staggering seven hundred in 2004.[19] The coverage itself was often sensationalized and alarmist. "[O]n January 8, 2003, the Associated Press ran a story with the headline 'Obesity at Age 20 Can Cut Life Span by 13 to 20 Years.' Only later did the story reveal that the obesity in question was at a BMI of 45 (that would be 340 pounds for a six-foot man), which affects less than 1 percent of the population."[20] No one, it seemed, considered the psychological impacts of putting fat people at the center of a firestorm of moral panic or stoking resentment and fear in thin people.

In 2012, research at Yale University outlined the impacts of a decade of anti-fat news coverage on thin people's attitudes. In the small study, researchers showed study participants a neutrally worded news story about obesity, paired with stereotypical images of fat people (wearing ill-fitting clothing, eating fast food) or images that sought to counter those stereotypes (a fat person working out or wearing more polished clothing). Afterward, researchers assessed participants' anti-fat bias. They found that those who viewed the "negative" stereotypical images of fat people reported higher levels of anti-fat bias. They also found that anti-fat bias wasn't correlated to income, age, ethnicity, or gender—or personal history of being the targets of anti-fat comments or treatment. Anti-fatness was correlated to body size. Thinner participants were more likely to express harsh judgments about fat people and to exhibit higher levels of explicit anti-fat bias. Today, according to Harvard University, four out of five Americans express some level of anti-fat bias, which continues to rise as other implicit biases stabilize or fall.[21] And between 2004 and 2010—peak years for the "obesity epidemic"—anti-fat bias rose a staggering 40 percent.[22]

While media coverage ballooned, so did research budgets. In 1993, the National Institutes of Health received $50 million for "obesity" research. By 2004, just eleven years later, they received $400 million.[23] As funding flowed into research, published papers skyrocketed. In 1999, fifty academic articles referenced "the obesity epidemic." In 2004, seven hundred articles were published—fourteen times as many as only five years earlier. Despite this wave of research, rates of obesity continued to climb. But deaths attributed to associated health conditions, like heart disease, declined. That is, more people may have had heart disease, but more of them were also surviving. According to the American Heart Association, between 2008 and 2018, "the annual death rate attributable to CHD declined 27.9 percent and the actual number of deaths declined 9.8 percent."[24] Even as Americans wrung their hands about the purported health risks of obesity—like heart disease—more Americans were surviving.

Still, elected officials at every level remained determined to pass policies to curb the spread of the "obesity epidemic." But few policy interventions had been proven to reduce the number of fat people, instead emphasizing existing beliefs that weight loss was a personal responsibility. And disproportionately, policies focused on weight loss in children. Across the country, governors signed new laws requiring calories to be printed on menus, requiring BMI "report cards" to be sent home to parents of school-age children, and increasing the number of instructional minutes devoted to physical education in schools. At the federal level, Congress overhauled school lunches. The Clinton Foundation's Alliance for a Healthier Generation pressured beverage manufacturers to remove soda from schools, negotiating a dropped class-action consumer lawsuit in return. These policies were largely met with praise, because they *sounded right* to many Americans who view fatness as the result of failed individual choices. Indeed, exercise and physical education have since been debunked as primary drivers of weight loss. Moreover, research found that most parents didn't believe their children's BMI report cards.[25]

While this wave of new fat-related policies appealed to the public's "common sense" ideas of weight loss, they were neither data-driven nor backed by sound scientific evidence. Rather than offering population-level proposals for a population-level trend, most were based on personal responsibility for fatness, not on what researchers say may influence body size: genetics, epigenetics, hormones, minority stress and oppression, poverty, individual behavior, mental health, the built environment, food access, and more. Despite these many factors, our policy solutions rely on outdated ideas of fat people as lazy, unintelligent, gluttonous, irresponsible, and noncompliant. A

2004 article from the *Georgetown Law Journal* laid out this tension at the time:

> Because obesity receives intense media and public attention, and is often an emotional issue, the public is likely to perceive it as a greater risk than it is. When the decision-making environment is so emotionally charged, policymakers may respond with inefficient, irrational, or even harmful policies. This makes careful scrutiny of the problem—including analysis of whether it is in fact a problem—and its solutions especially important.[26]

Researchers and clinicians like William Dietz had long pressed for fatness to be seen as a disease and later an epidemic in hopes of increasing public investment in the issue and in equally high hopes of destigmatizing a misunderstood body type. While the rhetorical shift toward an "obesity epidemic" in the late 1990s and early 2000s certainly drew public attention and concern, it didn't do the work that Dietz and others had hoped in terms of destigmatizing and demystifying fatness. Indeed, public health and policy interventions relied on moralizing constructions of "personal responsibility," undercutting any rhetoric of fatness being a "disease" beyond our control. Overwhelmingly, press coverage and public response alike prioritized condemnation over curiosity, disdain over empathy, fear over understanding, and bias over science.

Ultimately, while there is an observable change in body weights in the United States and around the world, our responses have largely furthered our cultural commitment to anti-fatness. Some scholars have argued that our response to the upward trend in American body weights constitutes what sociologist Natalie Boero terms a "postmodern epidemic," and what others call a moral panic. And that moral panic isn't about fat people's health: it's about fat people *existing* and *being seen*. After all, simple Instagram photos of fat people at the beach or eating a meal are met with allegations of "glorifying obesity." Those accusations can hardly be said to produce any beneficial change for fat people or our health. They are the direct result of bias and may also be a sign of moral panic.

Sociologist Stanley Cohen was the first to lay out a framework for understanding moral panics in his study of mods and rockers, *Folk Devils and Moral Panics*. Erich Goode and Nachman Ben-Yehuda later built on this work. In 1994, they established five core characteristics of a moral panic, synopsized here in a 2020 article in *PLOS One*:

> (1) **CONCERN**, where there is a heightened level of concern about certain groups or categories,
>
> (2) **HOSTILITY**, where one can observe an increase in hostility towards the "deviants" of "respectful society,"
>
> (3) **CONSENSUS**, where a consensus about the reality and serious-ness of a threat can be found,
>
> (4) **DISPROPORTIONALITY**, where public concern is in excess of what "should" be, and
>
> (5) **VOLATILITY**, where the panic is temporary and fleeting and though it might reoccur, the panic is not long lasting.[27]

While the "obesity epidemic" has been anything but fleeting— its half-life has now lasted more than two decades—our response to it meets many of Goode and Ben-Yehuda's other criteria for a moral panic. Our *concern* about the perceived scourge of obesity has skyrocketed in recent years, giving way to anti-fat *hostility*, as witnessed by growing levels of anti-fat bias. *Consensus* is evident in the near-complete lack of counternarratives in the face of over seven hundred national news articles about an obesity epidemic each year. And *disproportionality* is evidenced by media coverage and public-policy interventions, both of which opt for alarmism and often biased "common sense" solutions that depart from more instructive, nuanced research. At every turn, it seems, we've chosen panic and bias over empathy and problem-solving. Our bodies may not make up an epidemic, but increasingly, our biases do.

"FAT PEOPLE DON'T EXPERIENCE DISCRIMINATION."

Anti-fat discrimination is real, it deeply harms fat people, and it operates at alarming levels. But more than that, as of 2022, anti-fat discrimination is perfectly legal in forty-eight states.

Today, just two states have banned anti-fat discrimination: one through its state legislature and another through its court system. Back in 1976, Michigan became the first state to ban discrimination on the basis of size at the state level, adding weight to its nondiscrimination laws.[1] Twenty-four years later, San Francisco followed suit, passing a local nondiscrimination ordinance in 2000.[2] Other US cities have since banned weight-based discrimination: Santa Cruz, California; Urbana, Illinois; Binghamton, New York; and Madison, Wisconsin. And, in 2007, Massachusetts legislators introduced a bill that would ban anti-fat discrimination. That bill has been repeatedly reintroduced but has yet to pass.[3] Washington, DC, has added "personal appearance" to its nondiscrimination laws, but because it does not explicitly name size, it is unclear whether courts will interpret that law to extend to anti-fat discrimination.[4]

Advocates have found success in the courts too. In 2019, Washington State's Supreme Court ruled that it must protect fat people from discrimination under its existing nondiscrimination laws, determining that fatness qualified as an impairment under the state's definitions of disability.[5] Prior to that, courts had repeatedly ruled the opposite: disability nondiscrimination protections should not be interpreted to protect fat people from discrimination.[6] Whatever the legal grounds offered, employees often don't win even clear-cut cases of weight-based employment discrimination. The Borgata Hotel Casino & Spa in Atlantic City hired its "Borgata Babes" in part on the basis of their thinness. "The casino had a policy in which it monitored its waitresses' weight and issued discipline, including suspension, if the waitress gained too much weight—specifically, if they gained more than 7% of their body weight from when they were first hired."[7] Even when those employees are thin, as in the case of the Borgata Babes, courts uphold employers' practices of hiring, firing, promoting, and demoting employees on the basis of their weight.[8] Weight-based discrimination cases brought by thin plaintiffs often proceed further in the courts and receive more media attention than those brought by fat plaintiffs. Even in the fight to end anti-fat discrimination, thin people come out ahead.

Employment discrimination also creates significant pay gaps between fat and thin workers. In 2010, researchers issued two of the first reports to determine the economic impacts of anti-fatness in fat workers' wages. The first study found that men lost out on $2,646 each year. For fat women, that number nearly doubled: being fat cost us $4,879.[9] The second study, published in the *Journal of Applied Psychology*, found even more devastating results, which were summarized in *Time*: "'very thin' women earned $22,000 more a year, while 'very heavy' women earned almost $19,000 less."[10] A 25-pound increase in a worker's weight "predicted an annual salary loss of approximately $14,000 per year." Even a 13-pound gain led to a $9,000 loss in pay annually.[11]

Managers' attitudes toward fat employees and candidates are often nakedly biased. Some 45 percent of British employers reported that they were less likely to hire fat interviewees than thin ones.[12] A 2016 study in *Frontiers in Psychology* found that hiring managers' perceptions of candidates were significantly shaped by their weight and gender.[13] Anti-fatness also shapes what jobs managers are willing to offer fat people. A 2014 Vanderbilt University paper showed that fat women were more likely to work in lower-wage jobs that "emphasize physical activity, but they are less likely to work in jobs that emphasize public interaction."[14] When hiring a fat candidate, it seems, managers can't imagine making a fat person one of the public faces of their workplace. Instead, they shuffle us into exercise-intensive jobs popularly assumed to lead to weight loss. Fat employees know we're experiencing inequitable treatment too—and we've known for decades. A 1990 study in the *Journal of Vocational Behavior* compared reports of employment discrimination from fat and thin workers. Very fat subjects reported the highest levels of employment discrimination, in addition to disclosing more "school victimization, attempts to conceal weight, and lower self-confidence" than thin subjects.[15] A 2008 Yale University survey underscored those results, finding that among workers with BMIs of thirty-five or higher, 40 percent reported that they had personally experienced anti-fat discrimination at work.[16] Those researchers also found that anti-fatness was one of the four most common types of discrimination reported in the United States.[17]

The criminal justice system, too, is a pivotal site for anti-fatness, and one where it conspires with white supremacy, misogyny, and rape culture. A 2013 study found that when presented with a fat woman defendant and a thin woman defendant, thin men on juries were more likely to believe fat women were guilty and those fat women would reoffend.[18] A 2015 study in the *Journal of Interpersonal Violence* looked at how potential jurors behave in sexual assault cases when they believe anti-fat myths. It found that holding anti-fat beliefs "was the most significant predictor of victim blaming,"[19] but it only predicted victim blaming when the victim to be blamed was a fat person.

Anti-fatness is regularly deployed to uphold anti-Blackness in the criminal justice system. The roots of anti-fatness and anti-Blackness are intertwined, and so too are their effects. Perhaps its most grotesque use is in lending credence to racist police violence. After the filmed murder of Eric Garner by New York City police officers, police union attorney Stuart London defended Garner's killer, Daniel

Pantaleo. London argued that Garner's size was to blame for his death, not Pantaleo's taped actions. The *Washington Post* quoted London's arguments in an administrative hearing on Garner's murder:

> "He died from being morbidly obese," London declared, prompting shocked snickers and disgusted head shakes in the courtroom. Pantaleo, sitting with his attorneys, remained silent. "He was a ticking time bomb that resisted arrest. If he was put in a bear hug, it would have been the same outcome."[20]

In that moment, anti-fatness was a racist and strategic choice: the prevalence and popularity of anti-fatness allowed London to thinly veil a fundamentally inhumane and anti-Black argument. And so, even in the face of video evidence of his client's guilt, London blamed Garner for his own death. London's argument came two years after the passing of Heather Heyer, echoing neo-Nazi responses to her death. Heyer, a white woman, died while counterprotesting against white supremacists in Charlottesville, Virginia, during the Unite the Right rally. She was run down and killed by a white nationalist who drove his car into a crowd of antiracist protestors. After her death, white supremacists crowed online, hyper-focused on the late woman's size. The Nazi website *The Daily Stormer* published a post called "Heather Heyer: Woman Killed in Road Rage Incident Was a Fat, Childless 32-Year-Old Slut."[21] Whether Stuart London understood that he was upholding white supremacy in the criminal legal system or not, his defense strategy mirrored the rhetoric of white supremacist movement leaders.

Anti-fat discrimination extends to health care too. Fat people face overt prejudice and discriminatory attitudes from health-care providers, who exhibit high levels of explicit and implicit anti-fatness leveled at their fat patients. And those attitudes translate to less understanding and worse care from providers. Fat people receive shorter office visits, health-care providers develop less rapport with us, and many fat people face misdiagnosis of severe health conditions, like autoimmune disorders and cancers, because providers attribute symptoms to our weight. That, in turn, leads fat patients to mistrust doctors and avoid seeking health care.

That anti-fatness isn't just in our heads or just the work of a few particularly dedicated anti-fat trolls. Anti-fat bias in health care has been repeatedly shown to exist at alarming rates. A 2015 research review on medical anti-fatness found that providers held "strong negative attitudes and stereotypes" about fat patients, that there was substantial evidence that those attitudes shaped their decision-making and interpersonal behavior, and that provider biases "may impact the care they provide."[22]

Anti-fatness in medicine has been identified, rightly, as both an ethical issue and a barrier to effective patient care. In a 2018 study of first-year medical students, research published in the *AMA Journal of Ethics* found that 70 percent of future physicians held implicit bias in favor of thin people and against fat people. "While most students thought obesity is a disease (89%) or behavioral (88%), 74% thought it results from ignorance, and 28% thought people with obesity are lazy."[23] That same study found a simple intervention, like discussing an episode of *House* that depicted anti-fat bias, reduced anti-fat bias. Other research has shown that even less can make an impact. One study found that viewing a single seventeen-minute video on anti-fat bias also made modest reductions in provider prejudice.[24] Still, even these small steps are more than most medical schools are doing. In health care, anti-fatness can be a matter of life and death. Yet most medical schools fail to even acknowledge it, and few studies have even examined the effectiveness of medical training around treatment of fat patients.[25] So medical students' profound anti-fat biases go unchecked, and few acknowledge or express awareness of them.[26]

While health-care providers' levels of anti-fatness may seem especially high, they largely mirror anti-fatness in the general public. A large-scale 2012 study found that medical doctors' "implicit and explicit attitudes about weight follow the same general pattern seen in the very large public samples that hold strong implicit and explicit anti-fat bias. We conclude that implicit and explicit anti-fat bias is as pervasive among MDs as it is among most people in society."[27] That is, health-care providers are just as biased against fat people as any of us. But unlike most of the rest of us, they are in positions of significant power. Doctors' prejudices mean they provide fat patients with lesser care, in turn, leading fat patients to less accurate diagnoses and less effective treatments. While most of us express significant anti-fat bias, health-care providers hold the lives of fat people in their hands.

Fat people face discrimination in businesses, like stores and restaurants. In 2017, the owner of a Memphis salon allegedly hung a sign on the door informing customers of new pricing. "Sorry, but if you are overweight, pedicures will be $45 due to service fees for pedicurists. Thank you!"[28] A local news outlet reported the owner denied that he'd put up the sign and said it wasn't necessary: "[I] nstead of putting a sign up he's decided to just not service someone if they are severely overweight."[29] In 2008, Mississippi lawmakers went so far as to propose a law that would prohibit restaurants from serving fat customers.[30] It wouldn't have *allowed* restaurants to discriminate, it would have *required* them to. Its lead sponsor told *The Early Show* that he was trying to focus more attention on ending fatness. "It was a far-reaching bill, but you're trying to get people's attention to study the proper motive of obesity which is a concern to all of us. [. . .] Sometimes you have to go a little extreme to get the dialogue started."[31] Mississippi's House Public Health Committee chair, a fat person, killed the bill in committee.

Fat people aren't just excluded by policies or interpersonal interactions. We also navigate frustratingly inconsistent access to public spaces. From café chairs to bus benches, bathroom stalls to airplane seats, the built environment is reliably designed for thin, nondisabled people. Many restaurateurs never consider the needs of fat or disabled people in designing their spaces, leaving very fat people to roll the dice anytime we walk into a bar or restaurant.[32] Will we fit in their booths, or will we have to wedge ourselves in and leave with bruises? Will their chairs hold our weight or buckle beneath us? Will their tables be placed far enough apart to allow us to move freely, or will they have tables packed in tightly, leaving us to squeeze through, hoping we don't knock over water glasses or bump into other patrons? Even buying furniture for our own homes can be challenging. Many furniture manufacturers don't disclose how much weight their chairs can hold. Those that list limits often have a low weight capacity of 200 or 250 pounds. That may mean those companies have tested their furniture for how much it can reliably support. Or it may mean that those furniture companies *didn't* test their furniture, opting instead for a low weight number to protect themselves from legal liability. Either way, low weight limits leave fat people with unreliable information about what furniture can safely hold us. Exercise equipment, too, has low weight limits. High-end brands don't offer any more reliability in access. Popular stationary bicycle company Peloton says its product holds just 297 pounds.[33] In order to find furniture that safely supports our bodies, fat people often have to pay an upcharge, or "fat tax," for a limited range of disproportionately pricey, low-quality options. That fat tax is applied well beyond just furniture, requiring fat people to pay more for airplane seating, clothing, uniforms, exercise equipment, and more.

From perilous situations to daily inconveniences, anti-fatness shows up in many aspects of fat people's daily lives. Studies that look for discrimination against fat people don't just find it, they find it at distressing levels. By all accounts, anti-fat discrimination is very real and very prevalent. Still, many steadfastly refuse to believe it. One researcher wrote an article whose title summed up our strange relationship to anti-fatness: "Discrimination against fat people is so endemic, most of us don't even realise it's happening."[34] That is, it isn't that anti-fat discrimination doesn't exist—it clearly does and has been proven to have devastating effects—it's that anti-fat discrimination is so prevalent and ubiquitous many of us have a hard time identifying it. Like the air that we breathe, it is invisible to us, a natural part of our environment. It stops looking like harmful patterns of exclusion and starts to look like *just the way things work.*

Like so many systems of oppression, anti-fatness renders itself not invisible but natural, normal, and valuable. There is no question whether anti-fat discrimination exists. But most of us treat it as something that is acceptable, because we accept it. So the question here is: how long will others tolerate it? What will it take for people who aren't fat to stand up for people who are? And why do so many people, even those outside of positions of power, expect so much research to convince them of what fat people have been saying for decades: anti-fat discrimination is real and deeply harmful? Why wasn't it enough to believe fat people's experiences and do the work to change?

OPPORTUNITIES FOR ACTION

✦ *Advocate for nondiscrimination protections for fat people.* Join organizing efforts to ban discrimination against fat people under the law. If your workplace includes a nondiscrimination statement or human resources handbook, advocate to address anti-fat discrimination in both. Talk to your human resources department about ending any workplace wellness programs that provide bonuses to thin people on the basis of their weight or that charge extra premiums to fat people on the basis of ours.

✦ *Research the history and present of anti-Blackness and anti-fatness.* Start with Sabrina Strings's *Fearing the Black Body: The Racial Origins of Fat Phobia*, Da'Shaun Harrison's *Belly of the Beast: The Politics of Anti-Fatness as Anti-Blackness*, and Andrea Elizabeth Shaw's *The Embodiment of Disobedience: Fat Black Women's Unruly Political Bodies*.

✦ *Volunteer at and donate to fat organizations fighting anti-fat discrimination.* Support fat groups like the Fat Rose Collective (fatrose.org), the National Association to Advance Fat Acceptance (naafa.org), the Association for Size Diversity and Health (asdah.org), NOLOSE for fat queer and trans people committed to ending fat oppression (nolose.org), and Denmark's FedFront (fedfront.dk).

MYTH 14

"I DON'T LIKE GAINING WEIGHT, BUT I DON'T TREAT FAT PEOPLE DIFFERENTLY."

A friend welcomes me into her home, meets me with an iPad full of photographs—before and after pictures of weight-loss surgery. She tells me she's found surgeons locally who will perform Roux-en-Y and gastric-sleeve surgeries. She assures me they're very affordable, as evidenced by advertising marked "very affordable." She brightens when she shows me her research, proud of having done such a good deed. These aren't surgeons for her own weight-loss surgery: she's proposing them for mine.

We have been down this road countless times before. I have told her for years, no, I do not plan on getting weight-loss surgery. Sometimes I get into the specifics—the tens of thousands of dollars in costs, the high complication rates, the lifetime of adjustments after weight-loss surgery (no carbonated beverages, the dull pain that can come with drinking cold water). But today, I don't have it in me. I do not tell her that the "bikini body" she imagines for me would take years of surgeries to produce: first, constriction or amputation of my stomach, then a series of surgeries to remove excess skin, lift my breasts and buttocks, and erase any evidence of former fatness. I do not tell her about watching friends make their own decisions to get weight-loss surgery, first giddy with their newfound thinness

117

and the attention it brings, then quietly mortified when the weight they lost slowly, invariably returns. I do not tell her that, in this moment, I'm struggling to pay for my housing and car, much less the $15,000 to $35,000 for a procedure I never wanted.[1] I have told her all of these things before; saying them again likely won't stop her from bringing it up.

For any person, having surgery is a deeply personal decision, only heightened by the social stakes attached to weight-loss surgery. This does not occur to my friend: that suggesting medical procedures for another person may be unhelpful, even invasive. She thinks only of the glimmering life that she imagines for me in thinness—countless suitors, glamorous clothing, professional success, a life well lived. She believes a thin life to be a transformed one, moving ever closer to perfection in all things. I do not.

I try again to set a boundary. "I don't plan to get surgery, and I don't want to talk about this, pretty much ever," I say plainly. "I'd rather hear about you. How's work? How's life?" For a moment, she seems to bristle, then brightens when she shows off her new outfit. Later, she tells me about her renewed quest to lose weight, which she refers to as "getting healthy." She's joined Weight Watchers, she tells me. ("I've done it all, and this one just *works*.")

"I know what you'll say," she tells me confidentially. "But I don't have a problem with bigger girls, bigger people, I just don't like how *I* feel when I gain weight."

I don't have a problem with fat people; I just don't want to gain weight.

It's a sentiment I've heard countless times from countless people. I believe that they believe it. But too often, their assurances that they love fat people are paired with comments and behaviors that leave me feeling profoundly isolated and judged.

Most of us are bad judges of our own biases. We may think of ourselves as egalitarian, clear-headed, justice-minded, compassionate. Or we may think of ourselves as rational decision-makers who reliably treat others with respect. To think of ourselves as biased, even discriminatory, flies in the face of our images of ourselves. It pains us to sit with our biases, so we resist examining them. And because we don't examine them, we don't uproot them, leaving us with attitudes and practices that don't reflect our values or our self-images. Too often, we think of bias as a conscious choice, a worldview that we must first consciously opt into in order to perpetuate. If we haven't decided to be biased, we must not be. We cannot be. But the truth is the opposite: we're products of a profoundly biased society: one that perpetuates racism, misogyny, classism, ableism, anti-Blackness, anti-fatness, and more. So even without consciously choosing those biases, we reproduce them. The conscious choice, then, is *undoing* that bias.

This has been upheld by those who study implicit bias, a field that examines biases we may hold and act on, often unconsciously. We would like to think of ourselves as unbiased, above the fray of judgment and discrimination, certainly not so cruel or thoughtless as to treat our fat friends and family differently. But data sets on implicit bias paint a different picture, revealing that *most* of us hold powerful prejudices that shape our behavior, frequently without conscious intent. And most of us are inaccurate judges of our own biases. According to Stanford University's *Encyclopedia of Philosophy*, "What a person says is not necessarily a good representation of the whole of what she feels and thinks, nor of how she will behave."[2] None of us are especially effective arbiters of our own bias—and we can't proclaim with any certainty that we "don't treat fat people differently."

And most of us *do* treat fat people differently, usually worse, than we treat thin people. In a 2019 series of studies with American, British, and Indian participants, respondents believed fat people were "less evolved and less human than people without obesity." That tendency toward what researchers call "blatant dehumanization" also led to greater support of policies that would increase overt discrimination targeting fat people.[3] Whether we mean to or not, most of us have learned to stigmatize fatness, and that stigma often translates to both personal dislike of fat people and promotion of explicitly anti-fat rhetoric and policies. Holding anti-fat stereotypes is directly linked to negative body image—and those stereotypes may actually alleviate it. A 2014 study in the journal *Body Image* looked at thin white women who participated in "body surveillance," or heavy monitoring of the appearance of one's own body. The researchers' findings are deeply troubling:

> [E]ndorsing fat stereotypes appears protective against body dissatisfaction in normal weight women who extensively engage in body surveillance. For women who hold fat stereotypes and report high body surveillance, we propose that downward appearance comparison may create a contrast between themselves and the people with overweight whom they denigrate, thus improving body dissatisfaction.[4]

That is, anti-fat thin white women in the study reported *less* body dissatisfaction, which the researchers suggest may be a result of their biases. Endorsing anti-fatness provided comfort, easing their own negative body image. If the researchers' assertion holds true, these thin white women were willing to demonize and reject fat people in order to soothe their own negative self-image.

In anti-fatness, explicit bias abounds. Fat people face high levels of discrimination in employment, health care, transportation, and more, most of which is upheld in the US by courts and culture alike. Popular television shows, even feel-good comedies like *Parks and Recreation*, are rife with harsh jokes about fat characters' bodies. Even in movies that are "based on a true story" thin actors are cast to play fat historical figures in fat suits, often passing over fat actors in the process, presuming that audiences would rather see a thin actor, even in a fat role. And explicit bias shows up constantly in many fat people's lives. It shows up when thinner people pressure fat people to lose weight, often without knowing our histories with dieting and disordered eating. It shows up when others speculate on the relationships of fat people, proclaiming that thin partners and prospects are "out of our league." And it shows up when friends and family comment on other fat people's bodies, telling us precisely their thoughts about bodies like ours in the process.

Among all that explicit bias, implicit bias can prove more difficult to spot. Those with privilege assume that if we're not using slurs, publicly humiliating others, or telling oppressive jokes, that we are not biased. But anti-fat implicit bias is all around us, and many of us perpetuate it, intentionally or not. On bad days, many describe a negative body image by saying they "feel fat," without considering the ways those comments tell their fat friends that being fat means being unhappy, isolated, unloved, and unlovable. Many casually engage in diet talk with fat and thin people alike, talking endlessly about the lengths they'll go to in order to avoid looking like fat people such as me. When fat friends state the simple fact that we are fat, thinner friends rush to dissuade us, saying things like "Sweetie, no, you're not!" or "I don't see you that way," without realizing that they're responding to their own definition of fat—one that presumes fatness is inherently a failure—and that referring to one's own fatness can only be an expression of troublingly low self-esteem, rather than a statement of fact. Even common questions that seem positive, like asking someone if they've lost weight, are reminders that our bodies are being watched and that we are expected to move ever-closer to an elusive, perfect thinness. Perhaps the most frequent refrain of my life as a fat person is thinner people expressing a "concern for my health," frequently without knowing anything about it. Their concern for my personal health may be genuine, but it's also based in deeply regressive, inaccurate stereotypes about fat people—that we cannot be healthy, that we do not know *how* to be healthy, and that we need a thin person to teach us. It's an exchange that reliably oozes with condescension: I am meant to be grateful for this salvation, delivered to me by a noble and generous thin person. I am wretched, and I am being saved.

Implicit bias powers what psychologists call normative discontent, the idea that people socially express body dissatisfaction, especially with regard to their weight.[5] Normative discontent is buttressed by a series of powerful social scripts to which many of us have become accustomed: voicing disapproval of our own bodies and expecting others to do the same. The office breakroom, a dressing

room at a department store, and meals with friends all become sites
for expressing discontent with our bodies. "I hate my thighs." "I'm
not swimming; nobody needs to see me in a bathing suit." *"You* look
amazing; *I* look terrible." Comments like these abound, often seen
as a way of blowing off steam, releasing the disappointment we feel
about our own bodies, and hopefully making us feel better in the
process. Research shows, however, instead of making us feel better,
these exchanges can make matters worse. A small study in 2011 found
that 93 percent of women college students participated in negative
body talk, despite its negative outcomes.[6] "Women appear to believe that complaining about one's body size with peers can relieve
distress associated with body dissatisfaction. However, our findings
suggest that such talk is associated with *greater* body dissatisfaction
and thin-ideal internalization."[7] Notably, 90 percent of participants
in the study had BMIs in the "normal" and "underweight" categories.
Fat participants noted that hearing thin people complain about their
weight left them feeling isolated, insulted, and hurt. As one partici-
pant put it, "If you're fat, then what am I?"[8] Contrary to popular
assumptions, conversations about negative body image aren't limited
to women. Recent research has found that people of multiple genders
turn to normative discontent to alleviate their bad body image, even
though it doesn't.[9]

Counter to popular assumptions, what relieves the stress of negative body image is positive body talk. For college students of all
genders, positive body image and positive body talk are linked to
greater optimism, higher self-esteem, and stronger relationships.[10]
And women with positive body image experience higher levels of
sexual satisfaction.[11] One Notre Dame professor, Alexandra Corning,
conducted an online experiment in which she showed undergradu-
ates photos of two thin women and two fat women, with one of
each making positive statements about their bodies and one of each
making negative statements about their bodies. Students were then
asked to rate the likeability of each woman. The most likeable was
a fat woman, paired with the statement "I know I'm not perfect,

but I love the way I look. I know how to work with what I've got, and that's all that matters."[12] The statement is positive ("I love the way I look"), while also acknowledging and subtly reinforcing the stigma facing fat bodies ("I know how to work with what I've got," "I know I'm not perfect"). While fat students in the previous study reported feeling hurt by thin student's claims that they "felt fat," Corning's study suggests that students felt reassured by a fat woman acknowledging the social unacceptability of her body and embracing it. While ostensibly a liberatory statement, it is also one that reminds thinner students of their superiority and fatter students of their inferiority. Too often, in conversations about body image, fat people are props for soothing thin people's feelings, while our own needs are disregarded. Fat people get hurt; thin people get healed.

Of course, some of those engaging in biased behaviors are also dealing with eating disorders and body dysmorphic disorder. The relationship between anti-fatness and eating and body image disorders is a thorny one. While many eating disorders are reinforced by pervasive anti-fatness, not all are necessarily rooted in it. Clinicians, researchers, and those in recovery alike have been clear that disordered eating can be driven by a sense that we're losing control of our lives and that we can regain control by exerting it over the food we eat and the size of our bodies. While not every eating disorder or body image disorder is rooted in anti-fatness, people diagnosed with those disorders can still perpetuate it. Any one of us can be hurt and still hurt others. Disordered eating isn't inherently anti-fat, but using fat people as prompts for reassurance that you're "not that fat" is. Body dysmorphic disorder doesn't inherently harm fat people, but telling fat people how fat you "feel" does. And those fat people may also have eating disorders or body dysmorphic disorder themselves, so in the process of expressing your own disordered thoughts, you may be triggering a relapse in the fat person you're talking to. None of us needs to magically "overcome" our disordered eating or body image, but all of us have a responsibility to get support in a way that doesn't threaten someone else's dignity or healing. Disorders of eating and body image aren't necessarily anti-fat, but they also don't absolve those with diagnoses of the harm they can cause to the fat people around them.

The good news for all of us is some solutions are beginning to emerge. Researchers have begun to test interventions to reduce anti-fat bias. A 2016 German study found teaching students that body weight largely isn't within our control resulted in decreased anti-fat bias, especially in women.[13] As a strategy for change, however, this intervention falls short: it erases the experiences of those who *do* choose fatness and continues to imply fatness is inherently negative, requiring explanation and justification. A 2020 study offers a more promising, inclusive approach. Researchers conducted a randomized controlled trial testing methods of changing anti-fat attitudes. College student participants were assigned to two groups. In the first group, participants were told their anti-fat attitudes were in line with their values. The second group was told their anti-fat attitudes were inconsistent with their values. While neither group decreased their implicit anti-fat bias, the second group showed a statistically significant decrease in explicit anti-fatness.[14] We don't know how long the decrease lasts, but this simple intervention shows promise. At the very least, we know we can blunt, even briefly, the sharpest edges of anti-fatness. All we have to do is remind ourselves of our values and who we aspire to be. For most of us, anti-fatness isn't part of our self-image. It's up to us to hold ourselves—and one another—accountable, so that we can make that self-image true.

OPPORTUNITIES FOR ACTION

+ *Assess your own biases.* Remember that none of us are accurate judges of our own biases, in part because acknowledging our biases is hard. Look beyond your own assessment for a more accurate read. One readily available, free tool to assess anti-fat bias is Harvard University's Project Implicit (implicit.harvard.edu), which offers implicit bias tests on a range of topics, including anti-fatness.

✦ *Ask people who are fatter than you for feedback.* All of us,
regardless of size, can perpetuate anti-fatness. Ask friends,
family, and partners who are fatter than you for feedback on
how you can better support them, and if there are behaviors
they'd like you to limit. Conversations asking for feedback
are rarer than they should be, so they may need some time
to reflect. Be sure to leave the door open for feedback at a
later time.

✦ *Ask for consent before engaging in diet talk or negative body talk.*
Nonconsensual negative body talk can worsen body dysmorphic disorder, trigger relapses of eating disorders, and
deeply hurt the fat people around you. If you need to process with a trusted friend or family member, ask if they're
up for a conversation about dieting or bad body image first.

✦ *Say what you're really feeling, instead of perpetuating weight
stigma by saying you "feel fat."* As many fat activists have
pointed out, fat is not a feeling. It's not a temporary emotional state but a body type, a real body type that real
people have. Rather than using our bodies as a metaphor
for low self-esteem, say what you're really feeling. Try "I'm
having a bad body image day," "I feel bloated and sluggish,"
"I feel guilty for eating," or "I'm feeling insecure."

PART FOUR

"FAT PEOPLE SHOULD . . ."

"FAT PEOPLE SHOULDN'T CALL THEMSELVES FAT."

I am at the airport security checkpoint when I hear a small and tender seedling of a voice behind me. "Look at that fat lady!"

I turn around, meet the bright eyes of a three-year-old, and smile. Her mother's face is stormy, voice sharp. "Don't call her that."

"It's okay," I offer. At 340 pounds, my size is undeniable. "She's right. I am fat."

"No, she's not. That's not nice."

"Some people don't like to be called fat, but I really don't mind." I look to the girl. "You're right—I'm a fat lady," I say, puffing up my cheeks.

The child smiles tentatively before her mother cuts in again, her angular voice coming out in jagged shards. "Don't ever say that word. It's a bad word, and I never want to hear you say it again, do you understand me?"

The child bursts into tears. Her mother shoots me a serrated glance. She is a knife; I am her steel.

"Now look what you've done."

As a fat person, I have found this has become a regular feature of my life: trying to convince people who don't wear plus sizes that I am not deeply wounded by the word *fat*.

When I refer to my own body as fat, I'm met with a knee-jerk, syrupy insistence that *you're not fat!* When children observe plainly that my body is fat, their straight-size parents reliably make a scene, sharply disciplining them, insisting *fat* means pain, and that fat bodies are not to be seen, discussed, observed, or embraced. In so doing, they redact fat bodies from their children's worldview. And, even with the best of intentions, they create powerful sense memories for children who dare to say the unspeakable name of bodies like mine. Instead of learning that fat is a body type, to be named neutrally and normally as any other, they associate naming fatness with their own deep embarrassment, confusion, and a sense that they've broken a rule they only just learned existed. I try, and almost uniformly fail, to convince thin people that I do not mind the word *fat*—that I strongly prefer it to kid-glove euphemisms like "curvy" or "fluffy" or stigmatizing medical terms like "obese."

I am fat, yes. I am also tall, blonde, and thirty-eight years old. These are simple facts of my body, none more insulting to me than another. But what I call my body does not seem to matter to the majority of straight-size people I meet. They cannot seem to stand the thought that I describe myself as fat, so they run between my body and the word that describes it like a bodyguard taking a bullet.

When I talk to other very fat people, they often feel similarly. The hurt doesn't come in naming our bodies for what they are—it comes in the harm that is visited upon us for being visibly fat. It comes from the street harassment, the pervasive medical discrimination, and the reliable silence of thin people when we are bullied. But when I talk to thin people about the word *fat*, I find myself an unwitting archaeologist, excavating deep histories of fear and hurt, frozen in amber. The fat people I know don't mind being called fat, in large part because we are—what's the use in denying it? But straight-size people are disproportionately mortified, unable or unwilling to neutralize one of the harshest words they know. For those straight-size people so deeply wounded, the pain of being called fat seems to lie in its inaccuracy. I am the word's target, and they are its collateral damage.

Most of us have been called fat at one point or another. Sometimes it's said with malice. Sometimes contempt. At other times, it drips with pity or sags with emotion. But whoever we are, being called fat is often a feature of our lives. It's no wonder we've become so afraid of being called fat. Most of us have felt the word's sting, sharp enough to break the skin. Fat is a term that holds a great deal of power for a great number of people. It is hurled as a weapon, a ruthless mace tearing through too many of us. We respond with Pavlovian fear, overtaken by our own instincts to self-preserve. For some, being called fat just once is enough to trigger the onset or relapse of an eating disorder. For others, it leads to body dysmorphic disorder, in which the affected person obsesses endlessly over perceived flaws in their appearance, usually something minor or imperceptible to others.[1] For such a small word, the hurt it can cause is great.

Too often, *fat* is shorthand for being seen as unlovable, undesirable, unwanted, excluded. So many of us learn to distance ourselves from fatness and, by extension, fat people. We learn to eliminate words like *fat* so that we can forget the heavy judgments we make fat people shoulder. When others describe themselves as fat, we learn to dissuade them, assuming theirs is a statement of self-hatred, rather than a neutral descriptor of their bodies. And we learn quips like "you are not fat, you *have* fat," as if fat people can be divided from our own skin, like Solomon splitting a child. We find comfort in denying our skin, insisting there's some essential us that exists outside of the rolls, wrinkles, and perceived flaws so many of us long to eschew. It is easier to distance ourselves from our bodies than to embrace what we've so long been taught to disdain. So we find discomfort with the word *fat* and decide to quarantine it.

But disproportionately, we focus on the harm being called fat can cause people *who haven't been fat*. Even in talking about the word *fat*, we push actual fat people to the side, opting instead to center "fat shaming" aimed at people who aren't fat. Celebrities like Tyra Banks and Jessica Simpson are defended against fat shaming, not because appearance-based public humiliation is unacceptable or part of an infrastructure that seeks to sideline fat people at every turn but because *they simply weren't fat*.[2] Banks and Simpson had drifted from an extremely restrictive thin ideal, yes, but neither wore plus sizes.

Their fat shaming wasn't wrong because fat shaming is fundamentally wrong; it was wrong because they weren't fat. The implication, then, is that if they had been fat, such public humiliation would've been warranted. And that implication is borne out among the treatment of plus-size celebrities like Lizzo, Chrissy Metz, and Gabourey Sidibe, all of whom are regularly pilloried in the press and social media for being fat, with precious few thin people rushing to their defense. The logic of "fat shaming" then reveals itself: it's wrong to publicly humiliate someone for being fat only if they aren't actually fat.

The outrage around the word *fat* that comes from people who haven't been fat, however, comes from a different place than fat people's experiences with the word. In many thin folks' imaginations, being called fat seems to be among the worst size-related experiences a person can have. But nearly all of us have been called fat at one point or another. And for those of us who are undeniably fat, being called fat is just the beginning. We aren't just called fat; we're treated differently by individuals and institutions alike. Employers refuse to hire or promote us and frequently pay us less than our thin counterparts. Airlines won't transport us, and other passengers happily scapegoat us for policies that already target us. Restaurants won't seat us, and health-care providers refuse to care for us.

All of that discrimination happens, overwhelmingly, without any solidarity from the very thin people who object to the fat shaming of thin people. Theirs isn't an objection in solidarity; it's a defense of their privilege as thin people. And at the end of all that differential treatment, we're told "You're not fat; you're beautiful!" or "You're not fat; you *have* fat!" Our discrimination and harassment are sanctioned by thin people, who then insist we aren't fat, quietly cleaving us from our own bodies.

Those around me make it clear at every turn that I don't *have* fat; I *am* fat. Remarkably, unforgivably fat. I don't define myself by my fat body, but nearly everyone else seems to. And too often, their perceptions turn meeting my most basic needs into a minefield.

Denying that some of us *are* fat may feel comforting, especially for those who aren't universally regarded as fat. But to me, it feels like a denial of a fundamental life experience that has significantly impacted me. It's not just a denial of my size but a denial of the biased attitudes and overt discrimination fat people contend with all too often.

Saying that I am "not fat" or that I simply "have fat" lands as a refusal to believe a core part of my life experience. But acknowledging that anti-fat bias exists and hurts their fatter friends would require thinner people to grapple with the ways in which they have upheld and perpetuated that bias. It would require them to assess and explain their actions to the fat people they have harmed—work for which many are wholly unprepared. It would call up an earthquake that would shake their sense of self as good friends and egalitarians. It's hard to face the ways in which we may have hurt the ones we love. So instead of taking on that larger task, many thinner friends default to reassuring me that I "have fat."

But "you aren't fat, you *have* fat" doesn't just sting because of its refusal to acknowledge the all-too-real and all-too-prevalent anti-fat bias. It stings because it quietly encourages leaving that bias intact. This rhetorical reframe proposes that it's just fine to leave our prejudice unchallenged because we aren't fat people, not like them. Keep treating fat people however you want. It's okay. You can rest assured that you're not one of them. It's a quiet and troubling kind of gaslighting, albeit unintentional: repeating to fat people that our bodies, the most observable and surveilled parts of us, aren't actually who we are.

For the most part, I am not called fat as an insult by other fat people. I am called "fat pig" by a thin server under her breath at a buffet, even before eating. I am called "huge fucking heifer" by a muscular man leering out his car window. I am called "fat c***" by men I reject. And I am called "fat bitch" by a middle-aged woman shouting at me on the street. These moments strike me sometimes as laughable, other times as cutting. Either way, these moments pass.

Thin people are often surprised to learn that those are not the instances that hurt me. The moments that hurt most are when thin people use euphemisms while they harm me. A physician assistant says, "We don't usually have such sturdy patients," when she tells me she doesn't have a blood pressure cuff that will fit my arm. Unprompted, a stranger at a bus stop tells me, *Don't worry, a lot of men like a curvy girl.* In a waiting room, a stranger tells me, *Big girls shouldn't wear belts. They look disgusting.*

This, then, is what so many straight-size people fear: not a changing body but a subjugation to the thin person they once were, a thin person who readily passed judgments on fat people or who let others' judgments go uninterrogated and uninterrupted. The fear of being fat is the fear of joining an underclass that you have so readily dismissed, looked down on, looked past, or found yourself grateful not to be a part of. It is a fear of being seen as slothful, gluttonous, greedy, unambitious, unwanted, and, worst of all, unlovable. Fat has largely been weaponized by straight-size people—the very people it seems to hurt most deeply. And ultimately, thin people are terrified of being treated the way they have so often seen fat people treated or even the way they've treated fat people themselves.

In that way, thinness isn't just a matter of health or beauty or happiness. It is a cultural structure of power and dominance. And being called fat cuts so deeply because it hints at a dystopian future in which a thin person might lose their cultural upper hand.

Arguably, the greatest trick of anti-fat bias is its insistence that, regardless of health, genetics, environment, disability, or any other factors, thinness and weight loss are universal accomplishments. Even for thin people with disabilities or chronic health issues. Even for thin people who struggle to put on weight. Even for the thin people who can "eat whatever I want and never gain a pound." Even for cancer patients and others struggling with illness, who are told, "On the bright side, you look thinner than ever."

I have never known that sense of bodily accomplishment or the pride that comes with it. It must be excruciating to think of losing it.

I have gingerly shared this theory with thin friends whose faces reliably sink when they hear it. Some insist that they have never treated fat people poorly, even as they stare at my rolling stomach or give me tips on how to lose weight they never carried. Others concede, sure, some thin people treat fat people badly, but they don't take part. But not remembering treating fat people badly isn't necessarily a sign of having treated fat people well—it's just as likely a sign of having so deeply normalized poor treatment of fat people that we don't even remember when we've done it. After all, ignoring the abuse of fat people isn't an exception or the actions of a vocal minority; it is the status quo.

And ultimately, that is in itself a kind of marginalization. Insistently avoiding the word *fat* continues to stigmatize my body and insist that describing my skin must be an insult. And correcting me for calling myself fat is a seemingly kind way of snatching my identity and my body away from me. It is dominance in action. You clearly can't care for your wretched body, and you certainly can't describe it. And ultimately, avoiding the word *fat* preserves its power and pain, regardless of its use, context, or speaker.

For me, and for many other fat people, reclaiming the word *fat* is about reclaiming our very bodies, starting with the right to name them. *Fat* isn't a negative aspect of one's body any more than *tall* or *short*. It can, and should, be a neutral descriptor. We can, and should, treat it as such. That's what many fat people are trying to do, only to be interrupted or usurped by thinner people.

But whether you subscribe to *body positivity* or *body neutrality*, *eating disorder recovery* or *fat activism*, none of us can build movements or healing spaces for our bodies without acknowledging two key things. First, we must situate our own struggles in relation to who they're designed to harm. Yes, thin people can be deeply wounded by being called fat. But the reason the insult lands is that, on some level, straight-size people know how fat people are treated, and they long to hold onto the privileges of their proximity to thinness. Being called fat may hurt, but it only hurts because of how we publicly exclude, hurt, and harm people who are actually fat. And second, none of these movements can exist without body autonomy, including the right to name our own bodies and the experiences that spring from them.

Yes, *fat* is a term with baggage, especially with straight-size people. But while it may feel loaded to those straight-size people, it is a key step in the healing and liberation of many fat people. Thin people's discomfort with a word that has hurt them shouldn't stand in the way of the liberation of actual fat people.

So let us name our own bodies. Like anyone, fat people are just trying to exist in a body in this world—and thin people's insistence that they know what's best for us is too often a barrier to accomplishing that simple, onerous task.

Instead of opting for the tempting work of reassuring ourselves and those around us that we aren't fat, let's look at the root cause: how we think of, and treat, people who are fat. It's time to do better by ourselves and the fat people we love by not distancing ourselves from anti-fat bias but by dismantling it.

REFLECTION QUESTIONS

+ How do you feel when you say the word *fat*? What, if anything, does that word bring up for you? What personal experiences are those feelings tied to?
+ Often, we assume others will be offended or hurt by the same terms we are, but it's much rarer that we actually ask. Do you know how the fat people in your life feel about the word *fat*? Have you asked them?
+ Notice when you describe other people's size. Is their size relevant to your discussion of them? Why or why not? Do you know the words that person prefers to use for themself?

OPPORTUNITIES FOR ACTION

+ *Practice saying and hearing the word fat neutrally.* If we believe that fat people aren't inherently inferior to thin people, then our language can and should reflect that. And if we believe that our bodies are sovereign, our practices need to respect that sovereignty. So let yourself say fat. Say it again and again. Say it until its blade dulls, until it can't hurt you. Say it so you can stop hurting fat people.

✦ *Ask fat people how we want to be described.* Get comfortable asking fat people what words we use to describe our own bodies and what our boundaries are around talking about size. If you don't know someone well enough to have those conversations, don't describe their body. If it's unavoidable, mirror the language they use.

✦ *Manage your own discomfort.* If you feel uncomfortable with the words someone else uses to describe their body, remind yourself that your body is yours to describe, and theirs should be their own. Remember that your discomfort is yours to carry, not to project onto others or ask them to hold.

"PEOPLE WHO HAVE NEVER BEEN FAT HAVE 'INTERNALIZED FATPHOBIA.'"

I know that you have learned to hate your body.

I know the messages, the images, the comments, both cruel and well-intended. I know the sinking feeling of seeing your changing body in the mirror, the sharp pain as your clothes dig into newly soft flesh. I know it hurts, and the pain can sometimes feel unbearable. I know it is tempting to validate that pain by asserting that you are the intended target of an oppressive system. I also know that, if you have never been a fat person, the name for that pain is not "internalized fatphobia."

Internalized oppression is a long-standing concept in social sciences and social justice work, one that has been discussed for decades and one that transcends movements. Internalized oppression and its twin concept, internalized subordination, refer to the ways in which a group targeted by oppression begins to internalize the messages of their oppressors and begins to do the work of oppression for them.

Internalized oppression isn't a matter of low self-esteem or lacking confidence. It's a product of systemic oppression. In the *Texas Hispanic Journal of Law & Policy*, Laura Padilla maps out how internalized oppression takes root:

> Dominant players start the chain of oppression through racist and discriminatory behavior. . . . Those at the receiving end of

prejudice can experience physical and psychological harm, and over time, they internalize and act on negative perceptions about themselves and other members of their own group.[1]

That is, internalized oppression isn't just oppressive concepts that anyone can come to believe; it is a direct result of being the sustained target of discrimination and prejudice. Author and organizer Suzanne Pharr expanded on the complexities of internalized oppression in *In the Time of the Right*:

> Internalized oppression is more than low self-esteem, which implies an individualized mental health issue calling for an individualized therapeutic solution. . . . The damaging effect of stereotyping, blaming the victim, and scapegoating is not only that the general public accepts such negative beliefs, but that the targets of these beliefs also come to accept that there is something wrong with themselves and their people. . . . It is then a more simple task to dominate them, free of the threat of organized resistance.[2]

Internalized oppression has never been as simple or as innocuous as "low self-esteem." It also isn't as simple as any person—on the upside or downside of power—coming to believe or agree with oppressive ideas. Internalized oppression is an essential component of marginalizing a group of people, making them believe their oppression is deserved, normal, and natural and may even require their participation as their own oppressors. Similarly, the Texas A&M University Office for Diversity explains internalized oppression as "the result of people of targeted groups believing, acting on, or enforcing the dominant system of beliefs about themselves and members of their own group."[3]

Internalized oppression is a concept that, for decades, has been used to describe the experiences of people who are specifically targeted by a system of oppression. Women may have internalized misogyny; for men, it is simply misogyny. Similarly, when thin people come to believe terrible, judgmental things about fat people and weight gain, even when they extend those judgments to themselves, that isn't "internalized fatphobia" or "internalized anti-fatness." It's just anti-fatness. While *fatphobia* has become a popular term to describe anti-fat beliefs and behaviors, mental health advocates and Mad Pride activists have been clear: oppressive behaviors aren't the same as phobias. Phobias are real mental illnesses; conflating them with bigoted beliefs and behaviors invites further stigma and relies on ableist language. Writer Denarii Monroe expertly unpacked the politics of calling oppressive behaviors phobias in a 2016 piece for *Everyday Feminism*: "Regardless of good intentions, at the end of the day, it's not okay to build our righteous movements on the backs of other marginalized people. Further, in choosing inaccurate, inadequate language, we harm ourselves as well."[4] Accordingly, and as previously mentioned, throughout this chapter and this book, I'll be using the terms *anti-fatness* and *anti-fat bias* in place of *fatphobia*.

Internalized anti-fatness is what happens when *fat people* police our own behavior and the behaviors of other fat people, having experienced a lifetime of that policing from thinner people. Internalized anti-fatness is what happens when fat people strive to be seen working out and eating salads, praying that our compliance with thin people's wishes will spare us their scorn. It happens when we tell ourselves or other fat people that we should dress to look thinner, often using more palatable code words like "slimming" and "flattering." It happens when fat people accept street harassment, fat taxes, and medical bias as the natural and reasonable costs of daring to live in the only bodies we have. And yes, internalized anti-fatness is what happens when fat people come to believe the harsh and constant judgments that other people, predominantly thin people, hurl at us.

None of this means that you and other people who aren't fat can't struggle with your body image. Many do. Nor does it mean that the way you've been made to feel about your body is acceptable. Your suffering is just as real and valid as anyone's. But that doesn't mean that your experience is the same as people who are visibly, undeniably fat—those of us who are kicked off airplanes, even as paying customers; those of us whose doctors may refuse to treat us; those of us who are laughed out of eating disorder treatment because we "look like you haven't missed a meal in a while"; those of us who are denied jobs solely due to our size.

Yes, you can feel very real, very deep hurt. But that isn't the same thing as being systemically excluded from meeting your most basic needs because of your size. If you don't experience a particular kind of oppression, it isn't yours to internalize. And despite the pain endured by many straight-size people—that is, people who don't wear plus sizes—that pain isn't internalized oppression.

When I share this information with straight-size people, I'm met with a cacophony of objections: "That's your opinion." "You don't know what it's like to be me." "You don't know what I've been through." They're right; I don't. But those objections often come from thin people, particularly thin white people, who struggle to conceive of oppression unless they are the target of it. Many white men are inclined to think that oppression isn't real, having escaped its crushing grip. Many white women are inclined to think that oppression is real but that we are the target of all of it. And when we claim that space, we erase and displace the many people who are intended targets of oppressive systems: Black people, Indigenous people, People of Color, disabled people, trans people, and fat people. What you are feeling—that compulsion to object—might be a sign of what happens when your sense of centrality is challenged.

In some ways, the appropriation of internalized anti-fatness mimics how thin women have taken over body positivity,[5] a largely unintentional but deeply harmful coup that took a movement rooted in radical fat activism, appropriated it for thin people who already had immense cultural power, and wrote fat people out of our own movement.[6] Today, body positivity is defined more by thin women's struggles with self-esteem than it is by the radical fat activists who paved the way for it. And now, even as fat activists of color work toward collective liberation, thinner women are once again asserting themselves as those most oppressed, claiming that their insecurities are "internalized fatphobia," both placing themselves at the center of a system that specifically targets fat people and simultaneously speaking over the countless fat people who are deeply, constantly impacted by anti-fatness in individuals, public policy, doctor's offices, and more.

Instead of thanking fat activists, particularly fat activists of color, for the work that has offered them so much or working shoulder to shoulder with us to build a more just world, many thin women, particularly thin, white women, instead appropriate our work, then write us out of it. That isn't internalized oppression, it's learned supremacy.

Yes, I know the fear of becoming fat and then the fear of becoming fatter. I know the urge to starve yourself, to succumb to the siren song of disordered eating just so you can meet the promise of thinness. I know the pressure that you level against yourself.

I also know the pressure you level against me and people who look like me. I know the look on your face when you see a body like mine and think, with momentary but great relief, "At least I'm not that fat." I know the way you pray not to sit next to someone who looks like me on an airplane or a city bus. And I know the disgust you may quell when you see a body like mine with bare arms, legs, or torsos.

I know your pain. And I know that the depth of that pain doesn't justify replicating it, visiting it again upon people with less cultural power than you. Your pain can be, and is, honored. Women who are not fat are centered in the vast majority of conversations about body image, eating disorders, and weight stigma. And now, many are displacing fat people once again, claiming "internalized fatphobia," and once again centering themselves in a conversation about a system of oppression that specifically and primarily harms fat people.

I know that you may struggle with your body image despite ostensibly meeting the beauty standard in so many ways. That dissatisfaction is part of living in this world, part of having a body. I know it hurts. But I don't know how to explain to you that other people have different experiences, that they may have different needs, and that you may not have it the worst. I do not know how to convince you to acknowledge—regularly and readily, to yourself and others—that you can feel hurt and also hurt others. You can struggle with your body image and still benefit significantly from anti-fatness. You can dislike your body and still push fat people to the margins, even in the movements and spaces we create for ourselves. And when it comes to fat people, you often do.

Thin women make up the majority of doctors who have refused to treat me. A thin woman once removed a melon from my shopping cart, tsk-tsking that it contained too much sugar. Thin women aren't the exception to anti-fatness—too often, they're the rule.

So, no, people who have never been fat, who have never worn plus sizes, don't have internalized fatphobia. It isn't internalized, it's just fatphobia.

It is not your fault that you have learned to replicate oppression. You've been hailed into a system that tells you your body is an accomplishment, albeit a tenuous one. Your struggle to stay thin isn't because of oppression you've internalized, it's because of dominance. Because you see the ways fat people are regarded, treated, and tossed aside and because you likely know, by and large, that is not how bodies like yours are treated.

You may yearn to stay thin or get thinner, at least in part to avoid the discriminatory attitudes and actions that are so commonly leveled against fat people. You haven't internalized our oppression. You've learned to keep yourself out of the line of fire. And instead of making the world safer for all of us, regardless of size, you focus on keeping yourself small and maintaining the dominance you've been taught you earned.

Internalized dominance, like internalized oppression, is a long-standing concept that transcends movements for social justice. Where internalized oppression refers to the ways marginalized people take up the mantle of our own oppression, internalized dominance refers to the ways people with privilege internalize and enact the belief that they are naturally and justifiably superior to the marginalized communities they contrast.[7] According to the Canadian Race Relations Foundation, internalized dominance "is likely to involve feelings of superiority, normalcy and self-righteousness, together with guilt, fear, projection and denial of demonstrated inequity."[8]

Microaggressions are often rooted in internalized dominance, small and piercing reminders that marginalized people need to remember our place. Sometimes those messages are coded; sometimes they're explicit. And in a country with a self-proclaimed war on obesity, where so many of us are trying or have tried to lose weight, many of us have bought into internalized oppression or dominance, seeking to align ourselves with thinness at nearly any cost.

Learning about these concepts and learning to see your own complicity in oppression may make you uncomfortable. It should. All of us should be uncomfortable when we realize the ways we've asserted our power over others. And we should use that discomfort to power our own growth—not to push painful realizations aside but to grow through them, to become better, to make new mistakes, and to grow through them too.

If this doesn't sound like you, if you find your throat still crowded with objections, here are some examples of what internalized anti-fat dominance can look like. Read them carefully. Notice your own defensiveness and discomfort. Listen for what it's telling you.

+ Recommending diets, offering to be "gym buddies," or otherwise telling fat people to lose weight.
+ Insisting that your thinness is a hard-fought victory and suggesting that it should be rewarded with praise, healthier relationships, or better jobs.
+ Suggesting that fat people cover our arms, our bellies, our thighs, or otherwise offering style "advice" that suggests fat bodies cannot or should not be seen.
+ Wanting to lose weight so that you aren't perceived or treated the way that fat people are.
+ Correcting fat people when we describe our own bodies as "plus size" or "fat."

+ Bringing up fat people's size and making it clear that you disapprove under the auspices of being "concerned for our health."
+ Seeking to find a weight limit for body positivity or neutrality—finding the size at which thinner people can, once again, reject or judge fat people.

Most of us replicate internalized dominance without knowing or thinking about it. That's how power and privilege maintain themselves. They make us their unwitting foot soldiers. After all, if fat people come to believe that we are inferior and that we need fixing, is it any wonder that thin people come to believe that their bodies are beyond reproach and that their culturally superior position is earned?

Having internalized dominance to work through isn't an indictment of thin people's character or goodness; it's a reflection of a culture that reliably rewards thinness and consistently penalizes fatness. There are ways to uproot our biases and challenge our internalized dominance. After a lifetime of training, it comes to us as easily and naturally as breathing.

No, none of this is a reflection on your character. But what you do next is. So, what will you do? And who will you become?

"NO ONE IS ATTRACTED TO FAT PEOPLE. ANYONE WHO IS HAS A 'FAT FETISH.'"

I was in my twenties when a partner first kept me secret.

We had dated for months. She wasn't a one-night stand, and I wasn't a temporary regret. Still, she wanted to keep our relationship secret. The people in her life thought of her as straight, but she didn't foresee a problem bringing home a queer partner. What she worried about was being seen together as fat people. Both of us were fat, but she was substantially less fat than I was and worried aloud about others' reactions at seeing two fat women together. She wasn't predatory in her desire. She didn't disregard my humanity or treat me with disgust. She was just deeply afraid of what others would think. Afraid of the bias we would encounter. Afraid of judgment from her family and friends, how their estimation of her might fall if she was seen with a fat person. Ultimately, that pressure was too much for our relationship to hold. I loved her but left the relationship feeling deeply humiliated.

Being kept secret by partners isn't an uncommon experience among fat people. It's an experience that many of us have written and spoken about. In 2017, fat activist, author, and style blogger Stephanie Yeboah asked her Twitter followers about their experiences of dating while fat. One Twitter user responded with a story about someone she dated for four years but only ever saw in private. "He liked bigger girls he told me but still didn't wanna be seen with me in public."[1] Another went on a great first date with a guy whose friend later confirmed that he "really liked me but 'couldn't get past' the fact I wasn't slim."[2] Another user wrote, "It's either we're fetishized and they think they can be super dirty/impolite because we're just objects, or, because we're fat, we aren't seen as sexual at all. There is no middle ground."[3]

Anti-fatness exists in relationships, but not because, as so many wrongly believe, fat people are somehow categorically unlovable and undesirable. The prevalence of anti-fat bias has led to a popular misconception that no one is attracted to fat people, and the only ones who are must be predatory or somehow damaged. It has led to labeling of nearly any attraction to fat people as a "fat fetish," regardless of the nature of that relationship or how the fat person or people in it feel. Indeed, fetishes can be part of satisfying, consensual relationships. Predatory sexual behavior targeting fat people is a problem, yes, and it should be addressed without further driving stigma around sex, sexuality, and kink. Similarly, some fat people who don't experience romantic or sexual desire are met with insistence they have simply failed to attract a partner, likely because of their weight, and are now offering up asexuality as a kind of excuse. It's a response that is profoundly dismissive of the identities and experiences of fat asexual people. Stigma of fat sexualities means that our own narratives of our bodies and desire—or lack thereof—are frequently rewritten by those around us. Many fat people can, and do, engage in kink. Many fat people can, and do, identify as asexual or aromantic. Still, their accounts of their own sexualities are erased, rewritten by reductive assumptions about what fat people can and do desire.

Similarly dismissive assumptions also rewrite the desires of those who are attracted to fat people. If you like someone who is fat, the logic goes, there must be something wrong with you. It is an overtly cruel and deeply dehumanizing logic to look upon someone else, often with disgust, and ask: *Who could love you?*

The question is a rhetorical one. Nearly all of us know fat people who have fallen in love, fat people who get laid, fat people who get married, fat people who do some of those things or none of those things. We know that fat people can be desired, loved, cherished. *Who could love you?* isn't a question, it's a statement. *Who could love you? No one.*

Those who believe that fat people are categorically undesirable frequently lay claim to a belief that societal refusal to acknowledge fat attraction is biological, driven by some imagined, deeply heterosexual drive to procreate. The argument goes that people are hardwired to seek out partners for procreation, rooted in a biological drive to find the most suitable mate. It is a logic that was deployed in the 1990s around gay people: queer people *couldn't* exist, and if we did, we were biological anomalies, failures of the system designed to carry humans forward. Fat people are similarly framed here as a blight, an exception to a system that prizes the straightest and thinnest among us, who are in turn deemed the fittest to survive. This is now, as it was then, an effort to legitimate clear, naked judgment by seeking out roots in the natural world. As if a drive to stigmatize fat people was some kind of biological imperative, not a choice made by one person to treat another terribly. Not a choice by one person to treat another person as impossible to love. It is that stigma—*who could love you?*—that drives the perceived undesirability of fat people. Anti-fatness, not fatness itself, fosters stigma against the desire and desirability of fat bodies.

Anti-fatness regulates the kinds of bodies we see and trains us in who we are socially permitted or expected to be attracted to. In 1996, Stephen King's *Thinner* was adapted for the screen and released to audiences across the country. Its trailer was overtly stigmatizing of its main character, a fat man named Billy Halleck, played by thin actor Robert John Burke, who wore a fat suit for the role. "For Billy Halleck, life is sweet, bigger is better, and too much is never enough."[4] A thin, conventionally attractive blonde woman rubs her hands across his chest while he confesses, "I can't help it, Heidi. All I think about is food." The movie's central plot device is that Halleck runs over a

Roma woman in his car, whose father places a curse on Halleck that leads to dramatic weight loss. That same year, Eddie Murphy put on a fat suit to star in *The Nutty Professor*, a remake of a 1963 Jerry Lewis film by the same name. Murphy's remake ushered in a resurgence of profoundly anti-fat comedies that starred thin actors in fat suits, from *Shallow Hal* to Murphy's own *Norbit*. As in *Thinner*, *The Nutty Professor* was overtly anti-fat. Murphy played Sherman Klump, a fat man who the film's trailer depicts as a cartoonish stereotype of fatness. Klump empties a mason jar of candy into his mouth, spilling it on his body and the floor. He goes to a workout class, where he stands on a mini trampoline, a motionless fat Black man in a sea of thin white women working out. Klump's family members, also played by Murphy, proclaim, "I know what healthy is!" while pouring gravy over a plate piled high with food. "His love life was disastrous," proclaims the trailer voiceover.[5] Klump is pursued by a graduate student who looks up to him named Carla Purty, played by Jada Pinkett Smith. In both movies, fat men are depicted as broad stereotypes, gluttonous and jolly, but they are still depicted as desired and desirable. That same year, the hit comedy *Friends* released an episode called "The One with the Prom Video." In it, the cast flashed back to their younger years. For Monica Geller, played by thin actor Courteney Cox, that meant revisiting her days as a fat high schooler. In their video getting ready for the prom, Monica wears a high-necked, long-sleeved dress, waving to the camera with one hand while she holds a wrapped deli sandwich in the other, eliciting peals of laughter from the studio audience. When she hugs her thin friend, Rachel, she accidentally smears mayonnaise on her shoulder. (While the adult versions of the characters watch their teenage selves, Monica's friend, Joey, shouts, "Some girl ate Monica!" to more audience laughter.[6]) When teenage Monica's date arrives, he is fat, and we are told he's seen *Star Wars* over three hundred times. These are all signals to his undesirability. While *Thinner*'s Billy Halleck and *The Nutty Professor*'s Sherman Klump had "earned" thin, conventionally attractive partners, Monica, a fat woman, could only be desired by someone socially coded as a last resort.

That same year, a watershed year for anti-fat media portrayals, researchers studied the perceptions of fat people's relationships by thin, straight, white college students. Those student participants were provided with profiles of fictional fellow students, which included basic personal information as well as height and weight. Based on that profile, participants were asked to rate aspects of each fictional student's romantic and sexual life. Questions addressed sexual desire, fantasies, libido, sexual disorders, partners, experience, and perceived desirability. On nearly every measure, participants rated fat people as less desired and desirable than thin people. Fat women, in particular, bore the brunt of judgment. Participants saw fat women as "less sexually attractive, skilled, warm, and responsive, and perceived her as less likely to experience desire and various sexual behaviors" than their thin peers.[7] Thin women were believed to have three sexual partners; fat women were thought to have had one. Thin women were seen as moderately desirable among potential partners; fat women were seen as less than half as desirable. Even when compared to other fat people, fat women fared poorly. Fat women were seen as "less sexually attractive, skilled, warm, and responsive" than fat men.[8]

Of course, it's difficult to illustrate a definitive, causal relationship between media representation and widely held anti-fat beliefs. But research does seem to indicate that an increase in media representation can interrupt anti-fat beliefs. One 2015 study found that just *seeing fat men more regularly* increased attraction toward them in women who date men.[9] The politics of desirability are shaped by who we are allowed to see as desirable, which is in turn shaped by *who we are allowed to see*. And even when media representation of fat people is severely lacking, desire for fat people persists. In *A Billion Wicked Thoughts*, Ogi Ogas and Sai Gaddam analyzed history's largest data bank on pornography viewers. "For every search for a 'skinny' girl, there are almost three searches for a 'fat' girl."[10] Gay men's searches, too, revealed far more searches for "bears" (burly or fat men) than "twinks" (young, thin men).[11] Fat people are desired when we're presented as desirable; we're seen as sexual when we're presented as sexual, and even when media representation falls short, *we are still desired and desirable.*

But even without research, the belief and logic that fat people are impossible to desire is deeply biased on its own. It pathologizes attraction to fat people, not on the basis of biased or abusive relationship dynamics but on the basis of *simple attraction to a fat person.* While most of us readily accept that others may have a physical "type," we balk when their type is fat people or includes fat people. We assume that anyone attracted to a fat person must have a fat fetish, rendering fat people a bizarre and troubling subject of attraction and further stigmatizing kinks and fetishes in the process. Sometimes, our cultural judgment of people who are attracted to fat people tips into making assumptions about that person's character, trauma history, or mental health. We assume that attraction to thin people is normal, natural, so common as to go unspoken. But we assume that attraction to fat people is sinister, untrustworthy, suspect.

All of those assumptions lay the foundation for terrible experiences for fat people. Stigmatizing fat attraction leaves fat people to sort predatory attraction from consensual, meaningful interest on our own. Many fat people can recount deeply cruel and hurtful experiences from our love lives. Lindy West's *Shrill* recounted the writer's personal experiences as a fat woman. The book was later adapted to a television show of the same name, in which Aidy Bryant played a fat lead who was, in one relationship, kept a secret from her partner's friends and family, a troublingly common experience among fat people. One fat person wrote to *Teen Vogue* about a Bumble date with a man who told her she should disclose her size in her dating profile.[12] In 2016, fat people flooded Twitter with their experiences using the hashtag #FatSideStories, started by fat activist Ali Thompson (@Artists_Ali) and KC Slack (@femmina). Many revealed painful treatment at the hands of romantic and sexual partners. "Never being able to shake the feeling that when people show romantic interest they're just doing it as a cruel joke."[13] "My ex: 'you always gain weight when you're depressed and I'm just not attracted to you when you're unhappy.'"[14] "Date told me 'Let's go for a walk, you don't need dessert. I didn't before but now I think I'll have two."[15] "Learning that men showing basic decency isn't=showing romantic interest. Realizing how rarely you're treated this way."[16]

That is perhaps the greatest harm of the cruel, biased logic of insisting that fat people are impossible to desire, to want, to love. Fat people have been told this lie so often and so forcefully, that some of us struggle to believe anything else.

REFLECTION QUESTIONS

+ Have you dated anyone who's fatter than you?
+ What messages have you received about the desirability or attractiveness of fat people? Where did those messages come from? How have you carried those messages forward, and where have you interrupted them?
+ Do you notice others' judgments of fat people's romantic and sex lives? What do they say about fat people's sex lives? What do you do or say when those judgments come up?
+ Where do your assumptions about fat people's desirability show up in your interactions with or comments about fat people? How can you bring fewer assumptions to your expectations and treatment of fat people?
+ Read Caleb Luna's excellent "Treating My Friends like Lovers: The Politics of Desirability."[17] How do desirability politics show up in your non-romantic and non-sexual relationships with fat people?

"FAT PEOPLE SHOULD PAY FOR A SECOND AIRPLANE SEAT."

Kevin Smith made headlines in 2010—not for his movies or podcasts but for boarding an airplane. The director boarded his Southwest Airlines flight, stowed his bags, and took his seat. Once he was settled, a member of the flight crew approached Smith and informed him that he would be ejected from the flight. He had violated the airline's "customer of size" policy at the time, which *The Guardian* summarized: "[P]assengers who are unable to lower both armrests when seated should book another seat because of complaints [Southwest] has received from customers whose comfort has been ruined by the 'encroachment of a large seatmate.'"[1] So he was escorted past row after row of other passengers, excluded and publicly humiliated because of his body. Smith later tweeted that he was told he was a "safety risk." "I know I'm fat, but was Captain Leysath really justified in throwing me off a flight for which I was already seated?"[2]

Smith's experience sounds painful, but Amber Phillips's was dangerous. Phillips, also a filmmaker and podcaster, boarded a small, regional American Airlines flight. She found her seat next to a thin white woman who seemed agitated by the small plane's cramped seats and irritated that their arms had brushed together. Phillips, a fat Black woman, said the thin white passenger positioned herself to push Phillips further into the wall. When Phillips asked her to stop, the other passenger began to complain, saying that Phillips was being "mean." As the flight continued, her complaints escalated, culminating with an accusation that Phillips had assaulted her. By the time they landed, the American Airlines crew called the police to investigate the alleged assault. Police detained both passengers for questioning before releasing them. Phillips told the *Washington Post* she was "scared, upset and shaken": "White people literally need to stop calling the cops on Black people who make them uncomfortable. They're calling the cops like they need to speak to the manager or something. You're not allowed to call the cops for things that aren't true."[3]

Smith and Phillips learned what so many other fat passengers have: when you're fat, flying can be a minefield. Other passengers may loudly complain in front of us about what they believe to be fat people's burdensome bodies. Flight attendants, too, may decide that we are too fat to fly, escorting us from the plane and leaving us stranded without warning or recourse. And those around us may take our photograph or film us, making another viral sensation of a fat person who dares to think we could fly with the dignity that thin people do.[4]

Among the most persistent challenges of flying while fat is navigating the maze of airline policies about when and whether we'll be permitted to stay on a flight. Current policies for so-called passengers of size vary substantially from airline to airline, leaving fat passengers, especially larger fat passengers, to determine which airlines will allow us to keep our seats and which won't. Within the United States, domestic airlines have a patchwork of policies that require fat passengers to conduct extensive research to see if we'll be permitted to stay on the plane. In the years following its decision to eject Kevin Smith from a flight, Southwest Airlines rewrote its policy, becoming one of the least hostile airline policies, setting a very low bar for the industry. As of 2022, fat Southwest passengers must purchase a second seat but may call after their trip to request a refund, which will be provided.[5] Alaska Airlines requires that customers pay for a second seat if they "cannot comfortably fit within one seat with the armrests in the down position."[6] Fat passengers can call customer service to request a refund for the second seat after travel, but it will only be granted if the flight had at least one vacant seat. Hawaiian Airlines recommends that fat passengers buy a second seat but notes, if it's booked online, that second seat is "not guaranteed to be adjacent." Fat people must pay for a second seat, even if we cannot use it.

Some airlines don't even make available the information we most need in order to navigate their policies. Policies may require us to fit in a seat but never disclose that seat's width. United Airlines, for example, requires that passengers be able to buckle their seatbelt with one extension. They provide the length of the extender but not of the seatbelt itself, making it difficult for fat passengers to know for sure whether or not our measurements will pass muster.[7] If flight crew decide on the day of the flight that a fat passenger should have purchased a second seat, in order to stay on the flight, that fat passenger will need to pay for an additional ticket at the day-of rate. Spirit Airlines requires purchase of a second seat if a passenger "is unable to sit in a single seat with the armrests lowered" but doesn't disclose the distance between those armrests.[8] Conversely, Delta Airlines shares its measurements for seat width and legroom but does not disclose when or whether fat passengers may be deplaned.[9] American Airlines and JetBlue go one step further, disclosing neither their seat measurements nor their policies for removing fat passengers from flights.[10]

Airlines outside the US have a similarly mixed bag of policies. Recently, in trying to find a flight for a work trip to Ireland, I found most airlines do not publish their policies for the seating and treatment of fat passengers. The customer-service employees of three different international airlines couldn't tell me if they had a policy, which likely means they don't. If that's the case, the fate of fat passengers like me is left to the discretion of whoever happens to be the flight crew on our trip. Without guidance, flight attendants are left to decide on a course of action when faced with complaints from thin passengers, handling customer service and stopgap policy creation at once. Fat passengers' travel plans, and often our dignity, hang in the balance. If that flight attendant believes we should stay on the flight, we may stay. If they think we need to be deplaned, they will deplane us. But we won't know if we'll make the cut until the flight takes off.

Notably, Canada's airline policies offer a bright spot. In 2008, Canadian courts ordered airlines to let fat and disabled travelers fly for the price of one ticket without any additional upcharges. Airlines claimed the cost would be untenable, but the Council of Canadians with Disabilities found that it would cost the nation's largest air carriers less than one Canadian dollar per ticket.[11] Today, Canadian airlines, like buses, boats, and trains before them, provide fat and disabled transport for the same price as thin, nondisabled passengers.

Airline policies vary widely from carrier to carrier, country to country, but all of them have one thing in common: they prioritize the comfort and preferences of thin people over the needs and dignity of fat people. Thin passengers complaining is a frequent trigger for fat passengers being escorted from the plane, away from the disapproving gaze of thin passengers. Those complaints are sometimes lodged without recognition of the power the instigators hold. If they get their way, a fat passenger will be kicked off their flight. Sometimes, they won't be offered another flight. Other times, they won't be offered a refund. Thin passengers may not know the impact that their complaints have on fat passengers. But even if they don't, complaining to a flight attendant about another passenger's body in their presence is a cruel gesture of judgment. Most airline policies lend credence to that entitlement and prejudice, accepting complaints of thin passengers as issues of customer service and treating the needs of fat passengers as a nuisance. Those policies also set up a bizarre dynamic: one in which the fate of fat passengers rests with the discomfort and bias of whoever happens to sit next to us. Our ability to fly isn't determined by our ability to pay or our conduct on the flight, as it might be for thinner people. It's determined by exclusionary policies and callous complaints from passengers, usually ones who are thinner than us.

Our cultural conversations about flying while fat also reinforce anti-fat judgment. We talk about fat passengers with scorn, insisting that *if they don't like it, they can just lose weight.* In so doing, we imply that fat people are responsible for the discriminatory policies, not the airlines who wrote them. Many of us treat airplane seat sizes as some eternal, immutable truth, rather than the product of a series of design decisions made by major manufacturers like Airbus and Boeing. Notably, airline seats have been shrinking for decades. Forty years ago, the average seat pitch (an industry measurement to assess legroom) was between 31 and 35 inches. Today, it's 29 to 33 inches. Similarly, seats that once measured 18.5 inches across are now just 17 inches wide.[12] Bathrooms are shrinking too. In 2018, the *Wall Street Journal* reported, by their measurements, new model Southwest Airlines 737 bathrooms were 20 percent narrower than older jets, allowing for additional rows of cramped seats, and more tickets sold on each flight.[13] Still, when thin people are uncomfortable on a flight, instead of leveling their frustration at the manufacturers who built such small, uncomfortable seats or the airlines that oversell flights, they aim at the easiest target: the fat person sitting next to them.

Many of us readily blame fat people for the fate that befalls them, never reckoning with the ways at which our bodies are excluded and ignored. As it stands, most public spaces are built for a minority of bodies—bodies that are thin and nondisabled, as well as bodies that are white, cis, straight, and otherwise on the upside of power. But instead of asking why manufacturers continue to build seating and airplanes that work for only a fraction of people, we steadfastly focus on the people who pay the greatest price, literally and figuratively, for being excluded.

OPPORTUNITIES FOR ACTION

+ *Urge passage of the SEAT Act*,[14] which regulates minimum seat sizes for US airlines, by calling your congressional representative, if you are in the United States. Advocate, too, for a policy like Canada's "one person, one fare" approach.

+ *Don't complain to flight crew about fat people's bodies.* If you witness someone else complaining about a passenger, interrupt them. Make sure they know that their anti-fatness isn't welcome. Check in with the fat person they're targeting to make sure they're okay.

+ *Defend fat people in public, whether or not we're there.* Interrupt the readiness with which so many thin people judge and complain about us, and make it clear you'll support fat people all the time, not just when we're there to see it.

"SKINNY SHAMING IS JUST AS BAD AS FAT SHAMING."

Whatever the size or shape of its target, body shaming is unacceptable. Body shaming, the practice of demeaning someone by making negative comments on their body, is unquestionably wrong and unproductive. Yes, even when it's aimed at politicians with whom you might vehemently disagree, like Donald Trump, Chris Christie, or former Toronto mayor Rob Ford. Yes, even when it's aimed at people whom have committed morally repugnant acts. Yes, even when it's aimed at celebrities whose personas you find grating or whom you believe to be promoting unattainable standards of health or beauty. And yes, even when it's leveled at those whose bodies afford them the privilege of thinness. Our bodies are neither reflections of our character nor comeuppance for bad actions. Projecting moral meaning onto our appearance directly foments individual judgment and, in some cases, cultural bias. And body shaming doesn't create meaningful change. When leveled at political opponents, it derails more meaningful conversations about policies and behaviors, recasting them as bodily failures rather than failures of values or competency. When leveled at thin people, it does not lead to weight gain. When leveled at fat people, it does not lead to weight loss. Body shaming only produces isolation, pain and, yes, shame.

Regardless of size, that shame can haunt us for days, months, years. Its specter follows us into swimming pools and dressing rooms. It whispers to us at mealtimes that we're eating too much, not enough, not the right foods, not meeting the expectations of the prying eyes around us. It can curdle with alarming quickness into disordered eating patterns, diagnosable eating disorders, distorted body image, and body dysmorphic disorder.

There are cultural touchstones of our dual obsession with and revulsion by extreme thinness, particularly in recent decades. In the 2000s, memes like "only dogs like bones" lifted up thin women at the expense of very thin women. Catchphrases like "real women have curves" not only lifted up "curvy" smaller fat women and cast aspersions on very thin women but also played into the classic transphobic trope of debating what constitutes a "real woman." (Everyone who identifies as a woman is a "real woman," whatever their size, shape, gender identity, or gender expression.) In that same era, grocery store tabloids featured "best and worst beach bodies," a parade of fat and very thin celebrities designed to boost sales by disgusting and enthralling readers with dueling photographs of famous bodies with fat rolls or with protruding clavicles and hip bones. The message is clear: bodies like these are meant to be leered at. But in recent years, those cultural messages have begun to fade, tempered by a growing public conversation about the harms of body shaming and, in the case of tabloids, a customer base less willing to trumpet their disgust at bodies that deviate from a narrow standard of beauty. Body shaming persists, including skinny shaming. But these pop cultural prompts to shame thinner people are losing purchase in a social and political landscape that increasingly critiques body shaming. Today, thin celebrities' pithy responses to body shaming can receive as much or more attention and adulation than the initial shaming itself. According to analysis of Harvard University's Implicit Association Tests, in the same early 2000s and 2010s era, bias against fat people rose markedly.[1]

At the individual level, body shaming targeting fat and very thin people may look similar. But beyond that individual level, the two sharply diverge. After all, there is a profound distinction between individual shaming and institutional discrimination. No, thin people

shouldn't be told to "eat a sandwich," nor should the fact of their
bodies be described as "anorexic." Those individual aggressions
are harmful and inexcusable. But those individual, interpersonal
instances are different than being denied the ability to meet even
your most basic needs. The individual acts of shaming a thin person
and shaming a fat person may look similar in that moment. But
what differentiates them is all the moments leading up to that, and
all the moments after. After all, anti-fatness is a complex web of
institutional and public policies, cultural practices, personal beliefs,
individual actions, and more. Anti-fatness has historically been driven
by anti-Blackness, and today, is deployed to uphold systemic ableism,
misogyny, misogynoir, classism, and other systems of oppression. In
the immense structures and impacts of anti-fat bias, the individual
act of fat shaming plays only a relatively small part. It is the tip of
the iceberg—the thing many people choose to acknowledge, often
ignoring the jagged and perilous mass that lies just below the surface.

Being told to "eat something" or being called anorexic is jarring
and unkind, the kind of unbidden comment that can stay with you
for hours and days, if not longer. It is a different problem, though,
than consistent court rulings that it's not illegal to fire someone for
gaining weight or being fat, as US courts have repeatedly done.[2] It
is a different issue than persistent bias in the criminal justice system.
In 2017, a forty-nine-year-old taxi driver in Canada was charged
with the alleged sexual assault of a fat seventeen-year-old. During
the trial, Judge Jean-Paul Braun spoke about the assault. "She's a
young girl, 17. Maybe she's a little overweight but she has a pretty
face, no? [. . .] She was a bit flattered. Maybe it was the first time
he showed interest in her."[3] His words reinforced the experiences of
many fat survivors of sexual assault: reporting their assaults meant
being dismissed out of hand, their fat bodies proof positive that they
would be "flattered," not traumatized, by sexual assault. Anti-fat bias,
including the belief that fat people are too desperate for sexual attention to be understood to be victims of assault, is so commonplace
that it can be stated by a sitting judge in open court.

Shaming thin people is an individual aggression, not a systemic one. It is different from requiring job applicants to meet or fall below a certain BMI. Studies and reviews have found evidence for weight-based discrimination in employment at just about every stage of the employment process, from selection to compensation, promotion, discipline, and firing. In other words, fat workers may be not hired or not promoted, or may be fired, *simply because they are fat*—a phenomenon that hasn't been documented at scale among thin workers. Thin people are reliably paid more than fat people at work too. While randomized controlled studies haven't been conducted here, self-report surveys have. A 2018 survey of employed adults in the UK found that workers with "obese" BMIs earned £1,940 (or $2,512) less each year than those with "normal" BMIs.[4] That pay gap widens further when gender is factored in: fat women earned £8,919 ($11,547) less than men of the same weight. And regardless of gender, 43 percent of fat people and 28 percent of thin people reported that thinner colleagues' careers progressed more quickly than their own.[5] And fat people frequently report being turned down for jobs for which they are qualified, sometimes with hiring managers stating up front that they aren't being hired due to their size.[6]

In nearly every facet of public life, people who are considered "too thin" reliably receive more and greater access to resources than their counterparts who are considered "too fat." Thin people are not escorted off airplanes for the comfort of fatter passengers. Thinness is not reliably used as grounds for denial of health care by providers. And skinny shaming is different from being the target of a lengthy and grueling war on obesity. For over twenty years, the US has declared a "war on obesity," pouring countless dollars into stigmatizing fatness and "correcting" fat bodies. Notably, there is no "war on underweight."

Eating disorder advocates and researchers agree that skinny shaming is real but fundamentally different from institutional and systemic anti-fatness. Eating disorder researcher Melissa A. Fabello argues that "[n]ot all kinds of oppression or stigma are interchangeable, especially when considering the greater context in which that stigma exists and the very real consequences of it. We cannot claim that one experience is equal to another—even if they're both harmful."[7] Samantha Kwan, whose research focuses on sociology of the body, suggests the differences between skinny shaming and anti-fatness are shaped by how we reward those whose bodies fit within our existing beauty standards: "Women are encouraged to comply with the thin ideal, and they are often rewarded for doing so and sanctioned when they do not. There is plenty of research that shows that people hold unflattering stereotypes of overweight individuals. These include the assumptions that fat individuals are lazy and lack discipline and willpower."[8] When institutions and individuals reject fatness and reward thinness, fat shaming and skinny shaming come with very different stakes.

Beyond these concrete differences in scope and impact, the trouble with comparing anti-fatness and so-called skinny shaming is, in part, when and how "skinny shaming" is invoked. As countless fat people on the internet can attest, body shaming aimed at very thin people is primarily invoked in conversations *about* fat justice and liberation. It happens like clockwork: a fat person speaks to their own experience of anti-fatness, and another person, usually a thin person and frequently a stranger, insists that "skinny shaming isn't any better." The issue here isn't whether or not individuals are shamed by other individuals for being "too thin" (they are) or whether that's wrong (it is). In a world that roundly rejects fatness and fat people, that muffles or mocks our experiences, speaking up about our encounters with anti-fatness can take courage and fortitude because so many people can and do outright dismiss us. When a thin person pipes up with "skinny shaming is just as bad," it sends the message that not only haven't we been heard, we have been willfully misunderstood. It tells us that now the very people who most benefit from anti-fat bias—thin people—not only refuse to hear out our experiences but demand our advocacy on their behalf. And it introduces anti-fatness and body shaming of very thin people as competitors in some zero-sum game for attention and support. As if there were a limited supply of both. And as if each phenomenon wasn't a different head on the same predatory hydra, leaving so many of us in its wake. In truth, many of the policy changes and cultural shifts that fat activists advocate for would also benefit thin people, including very thin people targeted by body shaming. But invoking "skinny shaming" as a rejoinder to fat justice and liberation assumes the two are opposing forces and meeting the needs of fat people would somehow deny the needs of thin people.

Sometimes, skinny shaming is invoked blatantly as a contrarian argument, playing devil's advocate to a straw man. In those cases, body shaming of very thin people is introduced as a counterargument in fat justice and liberation spaces. But a counterargument to what? Fat activists, by and large, aren't advocating for shaming thin people. Quite the opposite: Many call for an end to appearance-based comments altogether, insisting that our individual bodies should not be fodder for discussion or assessment. Many fat activists and eating disorder recovery advocates seek to remove individual bodies from the public sphere, fighting tirelessly against the idea of commenting in praise or disparagement of anyone else's body. Certainly this approach is one that could benefit anyone who has fielded unwanted comments on their shape, size or appearance, including very thin people. These core tenets of much fat activism are often ignored when skinny shaming is invoked in fat spaces.

At other times, *skinny shaming is just as bad* is a straightforward derailing tactic: a way for thin people to draw attention away from conversations about fat justice and liberation or end their own discomfort with conversations that do not place thin experiences at their center. Signs that an invocation of skinny shaming may be simple derailing include: the person interjecting may not raise concerns of skinny shaming outside of spaces dedicated to fat people's liberation. They may not interrupt anti-fatness when they see it. And their comments may not address a broad phenomenon of skinny shaming, just an assertion of its existence and its severity. They do not illustrate its magnitude, cite sources on its impacts, or call for specific actions for remedy. Instead, their broad statements of discomfort seem to reveal a speaker who feels either uncomfortably decentered or wounded and unheard. Those are real challenges, but individual moments of shaming thin people shouldn't be treated in the same way as the web of policies, practices, and attitudes that leave fat people with lower incomes, less access to health care, and institutional discrimination at nearly every turn. And they cannot justify the bizarre and persistent assumption that addressing the needs of fat people necessitates ignoring the feelings of thin people. Thin people's discomfort in conversations about fat justice and liberation is understandable. Acknowledging the immensity of anti-fatness requires them to acknowledge some level of privilege based solely on the size of their bodies. That acknowledgment may feel like an abandonment of betrayal of the body shaming they have experienced. Acknowledging anti-fatness would require pulling themselves out of the center of the conversation long enough to acknowledge what they haven't experienced, the hardships they haven't lived. And all of that would require them to sit with their discomfort long enough to commit to combatting anti-fatness, to chart a path forward in their own growth and advocacy. In moments like these, thin people fail to acknowledge the harm of anti-fatness on its own terms, opting instead to interject their own experiences, bolstered by considerable privilege. Whether they intend it or not, they often unintentionally convey that fat people aren't worth sparing a few moments of their attention and that they will not support fat bodies, or the experiences born of them, if it means drawing attention, even momentarily, away from their own bodies.

Fat and very thin people alike can benefit from fighting body shaming, just as we all can benefit from supporting fat activism. We can, and must, fight anti-fatness, body shaming, and body policing shoulder to shoulder. But remember, even when thin people have experienced profound moments of body shaming, the institutions and systems in which they exist still confer them social privilege on the basis of their thinness. And remember, that privilege means fighting those fights together relies on the willingness of thin people to show up for experiences that do not tidily mirror their own.

That togetherness relies on thin people's willingness to advocate as strenuously for very fat people as they do for themselves. Many fat activists have asserted, loudly and repeatedly, that no one should be body shamed, regardless of their size. If we are to fight individual body shaming together, thin people need to interrogate their own complicity in anti-fatness, confront it when they see it, and allow fat people to speak to our experiences without drowning us out.

"ANTI-FATNESS IS THE LAST SOCIALLY ACCEPTABLE FORM OF DISCRIMINATION."

In a book full of myth busting, this may seem to be less a myth than a brutal truth. After all, the pages you've read so far are replete with stories of anti-fatness from individuals, institutions, families, and more. All are harsh; some are brutal. If you are new to examining the unvarnished experiences of fat people, the casual cruelty that follows so many of us may seem unthinkable. It may be jarring to hear that your fat colleague makes so much less money than you for doing the same job. You may find yourself tapping into a well of anger you didn't know was yours, so far beneath topsoil and clay, down in your bedrock. If you are a fat person new to situating your experiences alongside those of other fat people, particularly those who are fatter than you, you may find yourself awash in rage and despair.

The last socially acceptable form of discrimination comes from a good place, a deep and growing desire to confront pervasive anti-fatness. When it comes from a thin person, it is often an acknowledgment of the unkind and harmful treatment people like me face in bodies like ours. Those thin people are actively deciding to stretch beyond the mistrust of fat people they have so consistently been taught: the belief that there is always a fatal flaw that has led us to our failing bodies. The belief that thin people are the detectives to locate that flaw and solve its crime as only a thin person can. Those thin people are expressing outraged solidarity that anyone is being dismissed so callously, rejected so consistently, hurt so publicly in this day and age because of how they look. I appreciate the sentiment—it is a rare one. When it comes from a fat person, *the last socially acceptable form of discrimination* may signal that they are learning to embrace their body in a world that refuses it. They are acutely, increasingly aware of all the ways in which they are not desired, not respected, not embraced, somehow a spectacle and a specter all at once. Embracing a fat body is no small feat, especially in a world that believes our bodies can only be failures or blights and increasingly insists we should not exist at all.

And whatever your size, if you've felt those feelings: you're right. The ways in which fat people are treated are unacceptable. And the ways in which all of us, fat or thin, have become inured to that treatment, even replicating it ourselves, is awful. Whatever difficult emotions come with that realization—whether anger or despair, shock or frustration—those emotions are correct. Simply put, the way we collectively treat fat people is *wrong*.

Whatever the size and history of your body, if you are new to this conversation about fat experiences and fat justice, you may reach for superlatives to express the depth of your shock, sadness, anger, and frustration. You may find yourself insisting that *anti-fatness is the last socially acceptable form of discrimination*. That insistence comes from good intentions and righteous outrage. It comes from solidarity, from a newly catalyzed politics around fatness and bodies. It comes from a desire for radical, meaningful, and immediate change.

But that insistence is also false. It's false neither because it's not discriminatory (it is) nor because it's not socially acceptable (it is that too). It's false because anti-fatness is *far* from the last socially acceptable form of discrimination. And insistence that it is papers over the struggles of many other communities that are still contending with deeply rooted discriminatory attitudes, systems of oppression, and the daily work of maintaining some sense of self in a culture that so ruthlessly seeks to dehumanize many of us. Despite such laudable common sentiments, calling anti-fatness *the last socially acceptable form of discrimination* carries more weight than just those good intentions.

Whatever your intent, *the last socially acceptable form of discrimination* conveys more than what you mean. Sometimes, it tells those around you that among your family and friends, you believe most forms of discrimination aren't tolerated, except in this one instance. But the hallmarks of prejudice aren't always as pronounced as slurs, votes, or assaults. Discriminatory attitudes and behaviors often move quietly, having learned not to show their faces, making themselves known in less overt ways.

Sometimes, *the last acceptable form of discrimination* means your family and friends don't experience discrimination, because you walk through life together with similar experiences. The experiences of the people you love do not push you to see the long shadow of bigotry in your daily lives or theirs. Despite your best intentions, you have not seen its rough silhouette. You have not been pushed to strip away your own corrosive residue of bigotry, left behind by living in a society that insists there is none. *The last acceptable form of discrimination* is a gift, a sign of the carefully insulated company we are blessed to keep.

But at its core, *the last acceptable form of discrimination* reveals what you have and haven't lived, what you do and don't recall. It reveals that you may not recall the heartbreak of trying to find a home or a job for a family member who has recently been released from prison. You may not have found the glowering and frightened faces of strangers who assume their past makes them dangerous. You have not struggled to leverage your clean record to benefit someone you love, only to be thwarted by trapdoors of their deep, fearful assumptions. It may convey that you do not know or recall life as an immigrant in the United States. Your memories of Sheriff Joe Arpaio's tent cities are distant and faded.[1] You have not wondered how long it will be until your house is raided, your family wrested from the home you built together. You have not applied for a job only to find that you were undocumented all this time, your body an uninvited guest without a home of its own. It may even convey how quickly you have forgotten the white supremacists who marched through the streets of Charlottesville, Portland, Washington, DC. It can tell those around you that you are likely not transgender. You have not scraped together what little you have to pay bills on an income well below the poverty line, with no financial safety net from family that has rejected you. You have not listened to the reading of names at Trans Day of Remembrance, hearing of the deaths of person after person, murdered just for looking like you. You do not remember what it feels like to know you might be next. *The last acceptable form of discrimination* implies that you have reached the end of your learning. It tells me that your life is uncontested enough to let you believe that one day, oppression just ends. You do not know or remember the ways in which it is forced beneath the surface, the way it mutates in the swampy waters of our subconscious.

Beyond your good intentions, "the last acceptable form of discrimination" implies that you believe racism, sexism, homophobia, transphobia, ableism, classism are all completed chapters, and that they have closed for all of us. But our attitudes are not so simple, our intent not foundational, our history not so straightforward. It may convey to those around you that your intentions are good but unexplored and that you have yet to examine the depths of your own bias, beneath the easy and tempting defense of your own good heartedness.

Simply put, anti-fatness is not the last socially acceptable form of discrimination. There is no last form of oppression. Many systems of oppression are hard at work all around us, socially acceptable because they are socially accepted.

Racism, particularly anti-Black and anti-Indigenous racism, is foundational to the institutions and culture of the United States. From genocide to enslavement, racism has played a central role not only in the founding of the US, but throughout our institutions, invented and defended by predominantly white leadership. Racism was baked into the GI Bill, which awarded significant new benefits to white veterans but denied them to one million Black veterans.[2] It was central to the housing crisis of the late 2000s, during which Black and Latinx applicants were 2.8 times as likely to be denied a loan than white applicants. And if they were approved, Black and Latinx people were 2.4 times *more* likely to receive a predatory subprime loan.[3] From 2016 to the 2021 insurrection, white supremacist organizations played a proud and visible role in supporting then-president Donald Trump. And racism isn't just an issue in institutions—it deeply forms and shapes the lives of Black people, Indigenous people, and People of Color in the United States. "Adolescent Brain Cognitive Development (ABCD) Study," published in 2021 in *JAMA Pediatrics*, found that by ages ten and eleven, 10 percent of Black children report experiencing firsthand racial discrimination. At that same age, 20.5 percent of Native American children say their peers treat them unfairly because of their race.[4] These aren't just historic or academic harms—they are current and rampant.

Disabled people report high levels of discrimination. Among college-educated employees in white-collar jobs who have invisible disabilities—a segment of disabled people with considerable privilege, compared to their unemployed and blue-collar counterparts—more than one-third report having experienced bias or discrimination. Among college-educated white-collar employees with visible disabilities, that number rises to 44 percent.[5] On an institutional level, for disabled people, marriage equality still isn't a reality. For disabled Americans who rely on Social Security disability benefits, getting married means increasing their monthly income. If that monthly income exceeds a federal threshold (in 2022, $1,350 per month for disabled people who are sighted and $2,260 for those who are blind[6]), disabled people may paradoxically lose their benefits, driving many further into poverty. As Jordan Gwendolyn Davis, a disabled lesbian, put it in *The Advocate*: "Even if [my partner] and I can legally marry, we really don't have the option to. That is, we don't have the option to unless we want to risk losing the disability benefits that sustain our survival."[7] And the discrimination facing disabled people doesn't just impact some small sliver of us. According to the Centers for Disease Control and Prevention, more than one in four Americans have some kind of disability. For those sixty-five or older, that number rises to two in five, or 40 percent.[8]

Systems of oppression are all around us, producing broadly accepted discrimination against a wide range of communities. In recent years, according to the Institute for Social Policy and Understanding, Islamophobia in the United States is on the rise.[9] Between 1999 and 2017, the National Coalition for the Homeless reported 1,769 violent attacks targeting unhoused people, 476 of whom died as a result.[10] Formerly incarcerated people face pervasive barriers to employment, housing, voting rights, and basic needs.[11] Even in queer and trans spaces, the needs and experiences of asexual and intersex people are still sidelined, minimized, and dismissed. Those forms of discrimination may not feel "socially acceptable" to you. Your friends and family may turn up their noses at them, insisting that they have transcended these biases. But if we aren't actively tackling those forms of oppression, then we are accepting them. Our inaction itself renders them "socially acceptable," regardless of what we choose to say out loud in polite company. If these forms of discrimination exist without immediate, decisive, near-unanimous intervention, then they are being accepted. And if they are accepted enough to exist, then they are acceptable. Their very existence is proof positive of their acceptability.

In many of these cases, proclamations about the *last socially acceptable form of discrimination* pull our focus away from addressing those existing systems of oppression. And more than that, they draw our attention away from our own complicity in those systems. Many of us who are housed, for example, shrug our shoulders at those who aren't, as if our housing crisis wasn't created by a series of decisions by people—people like elected officials, developers, even ourselves. As a middle-class white person, I frequently hear friends and family condemn gentrification without grappling in any meaningful way with our own roles in driving gentrification and housing crises. We don't talk to the landlords in our families. We don't second-guess our decisions to buy homes in neighborhoods that are historically populated with lower-income communities, Black communities, and communities of color. We fail to reckon, too, with the bizarre lawlessness of buying homes on stolen land. Beyond housing, we talk ourselves out of the hard work of uprooting family members' racism. We make that racism acceptable when we tell ourselves *my uncle's never going to change, so why try?* Or *I meant well, so I can't be racist.* We condone racism, transphobia, and more when we tell ourselves *there's no point in arguing.* We permit all kinds of oppression when we justify and excuse others' perpetuation of them.

Calling anti-fatness "the last socially acceptable form of discrimination" doesn't just imply that other systems of oppression are somehow "fixed" and no longer operational—it also renders our complicity in those systems of oppression invisible, even to us.

Whatever our intentions, statements like "anti-fatness is the last socially acceptable form of discrimination" paper over the struggles of many communities—communities in which fat people exist. When we erase those communities, we also erase the fat people in them and reduce our conception of fatness to only those fat people who hew closest to the most privileged identities. If we imply that racism is no longer a problem, we erase the dual burdens of racism and anti-fatness placed on fat BIPOC. If we ignore ableism, we make invisible the 38 percent of disabled Americans who are fat.[12] And by slowly whittling away fat people who hold multiple marginalized identities, we are left primarily to focus on fat people with the greatest privilege: white fat people, wealthy fat people, nondisabled fat people, fat people with citizenship.

Like so many fat people, I deeply value the growth and solidarity of those closest to me, including those who proclaim that anti-fatness is *the last socially acceptable form of discrimination.* And as an organizer, I welcome more people to the movements for fat justice and liberation.

After all, movements are built to expand, not contract. I treasure the solidarity that so many newly politicized people, fat and thin alike, bring to their growing support of those who are fatter than they are. But I cannot let support of fat people like me—fat people with considerable privilege—come at the even unintended cost of their support for so many other marginalized communities. Their newfound intimacy with fat pain doesn't erase the deeper needs, the bodily safety, and the ignored voices of so many more. The countless people who know that, despite your best intentions, there is no *last oppression*. We can always find new ways to understand marginalized communities, new experiences to learn about, and systems of oppression we haven't yet explored. Like a virus or parasite, oppression mutates, adapting to its environment, finding hosts wherever it can. And as with any virus, meaning well is not a cure. It cannot simply be wished away.

OPPORTUNITIES FOR ACTION

+ *Practice stating your support for fat people without comparing communities or struggles.* Some ways to do that:
  - "Anti-fat bias is a troubling, insidious form of discrimination."
  - "Fat hate happens out in the open, and many of us think it's acceptable and deserved."
  - "I support fat people."
  - "Anti-fatness isn't welcome here."
+ *Read the work of fat writers who hold multiple marginalized identities.* If you like poetry, start with Caleb Luna's *Revenge Body*, Yesika Salgado's *Corazón*, or Rachel Wiley's *Nothing Is Okay*. If you like nonfiction, try Sonya Renee Taylor's *The Body Is Not an Apology*. Or you can support the work of organizations supporting fat people who hold multiple marginalized identities, like JerVae Anthony's Fat Black Liberation (fatblackliberation.com) or NOLOSE,

an organization of fat queer and trans people committed to
ending fat oppression (nolose.org). Expose yourself to the
work and stories of fat Black people, Indigenous people,
and People of Color; fat trans people; fat disabled people,
and more. Remember that multiple systems of oppression
operate at once, and many fat people are left to contend not
just with anti-fatness but with racism, xenophobia, ableism,
transphobia, Islamophobia, and other forms of bias.

ACKNOWLEDGMENTS

This book has been made possible by the hard work and extraordinary generosity of so many people. It wouldn't exist without my literary agent, Beth Vesel, and editor, Joanna Green. The outstanding staff team at Beacon Press made it possible for you to hear, read, or hold both this book and my last, *What We Don't Talk About When We Talk About Fat.*

Many of the ideas expressed here were shaped up by my excellent editor at *SELF*, Zahra Barnes, who is both a joy and an honor to work alongside. In writing this manuscript, I benefited greatly from the input and guidance of David McElhatton, Dan Casey, Rebecca Eisenberg, Daniel Alexander Jones, Jeanie Finlay, Sally Tamarkin, Virginia Sole-Smith, Talia Lavin, my niece, Rita, and my mom, Pam. My *Maintenance Phase* cohost, Michael Hobbes, allowed me the grace and space to finish this manuscript, picking up more than his fair share of work. And as ever, he did it with happiness, candor, and humor.

Like any movement work, this book simply wouldn't exist without generations of fat activists, thinkers, and artists, and it exists in dialogue with their work: Sonya Renee Taylor, Marilyn Wann, Roxane Gay, the late Cat Pausé, Saucye West, Jes Baker, Rachel Wiley, Sophia Carter-Kahn, April K. Quioh, Kivan Bay, Da'Shaun Harrison, Evette Dionne, Stacy Bias, Caleb Luna, Lesley Kinzel, Kate Harding, Marianne Kirby, Tigress Osborn, Shoog McDaniel, JerVae Anthony, Ash Nischuk, Mary Lambert, Shiloh George, Ijeoma Oluo, Lindy West, Ushshi Rahman, Cece Olisa, Esther Rothblum, Sondra Solovay, Charlotte Cooper, Stephanie Yeboah, Natalie

Boero, Paul Campos, Jessamyn Stanley, Yesika Salgado, and many, many more. I also owe a debt of gratitude to the organizations and projects that have fought and continue to fight for fat people: the Fat Underground, the New Haven Fat Liberation Front, FedFront, the National Association to Advance Fat Acceptance, the Association for Size Diversity and Health, NOLOSE, *The Body Is Not an Apology*, and more.

The data points offered in these pages wouldn't be possible without researchers working to understand how anti-fat bias operates, and on what scale—researchers like Rebecca Puhl and Sean Phelan, and journalists who cover their work, like Gina Kolata. It also wouldn't be possible without scholars like Natalie Boero, J. Eric Oliver, Amy Erdman Farrell, and Sabrina Strings, whose work has offered so much to movements built by and for fat people. Feedback and conversations with *Maintenance Phase* listeners, whether about their lived experiences or about their scholarly or scientific research, also substantially shaped this book.

Finally, this book was facilitated through the support of my family: Pam, Rusty, Chris, Bridget, Rita, Henry, Zack, and Gavin. It was bolstered by the support of dear friends like Abbott, Veazey, Rossi, Howell, Hill-Hart, Alice, Olivia, the Magpie family, Alejandro, Jessica, Maceo, Jennifer, Pidge, Emily, and Jeanie. And my sweet little dog, Finn Diesel, kept my spirits up while I wrote about tough stuff.

NOTES

INTRODUCTION

1. Denarii Monroe, "3 Reasons to Find a Better Term Than '-Phobia' to Describe Oppression," *Everyday Feminism*, October 7, 2016, https://everyday feminism.com/2016/10/find-a-better-term-than-phobia.

MYTH 1: "BEING FAT IS A CHOICE."

1. Rachel Paula Abrahamson, "Plus-Size Model Lost 240 Pounds and Kept It Off: Pics," *Us Weekly*, Oct. 15, 2017, https://www.usmagazine.com/celebrity-moms/news/plus-size-model-lost-240-pounds-and-kept-it-off-w203492.

2. Abrahamson, "Plus-Size Model Lost 240 Pounds and Kept It Off."

3. Abrahamson, "Plus-Size Model Lost 240 Pounds and Kept It Off."

4. Abrahamson, "Plus-Size Model Lost 240 Pounds and Kept It Off."

5. J. G. Bacon, K. E. Scheltema, and B. E. Robinson, "Fat Phobia Scale Revisited: The Short Form," *International Journal of Obesity* 25, no. 2 (Mar. 25, 2001): 252–57, https://doi.org/10.1038/sj.ijo.0801537.

6. David B. Allison, Vincent C. Basile, and Harold E. Yuker, "The Measurement of Attitudes Toward and Beliefs About Obese Persons," *International Journal of Eating Disorders* 10, no. 5 (Sept. 1991): 599–607, https://doi.org/10.1002/1098-108X(199109)10:5%3C599::AID-EAT2260100512%3E3.0.CO;2-%23.

7. Gina Kolata, "One Weight-Loss Approach Fits All? No, Not Even Close," *New York Times*, Dec. 12, 2016, https://www.nytimes.com/2016/12/12/health/weight-loss-obesity.html.

8. Gina Kolata, "Americans Blame Obesity on Willpower, Despite Evidence It's Genetic," *New York Times*, Nov. 1, 2016, https://www.nytimes.com/2016/11/01/health/americans-obesity-willpower-genetics-study.html.

9. "Lipoedema," NHS, https://www.nhs.uk/conditions/lipoedema, accessed Feb. 22, 2022.

10. Philipp Kruppa, Iakovos Georgiou, Niklas Biermann, Lukas Prantl, Peter Klein-Weigel, and Mojtaba Ghods, "Lipedema—Pathogenesis, Diagnosis, and Treatment Options," *Deutsches Ärzteblatt International*, June 1, 2020, https://doi.org/10.3238/arztebl.2020.0396.

11. "Polycystic Ovary Syndrome (PCOS)," Johns Hopkins Medicine, https://www.hopkinsmedicine.org/health/conditions-and-diseases/polycystic-ovary-syndrome-pcos, accessed Feb. 22, 2022.

12. "PCOS (Polycystic Ovary Syndrome) and Diabetes," Centers for Disease Control and Prevention (CDC), Mar. 24, 2020, https://www.cdc.gov/diabetes/basics/pcos.html.

13. David Russell-Jones and Rehman Khan, "Insulin-Associated Weight Gain in Diabetes—Causes, Effects and Coping Strategies," *Diabetes, Obesity and Metabolism* 9, no. 6 (Dec. 15, 2006): 799–812, https://doi.org/10.1111/j.1463-1326.2006.00686.x.

14. "10 Diabetes Medications That Cause Weight Gain (or Loss)," GoodRx, https://www.goodrx.com/conditions/diabetes/diabetes-medications-that-can-cause-weight-gain, accessed Feb. 22, 2022.

15. "Statistics About Diabetes," ADA, https://www.diabetes.org/about-us/statistics/about-diabetes, accessed Feb. 22, 2022.

16. "Obesity Stigma Prevalent in Online News Coverage," *YaleNews*, Yale University, Nov. 18, 2021, https://news.yale.edu/2011/05/05/obesity-stigma-prevalent-online-news-coverage.

17. "Obesity Stigma Prevalent in Online News Coverage," *YaleNews*.

18. Rebecca M. Puhl, Jamie Lee Peterson, Jenny A. DePierre, and Joerg Luedicke, "Headless, Hungry, and Unhealthy: A Video Content Analysis of Obese Persons Portrayed in Online News," *Journal of Health Communication* 18, no. 6 (Feb. 19, 2013): 686–702, https://doi.org/10.1080/10810730.2012.743631.

19. Sarah E. Gollust, Ijeoma Eboh, and Colleen L. Barry, "Picturing Obesity: Analyzing the Social Epidemiology of Obesity Conveyed Through US News Media Images," *Social Science & Medicine* 74, no. 10 (Mar. 6, 2012): 1544–51, https://doi.org/10.1016/j.socscimed.2012.01.021.

20. Rebecca M. Puhl, Joerg Luedicke, and Chelsea A. Heuer, "The Stigmatizing Effect of Visual Media Portrayals of Obese Persons on Public Attitudes: Does Race or Gender Matter?" *Journal of Health Communication* 18, no. 7 (Apr. 11, 2013): 805–26, https://doi.org/10.1080/10810730.2012.757393.

21. Georgina Johnstone and Sharon L. Grant, "Weight Stigmatisation in Antiobesity Campaigns: The Role of Images," *Health Promotion Journal of Australia* 30, no. 1 (Aug. 5, 2018): 37–46, https://doi.org/10.1002/hpja.183.

22. Inge Kersbergen and Eric Robinson, "Blatant Dehumanization of People with Obesity," *Obesity* 27, no. 6 (Apr. 2, 2019): 1005–12, https://doi.org/10.1002/oby.22460.

23. Gina Kolata, "After 'the Biggest Loser,' Their Bodies Fought to Regain Weight," *New York Times*, May 2, 2016, https://www.nytimes.com/2016/05/02/health/biggest-loser-weight-loss.html.

24. Michael R. Lowe, Sapna D. Doshi, Shawn N. Katterman, and Emily H. Feig, "Dieting and Restrained Eating as Prospective Predictors of Weight Gain," *Frontiers in Psychology* 4 (Sept. 2, 2013), https://doi.org/10.3389/fpsyg.2013.00577.

25. Alison Fildes, Judith Charlton, Caroline Rudisill, Peter Littlejohns, A. Toby Prevost, and Martin C. Gulliford, "Probability of an Obese Person Attaining Normal Body Weight: Cohort Study Using Electronic Health Records," *American Journal of Public Health* 105, no. 9 (Sept. 2015), https://doi.org/10.2105/ajph.2015.302773.

26. Michael Hobbes, "Everything You Know About Obesity Is Wrong," *HuffPost*, Sept. 19, 2018, https://highline.huffingtonpost.com/articles/en/everything-you-know-about-obesity-is-wrong.

27. Bruce Owens Grimm, "A Desire for Fat," Lit Haunts, *Medium*, Nov. 12, 2019, https://bruceowensgrimm.medium.com/a-desire-for-fat-89f81be3f258.

28. Grimm, "A Desire for Fat."

29. Caleb Luna (@chairbreaker), "As queers, we saw the failures in the 'born this way' argument decades ago. It doesn't need to not be our fault for it to be okay to exist. I choose queerness every day. I choose fatness every day. And those are both legitimate and desirable choices that improve my life," Twitter, Jan. 5, 2022, 3:39 p.m., https://twitter.com/chairbreaker_/status/1478826060682711042.

MYTH 2: "ANY FAT PERSON CAN BECOME THIN IF THEY TRY HARD ENOUGH."

1. Priya Sumithran, Luke A. Prendergast, Elizabeth Delbridge, Katrina Purcell, Arthur Shulkes, Adamandia Kriketos, and Joseph Proietto, "Long-Term Persistence of Hormonal Adaptations to Weight Loss," *New England Journal of Medicine* 365, no. 17 (Oct. 27, 2011): 1597–1604, https://doi.org/10.1056/nejmoa1105816.

2. Olga Gruzdeva, Daria Borodkina, Evgenya Uchasova, Yulia Dyleva, and Olga Barbarash, "Leptin Resistance: Underlying Mechanisms and Diagnosis," *Diabetes, Metabolic Syndrome and Obesity: Targets and Therapy* Volume 12 (Jan. 25, 2019): 191–98, https://doi.org/10.2147/dmso.s182406.

3. Andrea G. Izquierdo, Ana B. Crujeiras, Felipe F. Casanueva, and Marcos C. Carreira, "Leptin, Obesity, and Leptin Resistance: Where Are We 25 Years Later?" *Nutrients* 11, no. 11 (Nov. 8, 2019): 2704, https://doi.org/10.3390/nu11112704.

4. Marsha McCulloch, "Appetite Hormones," *Today's Dietitian*, July 2015, https://www.todaysdietitian.com/newarchives/070115p26.shtml.

5. Danielle Kappele, "Why Willpower Isn't Enough to Keep the Pounds Off," CBC News, Dec. 23, 2016, https://www.cbc.ca/news/health/why-willpower-isn-t-enough-to-keep-the-pounds-off-1.3907411.

6. Alison B. Evert and Marion J. Franz, "Why Weight Loss Maintenance Is Difficult," *Diabetes Spectrum* 30, no. 3 (Aug. 1, 2017): 153–56, https://doi.org/10.2337/ds017-0025.

7. Robert Ross and Ian Janssen, "Physical Activity, Total and Regional Obesity: Dose-Response Considerations," *Medicine and Science in Sports and Exercise* 33, no. 6 (June 2001), https://doi.org/10.1097/00005768-200106001-00023.

8. Rena R. Wing, "Physical Activity in the Treatment of the Adulthood Overweight and Obesity: Current Evidence and Research Issues," *Medicine & Science in Sports & Exercise* 31, no. Supplement 11 (Nov. 1999), https://doi.org /10.1097/00005768-199911001-00010.

9. Kelly A. Shaw, Hanni C. Gennat, Peter O'Rourke, and Chris Del Mar, "Exercise for Overweight or Obesity," *Cochrane Database of Systematic Reviews*, Oct. 18, 2006, https://doi.org/10.1002/14651858.cd003817.pub3.

10. Robert H. Shmerling, "When Dieting Doesn't Work," *Harvard Health*, May 26, 2020, https://www.health.harvard.edu/blog/when-dieting -doesnt-work-2020052519889.

11. Long Ge, Behnam Sadeghirad, Geoff D. Ball, Bruno R. da Costa, Christine L. Hitchcock, Anton Svendrovski, Ruhi Kiflen et al., "Comparison of Dietary Macronutrient Patterns of 14 Popular Named Dietary Programmes for Weight and Cardiovascular Risk Factor Reduction in Adults: Systematic Review and Network Meta-Analysis of Randomised Trials," *British Medical Journal (BMJ)*, Apr. 1, 2020, m696, https://doi.org/10.1136/bmj.m696.

12. Long Ge et al., "Comparison of Dietary Macronutrient Patterns of 14 Popular Named Dietary Programmes for Weight and Cardiovascular Risk Factor Reduction in Adults."

13. Stuart Wolpert, "Dieting Does Not Work, UCLA Researchers Report," UCLA, Apr. 3, 2007, https://newsroom.ucla.edu/releases/Dieting-Does -Not-Work-UCLA-Researchers-7832.

14. D. Crawford, R. W. Jeffery, and S. A. French, "Can Anyone Successfully Control Their Weight? Findings of a Three Year Community-Based Study of Men and Women," *International Journal of Obesity* 24, no. 9 (Sept. 24, 2000): 1107–10, https://doi.org/10.1038/sj.ijo.0801374.

15. K. H. Pietiläinen, S. E. Saarni, J. Kaprio, and A. Rissanen, "Does Dieting Make You Fat? A Twin Study," *International Journal of Obesity* 36, no. 3 (Mar. 2012): 456–64, https://doi.org/10.1038/ijo.2011.160.

16. Mohsen Mazidi, Niki Katsiki, Dimitri P. Mikhailidis, Naveed Sattar, and Maciej Banach, "Lower Carbohydrate Diets and All-Cause and Cause-Specific Mortality: A Population-Based Cohort Study and Pooling of Prospective Studies," *European Heart Journal* 40, no. 34 (2019): 2870–79, https://doi .org/10.1093/eurheartj/ehz174.

17. Ana Sandolu, "Low-Carb Diets 'Are Unsafe and Should Be Avoided'," *Medical News Today*, Aug. 28, 2018, https://www.medicalnewstoday.com/articles /322881#Why-low-carb-diets-should-be-avoided.

18. K. Aleisha Fetters, "Why Low-Fat Diets Don't Work," *U.S. News & World Report*, Nov. 20, 2015, https://health.usnews.com/health-news/health -wellness/articles/2015/11/20/why-low-fat-diets-dont-work.

19. Shirley A. Beresford, Karen C. Johnson, Cheryl Ritenbaugh, Norman L. Lasser, Linda G. Snetselaar, Henry R. Black, Garnet L. Anderson et al., "Low-Fat Dietary Pattern and Risk of Colorectal Cancer," *Journal of the American*

Medical Association (*JAMA*) 295, no. 6 (Feb. 8, 2006): 643, https://doi.org/10 .1001/jama.295.6.643.

20. Ross L. Prentice, Bette Caan, Rowan T. Chlebowski, Ruth Patterson, Lewis H. Kuller, Judith K. Ockene, Karen L. Margolis et al., "Low-Fat Dietary Pattern and Risk of Invasive Breast Cancer," *JAMA* 295, no. 6 (Feb. 8, 2006): 629, https://doi.org/10.1001/jama.295.6.629.

21. Barbara V. Howard, Linda Van Horn, Judith Hsia, JoAnn E. Manson, Marcia L. Stefanick, Sylvia Wassertheil-Smoller, Lewis H. Kuller et al., "Low-Fat Dietary Pattern and Risk of Cardiovascular Disease," *JAMA* 295, no. 6 (Feb. 8, 2006): 655, https://doi.org/10.1001/jama.295.6.655.

22. Max Wishnofsky, "Caloric Equivalents of Gained or Lost Weight," *American Journal of Clinical Nutrition* 6, no. 5 (1958): 542–46, https://doi. org/10.1093/ajcn/6.5.542.

23. Maurice E. Shils and Moshe Shike, eds., *Modern Nutrition in Health and Disease* (Philadelphia: Lippincott Williams & Wilkins, 2006).

24. Diana M. Thomas, M. Cristina Gonzalez, Andrea Z. Pereira, Leanne M. Redman, and Steven B. Heymsfield, "Time to Correctly Predict the Amount of Weight Loss with Dieting," *Journal of the Academy of Nutrition and Dietetics* 114, no. 6 (Mar. 31, 2014): 857–61, https://doi.org/10.1016/j .jand.2014.02.003.

25. Brian Elbel, Rogan Kersh, Victoria L. Brescoll, and L. Beth Dixon, "Calorie Labeling and Food Choices: A First Look at the Effects on Low-Income People in New York City," *Health Affairs* 28, no. Supplement 1 (2009), https://doi.org/10.1377/hlthaff.28.6.w1110.

26. Tamara Duker Freuman, "Who Actually Needs a 2,000-Calorie Diet?" *U.S. News & World Report*, June 14, 2016, https://health.usnews.com /health-news/blogs/eat-run/articles/2016-06-14/who-actually-needs-a-2-000 -calorie-diet.

27. Marion Nestle, "Why Does the FDA Recommend 2,000 Calories per Day?" *The Atlantic*, Aug. 4, 2011, https://www.theatlantic.com/health /archive/2011/08/why-does-the-fda-recommend-2-000-calories-per-day /243092.

28. Giles Yeo, *Why Calories Don't Count: How We Got the Science of Weight Loss Wrong* (New York: Simon & Schuster, 2021), 32.

29. K. Aleisha Fetters, "What Happens to Your Body When You Go on an Extreme Diet?" *U.S. News & World Report*, Aug. 3, 2021, https://health.usnews .com/wellness/articles/what-happens-to-your-body-when-you-go-on-an -extreme-diet.

30. Claudia McNeilly, "Why Instagram's Favorite Diet—'Teatoxing'— Won't Actually Help You Lose Weight," *Teen Vogue*, Jan. 15, 2016, https:// www.teenvogue.com/story/tea-detox-teatox-bad-for-health-dangers.

31. Hiroshi Noto, Atsushi Goto, Tetsuro Tsujimoto, and Mitsuhiko Noda, "Low-Carbohydrate Diets and All-Cause Mortality: A Systematic

Review and Meta-Analysis of Observational Studies," *PLOS One* 8, no. 1 (Jan. 25, 2013), https://doi.org/10.1371/journal.pone.0055030.

32. F. Xavier Pi-Sunyer, "Short-Term Medical Benefits and Adverse Effects of Weight Loss," *Annals of Internal Medicine* 119, no. 7 (Oct. 1, 1993): 722, https://doi.org/10.7326/0003-4819-119-7_part_2-199310011-00019.

33. Huajie Zou, Ping Yin, Liegang Liu, Wenhua Liu, Zeqing Zhang, Yan Yang, Wenjun Li, Qunchuan Zong, and Xuefeng Yu, "Body-Weight Fluctuation Was Associated with Increased Risk for Cardiovascular Disease, All-Cause and Cardiovascular Mortality: A Systematic Review and Meta-Analysis," *Frontiers in Endocrinology* 10 (Nov. 8, 2019), https://doi.org/10.3389/fendo.2019 .00728.

34. Gina Kolata, "After 'The Biggest Loser,' Their Bodies Fought to Regain Weight," *New York Times*, May 2, 2016, https://www.nytimes.com/2016 /05/02/health/biggest-loser-weight-loss.html.

35. "Disordered Eating & Dieting," National Eating Disorders Collaboration, https://nedc.com.au/eating-disorders/eating-disorders-explained /disordered-eating-and-dieting, accessed Mar. 12, 2022.

36. "Ugly Laws," Eugenics Archives, Social Sciences and Humanities Research Council of Canada, https://eugenicsarchive.ca/discover/connections /54d39e27f8a0ea4706000009, accessed Mar. 12, 2022.

MYTH 3: "PARENTS ARE RESPONSIBLE FOR THEIR CHILD'S WEIGHT."

1. Nadeem Badshah, "Two Teenagers Placed in Foster Care After Weight Loss Plan Fails," *The Guardian*, Mar. 11, 2021, https://www.theguardian.com /society/2021/mar/10/two-teenagers-placed-in-foster-care-after-weight-loss -plan-fails.

2. Ryan Jaslow, "Obese Third-Grader Taken from Family: Did State Go Too Far?" CBS News, Nov. 28, 2011, https://www.cbsnews.com/news/obese -third-grader-taken-from-family-did-state-go-too-far.

3. Ryan Jaslow, "Five-Year-Old's Removal from Family Spotlights Obesity Intervention." CBS News, Dec. 5, 2011, https://www.cbsnews.com/news/five -year-olds-removal-from-family-spotlights-obesity-intervention.

4. Lindsey Murtagh and David S. Ludwig, "State Intervention in Life-Threatening Childhood Obesity," *JAMA* 306, no. 2 (July 13, 2011), https:// doi.org/10.1001/jama.2011.903.

5. Nadeem Badshah, "Two Teenagers Placed in Foster Care After Weight Loss Plan Fails."

6. "Body Mass Index (BMI) Measurement in Schools," CDC, Jan. 25, 2017, https://www.cdc.gov/healthyschools/obesity/bmi/bmi_measurement _schools.htm.

7. Kristine A. Madsen, Hannah R. Thompson, Jennifer Linchey, Lorrene D. Ritchie, Shalika Gupta, Dianne Neumark-Sztainer, Patricia B. Crawford, Charles E. McCulloch, and Ana Ibarra-Castro, "Effect of School-Based Body Mass Index Reporting in California Public Schools," *JAMA Pediatrics* 175,

no. 3 (Nov. 16, 2020): 251, https://doi.org/10.1001/jamapediatrics.2020.4768; "Digest of Education Statistics," National Center for Education Statistics (NCES), US Department of Education, https://nces.ed.gov/programs/digest /d17/tables/dt17_101.40.asp, accessed Feb. 27, 2022.

    8. Kristine A. Madsen et al., "Effect of School-Based Body Mass Index Reporting in California Public Schools."

    9. Renee Engeln, "Schools Should Stop Giving Kids BMI Report Cards," *Psychology Today*, Nov. 12, 2020, https://www.psychologytoday.com/us/blog /beauty-sick/202012/schools-should-stop-giving-kids-bmi-report-cards.

    10. Hilary Whyte and S. M. Findlay, "Dieting in Adolescence," *Paediatrics & Child Health* 9, no. 7 (Sept. 2004): 487–91, https://doi.org/10.1093/pch/9.7.487.

    11. Whyte and Findlay, "Dieting in Adolescence."

    12. "Calls to Set Up Fat Camps for Obese Children in Scotland," *The Scotsman*, Dec. 6, 2016, https://www.scotsman.com/news/politics/calls-set -fat-camps-obese-children-scotland-1461399.

    13. Caroline Davies, "NHS to Set Up 15 Special Clinics in England for Severely Obese Children," *The Guardian*, Nov. 16, 2021, https://www.the guardian.com/society/2021/nov/16/nhs-15-special-clinics-england-severely -obese-children.

    14. Eleanor Hayward, "Thousands of Overweight Children Are to Be Sent to NHS Clinics in Bid to Tackle Obesity Crisis," *Daily Mail Online*, Nov. 16, 2021, https://www.dailymail.co.uk/news/article-10205945/Thousands -overweight-children-sent-NHS-clinics-bid-tackle-obesity-crisis.html.

    15. Stephanie Mansfield, "The Fat Farm," *Washington Post*, July 13, 1980, https://www.washingtonpost.com/archive/politics/1980/07/13/the-fat-farm /27f15cf4-b5f6-4509-b9e0-11b55878f355.

    16. P. J. Gately, C. B. Cooke, R. J. Butterly, P. Mackreth, and S. Carroll, "The Effects of a Children's Summer Camp Programme on Weight Loss, with a 10 Month Follow-Up," *International Journal of Obesity* 24, no. 11 (Nov. 2000): 1445–52, https://doi.org/10.1038/sj.ijo.0801405.

    17. "Pediatric and Adolescent Bariatric Surgery," Children's National Hospital, https://childrensnational.org/departments/bariatric-surgery-program, accessed Feb. 27, 2022.

    18. Mohammed Al Mohaidly, Ahmed Suliman, and Horia Malawi, "Laparoscopic Sleeve Gastrectomy for a Two-and Half Year Old Morbidly Obese Child," *International Journal of Surgery Case Reports* 4, no. 11 (Sept. 12, 2013): 1057–60, https://doi.org/10.1016/j.ijscr.2013.07.033.

    19. "Clinical Commissioning Policy: Obesity Surgery for Children with Severe Complex Obesity," NHS England Specialised Services Clinical Reference Group for Severe and Complex Obesity, Apr. 2017, https://www.england .nhs.uk/wp-content/uploads/2017/04/16053p-obesity-surgery-children-severe -complex-obesity.pdf.

    20. Roberto A. Ferdman, "Why Diets Don't Actually Work, According to a Researcher Who Has Studied Them for Decades," *Washington Post*, Nov. 25,

2021, https://www.washingtonpost.com/news/wonk/wp/2015/05/04/why-diets
-dont-actually-work-according-to-a-researcher-who-has-studied-them-for
-decades.

21. Gina Kolata, "One Weight-Loss Approach Fits All? No, Not Even
Close," *New York Times*, Dec. 12, 2016, https://www.nytimes.com/2016/12/12
/health/weight-loss-obesity.html.

22. Caryn Bell, Jordan Kerr, and Jessica Young, "Associations Between
Obesity, Obesogenic Environments, and Structural Racism Vary by County-
Level Racial Composition," *International Journal of Environmental Research and
Public Health* 16, no. 5 (Mar. 9, 2019): 861, https://doi.org/10.3390/ijerph
16050861.

23. Adam Cohen, "Introduction," *Imbeciles: The Supreme Court, American
Eugenics, and the Sterilization of Carrie Buck* (New York: Penguin Press, 2017).

24. Ellen J. Kennedy, "On Indigenous Peoples Day, Recalling Forced
Sterilizations of Native American Women," *MinnPost*, Oct. 14, 2019, https://
www.minnpost.com/community-voices/2019/10/on-indigenous-peoples
-day-recalling-forced-sterilizations-of-native-american-women.

25. Kennedy, "On Indigenous Peoples Day, Recalling Forced Sterilizations of Native American Women."

26. "California Launches Program to Compensate Survivors of State-
Sponsored Sterilization," Office of Governor Gavin Newsom, State of California, Dec. 31, 2021, https://www.gov.ca.gov/2021/12/31/california-launches
-program-to-compensate-survivors-of-state-sponsored-sterilization.

27. Sarah Mizes-Tan, "For Decades, California Forcibly Sterilized
Women Under Eugenics Law. Now, the State Will Pay Survivors," *Cap Radio*,
July 20, 2021, https://www.capradio.org/articles/2021/07/20/for-decades
-california-forcibly-sterilized-women-under-eugenics-law-now-the-state-will
-pay-survivors.

28. Jo Yurcaba, "Texas AG Says Transition Care for Minors Is Child Abuse
Under State Law," NBCNews.com, Feb. 22, 2022, https://www.nbcnews.com
/nbc-out/out-politics-and-policy/texas-ag-says-transition-care-minors-child
-abuse-state-law-rcna17176.

29. Jo Yurcaba, "Texas Governor Calls on Citizens to Report Parents of
Transgender Kids for Abuse," NBCNews.com, Feb. 23, 2022, https://www
.nbcnews.com/nbc-out/out-politics-and-policy/texas-governor-calls-citizens
-report-parents-transgender-kids-abuse-rcna17455.

30. Frank Edwards, Sara Wakefield, Kieran Healy, and Christopher
Wildeman, "Contact with Child Protective Services Is Pervasive but Un-
equally Distributed by Race and Ethnicity in Large US Counties," *Proceedings
of the National Academy of Sciences* 118, no. 30 (July 19, 2021), https://doi.org
/10.1073/pnas.2106272118.

31. Chris Gottlieb, "We Must Stop Separating Black Families with Child
Welfare," *Time*, Mar. 17, 2021, https://time.com/5946929/child-welfare-black
-families.

32. William Wan, "What Separation from Parents Does to Children: 'The Effect Is Catastrophic,'" *Washington Post*, June 19, 2018, https://www .washingtonpost.com/national/health-science/what-separation-from-parents -does-to-children-the-effect-is-catastrophic/2018/06/18/cooc3oec-732c-11e8 -805c-4b67019fcfe4_story.html.

33. Eliot Marshall, "Childhood Neglect Erodes the Brain," *Science*, Jan. 26, 2015, https://www.science.org/content/article/childhood-neglect-erodes-brain.

34. Sasha Aslanian, "Researchers Still Learning from Romania's Orphans," NPR, Sept. 16, 2006, https://www.npr.org/templates/story/story.php?storyId =6089477.

35. Sven R. Silburn, Stephen R. Zubrick, David M. Lawrence, Francis G. Mitrou, John A. De Maio, Eve Blair, Adele Cox et al., "The Intergenerational Effects of Forced Separation on the Social and Emotional Wellbeing of Aboriginal Children and Young People," Australian Institute of Family Studies, *Family Matters* 75 (2006): 10–17; https://aifs.gov.au/sites/default/files/publication -documents/rr21.pdf.

36. Zhengkui Liu, Xinying Li, and Xiaojia Ge, "Left Too Early: The Effects of Age at Separation from Parents on Chinese Rural Children's Symptoms of Anxiety and Depression," *American Journal of Public Health* 99, no. 11 (Sept. 20, 2011): 2049–54, https://doi.org/10.2105/ajph.2008.150474.

37. Joseph J. Doyle, "Child Protection and Child Outcomes: Measuring the Effects of Foster Care," *American Economic Review* 97, no. 5 (Dec. 2007): 1583–1610, https://doi.org/10.1257/aer.97.5.1583.

38. Stephanie Carnes, "The Trauma of Family Separation Will Haunt Children for Decades," *HuffPost*, June 22, 2018, https://www.huffpost.com/entry /opinion-carnes-family-separation-trauma_n_5b2bf535e4b00295f15a96b2.

MYTH 4: "THIN PEOPLE SHOULD HELP FAT PEOPLE LOSE WEIGHT."

1. Kelli E. Friedman, Simona K. Reichmann, Philip R. Costanzo, Arnaldo Zelli, Jamile A. Ashmore, and Gerard J. Musante, "Weight Stigmatization and Ideological Beliefs: Relation to Psychological Functioning in Obese Adults," *Obesity Research* 13, no. 5 (May 2005): 907–16, https://doi.org/10.1038/oby .2005.105.

2. Sabrina Strings, *Fearing the Black Body: The Racial Origins of Fat Phobia* (New York: New York University Press, 2019).

MYTH 5: "WEIGHT LOSS IS THE RESULT OF HEALTHY CHOICES AND SHOULD BE CELEBRATED."

1. Adele (@adele), "Thank you for the birthday love," Instagram, May 6, 2020, https://www.instagram.com/p/B_1VGc5AsoZ.

2. "Adele Monologue—SNL," *Saturday Night Live*, Oct. 24, 2020, available at YouTube, https://www.youtube.com/watch?v=LlWs87C2B7Q.

3. "Bubba Smith, NFL Star and 'Police Academy' Actor, Found Dead at Home," *Los Angeles Times*, Aug. 3, 2011, https://latimesblogs.latimes.com

/lanow/2011/08/bubba-smith-nfl-star-police-academy-actor-found-dead
-home.html.

4. "Bubba Smith Died of Drug Intoxication, Coroner Says," *Los Angeles
Times*, Nov. 2, 2011, https://latimesblogs.latimes.com/lanow/2011/11/bubba
-smith-died-of-drug-intoxication-other-factors-coroner-says.html.

MYTH 6: "OBESITY IS THE LEADING CAUSE OF DEATH IN THE UNITED STATES."

1. Bruno Latour, *Pandora's Hope: Essays on the Reality of Science Studies*
(Cambridge, MA: Harvard University Press, 1999), 304.

2. Ali H. Mokdad, "Actual Causes of Death in the United States, 2000,"
JAMA 291, no. 10 (Mar. 10, 2004): 1238, https://doi.org/10.1001/jama.291
.10.1238.

3. Gina Kolata, "Data on Deaths from Obesity Is Inflated, U.S. Agency
Says," *New York Times*, Nov. 24, 2004, https://www.nytimes.com/2004/11/24
/health/data-on-deaths-from-obesity-is-inflated-us-agency-says.html.

4. David B. Allison, "Annual Deaths Attributable to Obesity in the United
States," *JAMA* 282, no. 16 (Oct. 27, 1999): 1530, https://doi.org/10.1001/jama
.282.16.1530.

5. Michael Gard, *The End of the Obesity Epidemic* (New York: Routledge,
2011), 16.

6. Allison, "Annual Deaths Attributable to Obesity in the United States."

7. Allison, "Annual Deaths Attributable to Obesity in the United States."

8. J. Eric Oliver, *Fat Politics: The Real Story Behind America's Obesity Epidemic* (Toronto: Oxford University Press Canada, 2006), 25.

9. Oliver, *Fat Politics*, 3–4.

10. "Correction: Actual Causes of Death in the United States, 2000,"
JAMA 293, no. 3 (Jan. 19, 2005): 293, https://doi.org/10.1001/jama.293.3.293.

11. Katherine M. Flegal, "Excess Deaths Associated with Underweight,
Overweight, and Obesity," *JAMA* 293, no. 15 (Apr. 20, 2005): 1861, https://
doi.org/10.1001/jama.293.15.1861.

12. Rosie Mestel, "Weighty Death Toll Downplayed," *Los Angeles Times*,
Apr. 20, 2005, https://www.latimes.com/archives/la-xpm-2005-apr-20-sci
-overweight20-story.html.

13. "Overweight & Obesity," CDC, 2005, http://web.archive.org/web
/20050829103423/http:/www.cdc.gov/PDF/Frequently_Asked_Questions
_About_Calculating_Obesity-Related_Risk.pdf.

14. Mestel,"Weighty Death Toll Downplayed."

15. Katherine M. Flegal, "The Obesity Wars and the Education of a Researcher: A Personal Account," *Progress in Cardiovascular Diseases* 67 (2021):
75–79, https://doi.org/10.1016/j.pcad.2021.06.009.

16. Flegal, "The Obesity Wars and the Education of a Researcher."

17. Flegal, "The Obesity Wars and the Education of a Researcher."

MYTH 7: "THE BMI IS AN OBJECTIVE MEASURE OF SIZE AND HEALTH."

1. "Body Mass Index (BMI)," CDC, June 7, 2021, https://www.cdc.gov
/healthyweight/assessing/bmi/index.html.

2. "Adolphe Quetelet," *Encyclopædia Britannica*, https://www.britannica
.com/biography/Adolphe-Quetelet, accessed Feb. 7, 2022.

3. Rutledge M. Dennis, "Social Darwinism, Scientific Racism, and the
Metaphysics of Race," *Journal of Negro Education* 64, no. 3 (1995): 243, https://
doi.org/10.2307/2967206.

4. Adalbert Albrecht, "Cesare Lombroso. A Glance at His Life Work,"
Journal of the American Institute of Criminal Law and Criminology 1, no. 2 (1910):
71, https://doi.org/10.2307/1133036.

5. Matt Simon, "Fantastically Wrong: The Scientist Who Seriously Believed Criminals Were Part Ape," *Wired*, Nov. 12, 2014, https://www.wired
.com/2014/11/fantastically-wrong-criminal-anthropology.

6. "Anthropometry," *Encyclopædia Britannica*, https://www.britannica.com
/science/anthropometry, accessed Feb. 7, 2022.

7. "Phrenology," *Encyclopædia Britannica*, https://www.britannica.com
/topic/phrenology, accessed Feb. 7, 2022.

8. "Quetelet, Adolphe," Eugenics Archives, Social Sciences and Humanities
Research Council of Canada, http://eugenicsarchive.ca/discover/connections
/5233cb0f5c2ec5000000009c, accessed Feb. 7, 2022.

9. Timothy F. Murphy and Marc A. Lappe, eds., *Justice and the Human
Genome Project* (Los Angeles: University of California Press, 1994), 18.

10. Sylvia Karasu, "Adolphe Quetelet and the Evolution of Body Mass
Index," *Psychology Today*, Mar. 18, 2016, https://www.psychologytoday.com/us
/blog/the-gravity-weight/201603/adolphe-quetelet-and-the-evolution-body
-mass-index-bmi.

11. Karasu, "Adolphe Quetelet and the Evolution of Body Mass Index."

12. Karasu, "Adolphe Quetelet and the Evolution of Body Mass Index."

13. A. Keys, F. Fidanza, M. J. Karvonen, N. Kimura, and H. L. Taylor,
"Indices of Relative Weight and Obesity," *International Journal of Epidemiology*
43, no. 3 (June 1, 2014): 655–65, https://doi.org/10.1093/ije/dyu058.

14. Keys et al., "Indices of Relative Weight and Obesity."

15. Mahbubur Rahman and Abbey B. Berenson, "Accuracy of Current
Body Mass Index Obesity Classification for White, Black, and Hispanic
Reproductive-Age Women," *Obstetrics & Gynecology* 115, no. 5 (2010): 982–88,
https://doi.org/10.1097/aog.ob013e3181da9423.

16. Marina Komaroff, "For Researchers on Obesity: Historical Review of
Extra Body Weight Definitions," *Journal of Obesity* 2016 (2016): 1–9, https://
doi.org/10.1155/2016/2460285.

17. "The National Institutes of Health Consensus Development Program:
Health Implications of Obesity," National Institutes of Health, US Department
of Health and Human Services, Feb. 11, 1985, https://consensus.nih.gov/1985
/1985Obesity049html.htm.

18. Komaroff, "For Researchers on Obesity."

19. Ray Moynihan, "Obesity Task Force Linked to Who Takes 'Millions' from Drug Firms," *BMJ* 332, no. 7555 (June 17, 2006), https://doi.org/10.1136/bmj.332.7555.1412-a.

20. Moynihan, "Obesity Task Force Linked to Who Takes 'Millions' from Drug Firms."

21. Anne McDermott and Elizabeth Cohen, "Who's Fat? New Definition Adopted," CNN Interactive, June 17, 1998, http://www.cnn.com/HEALTH/9806/17/weight.guidelines.

22. A. Janet Tomiyama, Deborah Carr, Ellen M. Granberg, Brenda Major, Eric Robinson, Angelina R. Sutin, and Alexandra Brewis, "How and Why Weight Stigma Drives the Obesity 'Epidemic' and Harms Health," *BMC Medicine* 16, no. 1 (Aug. 15, 2018), https://doi.org/10.1186/s12916-018-1116-5.

23. Gina Kolata, "Why Do Obese Patients Get Worse Care? Many Doctors Don't See Past the Fat," *New York Times*, Sept. 26, 2016, https://www.nytimes.com/2016/09/26/health/obese-patients-health-care.html.

24. M. A. Green, M. Strong, F. Razak, S. V. Subramanian, C. Relton, and P. Bissell, "Who Are the Obese? A Cluster Analysis Exploring Subgroups of the Obese," *Journal of Public Health* 38, no. 2 (Apr. 18, 2015): 258–64, https://doi.org/10.1093/pubmed/fdv040.

25. Gina Kolata, "One Weight-Loss Approach Fits All? No, Not Even Close," *New York Times*, Dec. 12, 2016, https://www.nytimes.com/2016/12/12/health/weight-loss-obesity.html.

26. Karasu, "Adolphe Quetelet and the Evolution of Body Mass Index."

27. "Widely Used Body Fat Measurements Overestimate Fatness in African-Americans, Study Finds," *ScienceDaily*, June 22, 2009, https://www.sciencedaily.com/releases/2009/06/090611142407.htm.

28. Susan B. Racette, Susan S. Deusinger, and Robert H Deusinger, "Obesity: Overview of Prevalence, Etiology, and Treatment," *Physical Therapy* 83, no. 3 (2003): 276–88. https://doi.org/10.1093/ptj/83.3.276.

29. "Global Obesity Levels—Obesity—Procon.org," *Obesity*, Apr. 20, 2020, https://obesity.procon.org/global-obesity-levels.

30. A. S. Jackson, P. R. Stanforth, J. Gagnon, T. Rankinen, A. S. Leon, D. C. Rao, J. S. Skinner, C. Bouchard, and J. H. Wilmore, "The Effect of Sex, Age and Race on Estimating Percentage Body Fat from Body Mass Index: The Heritage Family Study," *International Journal of Obesity* 26, no. 6 (May 30, 2002): 789–96, https://doi.org/10.1038/sj.ijo.0802006.

31. "Vaginoplasty/Vulvoplasty," Transfeminine Bottom Surgery, University of Utah Health, https://healthcare.utah.edu/transgender-health/gender-affirmation-surgery/vaginoplasty.php, accessed Feb. 8, 2022.

32. Jody L. Herman, Taylor N. T. Brown, and Ann P. Haas, "Suicide Thoughts and Attempts Among Transgender Adults," Williams Institute, UCLA, Apr. 9, 2020, https://williamsinstitute.law.ucla.edu/publications/suicidality-transgender-adults.

33. V. Hainer and I. Aldhoon-Hainerova, "Obesity Paradox Does Exist," *Diabetes Care* 36, no. Supplement_2 (July 17, 2013), https://doi.org/10.2337/dcs13-2023.

34. Su-Min Jeong, Kyungdo Han, Dahye Kim, Sang Youl Rhee, Wooyoung Jang, and Dong Wook Shin, "Body Mass Index, Diabetes, and the Risk of Parkinson's Disease," *Movement Disorders* 35, no. 2 (Nov. 30, 2019): 236–44, https://doi.org/10.1002/mds.27922.

35. Andria Bianchi and Maria Ricupero, "Questioning the Ethics of Promoting Weight Loss in Clinical Practice," *Canadian Journal of Bioethics* 3, no. 1 (2020): 95–98, https://doi.org/10.7202/1070228ar.

36. Erika Aparecida Silveira, Lorena Pereira de Souza Rosa, Annelisa Silva de Carvalho Santos, Camila Kellen de Souza Cardoso, and Matias Noll, "Type 2 Diabetes Mellitus in Class II and III Obesity: Prevalence, Associated Factors, and Correlation Between Glycemic Parameters and Body Mass Index," *International Journal of Environmental Research and Public Health* 17, no. 11 (2020): 3930, https://doi.org/10.3390/ijerph17113930.

37. Cameron Razieh, Francesco Zaccardi, Melanie J. Davies, Kamlesh Khunti, and Thomas Yates, "Body Mass Index and the Risk of Covid-19 Across Ethnic Groups: Analysis of UK Biobank," *Diabetes, Obesity and Metabolism* 22, no. 10 (June 29, 2020): 1953–54, https://doi.org/10.1111/dom.14125.

38. Alexandra Sifferlin, "Five Things You're Getting Wrong About Weight and Weight Loss," *Time*, July 31, 2013, https://healthland.time.com/2013/07/31/five-things-youre-getting-wrong-about-weight-and-weight-loss.

MYTH 8: "DOCTORS ARE UNBIASED JUDGES OF FAT PEOPLE'S HEALTH."
1. "Ellen Maud Bennett Obituary," *Times Colonist*, July 14, 2018, https://www.legacy.com/ca/obituaries/timescolonist/name/ellen-bennett-obituary?pid=189588876.

2. Ashifa Kassam, "Canadian Woman Uses Own Obituary to Rail Against Fat-Shaming," *The Guardian*, July 30, 2018, https://www.theguardian.com/world/2018/jul/30/canada-ellen-maud-bennett-obituary-fat-shaming.

3. Maya Dusenbery, "Doctors Told Her She Was Just Fat. She Actually Had Cancer," *Cosmopolitan*, Feb. 19, 2021, https://www.cosmopolitan.com/health-fitness/a19608429/medical-fatshaming.

4. Gina Kolata, "Why Do Obese Patients Get Worse Care? Many Doctors Don't See Past the Fat," *New York Times*, Sept. 26, 2016, https://www.nytimes.com/2016/09/26/health/obese-patients-health-care.html.

5. "Can Scoliosis Occur Later in Life?" Colorado Center of Orthopaedic Excellence, admin https://ccoe.us/wp-content/uploads/2021/04/ccoe_otc_lg.svg, Aug. 13, 2019, https://ccoe.us/general/can-scoliosis-occur-later-in-life.

6. Ryan S. Darby, Nicole E. Henniger, and Christine R. Harris, "Reactions to Physician-Inspired Shame and Guilt," *Basic and Applied Social Psychology* 36, no. 1 (Feb. 10, 2014): 9–26, https://doi.org/10.1080/01973533.2013.856782.

7. Kimberly A. Gudzune, Mary Margaret Huizinga, Mary Catherine Beach, and Lisa A. Cooper, "Obese Patients Overestimate Physicians' Attitudes of Respect," *Patient Education and Counseling* 88, no. 1 (2012): 23–28, https://doi.org/10.1016/j.pec.2011.12.010.

8. Angela S. Alberga, Iyoma Y. Edache, Mary Forhan, and Shelly Russell-Mayhew, "Weight Bias and Health Care Utilization: A Scoping Review," *Primary Health Care Research & Development* 20 (July 22, 2019), https://doi.org/10.1017/s1463423619000227.

9. Lisa Esposito, "Black Women and Breast Cancer: Disparities Continue," *U.S. News & World Report*, Oct. 23, 2015, https://health.usnews.com/health-news/patient-advice/articles/2015/10/23/black-women-and-breast-cancer-disparities-continue.

10. Sandhya Somashekhar, "The Disturbing Reason Some African American Patients May Be Undertreated for Pain," *Washington Post*, Oct. 26, 2021, https://www.washingtonpost.com/news/to-your-health/wp/2016/04/04/do-blacks-feel-less-pain-than-whites-their-doctors-may-think-so/?noredirect=on.

11. Tyler G. Martinson, Shruti Ramachandran, Rebecca Lindner, Tamar Reisman, and Joshua D. Safer, "High Body Mass Index Is a Significant Barrier to Gender-Confirmation Surgery for Transgender and Gender-Nonbinary Individuals," *Endocrine Practice* 26, no. 1 (Jan. 1, 2020): 6–15, https://doi.org/10.4158/ep-2019-0345.

12. "New Report Reveals Rampant Discrimination Against Transgender People by Health Providers, High HIV Rates and Widespread Lack of Access to Necessary Care," National LGBTQ Task Force, Oct. 13, 2010, https://www.thetaskforce.org/new-report-reveals-rampant-discrimination-against-transgender-people-by-health-providers-high-hiv-rates-and-widespread-lack-of-access-to-necessary-care-2.

13. M. R. Hebl and J. Xu, "Weighing the Care: Physicians' Reactions to the Size of a Patient," *International Journal of Obesity* 25, no. 8 (Aug. 2, 2001): 1246–52, https://doi.org/10.1038/sj.ijo.0801681.

14. Gary D. Foster et al., "Primary Care Physicians' Attitudes About Obesity and Its Treatment," *Obesity Research* 11, no. 10 (2003): 1168–77, https://doi.org/10.1038/oby.2003.161.

15. Marlene B. Schwartz et al., "Weight Bias Among Health Professionals Specializing in Obesity," *Obesity Research* 11, no. 9 (2012): 1033–39, https://doi.org/10.1038/oby.2003.142.

16. Kimberly A. Gudzune, Mary Catherine Beach, Debra L. Roter, and Lisa A. Cooper, "Physicians Build Less Rapport with Obese Patients," *Obesity* 21, no. 10 (Oct. 6, 2013): 2146–52, https://doi.org/10.1002/oby.20384.

17. Hebl and Xu, "Weighing the Care: Physicians' Reactions to the Size of a Patient."

18. Anne Tanneberger and Cristina Ciupitu-Plath, "Nurses' Weight Bias in Caring for Obese Patients: Do Weight Controllability Beliefs Influence the

Provision of Care to Obese Patients?" *Clinical Nursing Research* 27, no. 4 (Jan. 4, 2017): 414–32, https://doi.org/10.1177/1054773816687443.

19. A. Janet Tomiyama, Deborah Carr, Ellen M. Granberg, Brenda Major, Eric Robinson, Angelina R. Sutin, and Alexandra Brewis, "How and Why Weight Stigma Drives the Obesity 'Epidemic' and Harms Health," *BMC Medicine* 16, no. 1 (Aug. 15, 2018), https://doi.org/10.1186/s12916-018-1116-5.

20. Pamela Ward and Deborah McPhail, "A Shared Vision for Reducing Fat Shame and Blame in Reproductive Care," *Women's Reproductive Health* 6, no. 4 (Oct. 18, 2019): 265–70, https://doi.org/10.1080/23293691.2019.1653582.

21. Ruth E. Zielinski, "BMI and Pregnancy/Childbirth: Risk Reduction or Fat Shaming?" *Women's Reproductive Health* 6, no. 4 (Oct. 18, 2019): 242–44, https://doi.org/10.1080/23293691.2019.1653580.

22. Rebecca Puhl, Christopher Wharton, and Chelsea Heuer, "Weight Bias Among Dietetics Students: Implications for Treatment Practices," *Journal of the American Dietetic Association* 109, no. 3 (Mar. 2009): 438–44, https://doi.org/10.1016/j.jada.2008.11.034.

23. "Lesbian, Gay, Bisexual, and Transgender Health," *Healthy People 2020*, Office of Disease Prevention and Health Promotion, https://www.healthypeople.gov/2020/topics-objectives/topic/lesbian-gay-bisexual-and-transgender-health, accessed Feb. 17, 2022.

24. Sean M. Phelan, John F. Dovidio, Rebecca M. Puhl, Diana J. Burgess, David B. Nelson, Mark W. Yeazel, Rachel Hardeman, Sylvia Perry, and Michelle Ryn, "Implicit and Explicit Weight Bias in a National Sample of 4,732 Medical Students: The Medical Student Changes Study," *Obesity* 22, no. 4 (Apr. 9, 2014): 1201–8, https://doi.org/10.1002/oby.20687.

25. "Do Doctors Dislike Overweight Patients?" VA Research Currents, US Department of Veterans Affairs, Aug. 3, 2015, https://www.research.va.gov/currents/0815-2.cfm.

26. Sean M. Phelan, Rebecca M. Puhl, Sara E. Burke, Rachel Hardeman, John F. Dovidio, David B. Nelson, Julia Przedworski et al., "The Mixed Impact of Medical School on Medical Students' Implicit and Explicit Weight Bias," *Medical Education* 49, no. 10 (Sept. 18, 2015): 983–92, https://doi.org/10.1111/medu.12770.

27. J. G. Bacon, K. E. Scheltema, and B. E. Robinson, "Fat Phobia Scale Revisited: The Short Form," *International Journal of Obesity* 25, no. 2 (Mar. 25, 2001): 252–57, https://doi.org/10.1038/sj.ijo.0801537.

28. David B. Allison, Vincent C. Basile, and Harold E. Yuker, "The Measurement of Attitudes Toward and Beliefs About Obese Persons," *International Journal of Eating Disorders* 10, no. 5 (Sept. 1991): 599–607, https://doi.org/10.1002/1098-108x(199109)10:5<599::aid-eat2260100512>3.0.co;2-#.

29. Joseph Mitchell Magness, "Figure Rating Scales: A Novel Measure of Weight Bias," *eGrove*, https://egrove.olemiss.edu/cgi/viewcontent.cgi?article=1793&context=etd, accessed Feb. 17, 2022.

30. "Project Implicit: Take a Test," Project Implicit, Harvard University, https://implicit.harvard.edu/implicit/takeatest.html, accessed Feb. 17, 2022.

MYTH 9: "FAT PEOPLE ARE EMOTIONALLY DAMAGED AND COPE BY 'EATING THEIR FEELINGS.'"

1. Rachel Rosenblit, "Weight Watchers Founder Jean Nidetch Was a 'Well-Fluencer' Long Before Those Existed. One Writer Is Giving the Trailblazer Her Due," *Washington Post*, Apr. 15, 2020, https://www.washingtonpost.com /entertainment/books/weight-watchers-founder-jean-nidetch-was-a-well -fluencer-long-before-those-existed-one-writer-is-giving-the-trailblazer-her -due/2020/04/15/1ba5fa9c-7f19-11ea-a3ee-13e1ae0a3571_story.html.

2. Robert D. McFadden, "Jean Nidetch, a Founder of Weight Watchers, Dies at 91," *New York Times*, Apr. 29, 2015, https://www.nytimes.com/2015 /04/30/business/jean-nidetch-dies-at-91-co-founder-of-weight-watchers-and -dynamic-speaker.html.

3. Rachel Zimmerman, "A Weight Watching Life, and (Maybe) a Post-Diet Era," WBUR News, May 1, 2015, https://www.wbur.org/news/2015/05 /01/weight-watchers-post-diet-era.

4. Veronica Horwell, "Jean Nidetch Obituary," *The Guardian*, May 1, 2015, https://www.theguardian.com/lifeandstyle/2015/may/01/jean-nidetch.

5. Russell Marx, "New in the DSM-5: Binge Eating Disorder," National Eating Disorders Association, Feb. 21, 2018, https://www.nationaleating disorders.org/blog/new-dsm-5-binge-eating-disorder.

6. *Management and Outcomes of Binge-Eating Disorder* (Rockville, MD: Agency for Healthcare Research and Quality, 2015); table of diagnostic criteria available at https://www.ncbi.nlm.nih.gov/books/NBK338301/table /introduction.t1.

7. Vincent Felitti, Kathy Jakstis, Victoria Pepper, and Albert Ray, "Obesity: Problem, Solution, or Both?" *Permanente Journal* 14, no. 1 (2010), https:// doi.org/10.7812/tpp/09-107.

8. Lorenzo Benet, "Sure, Oprah Slimmed Down Fast, but Liquid Diets Aren't Right For [sic]," *Chicago Tribune*, Dec. 27, 1988, https://www.chicago tribune.com/news/ct-xpm-1988-12-28-8802280291-story.html.

9. Bessel A. Van der Kolk, "What's Love Got to Do with It?" *The Body Keeps the Score: Brain, Mind, and Body in the Healing of Trauma* (New York: Penguin Books, 2014).

10. "ACEs and Obesity," STOP Obesity Alliance: Strategies to Overcome and Prevent Obesity, Milken Institute School of Public Health, George Washington University, Apr. 30, 2017, https://stop.publichealth.gwu.edu/LFD -apr17.

11. Blanca M. Herrera, Sarah Keildson, and Cecilia M. Lindgren, "Genetics and Epigenetics of Obesity," *Maturitas* 69, no. 1 (May 2011): 41–49, https:// doi.org/10.1016/j.maturitas.2011.02.018.

12. Stephanie E. King and Michael K. Skinner, "Epigenetic Transgenerational Inheritance of Obesity Susceptibility," *Trends in Endocrinology & Metabolism* 31, no. 7 (July 2020): 478–94, https://doi.org/10.1016/j.tem.2020 .02.009.

13. A. Janet Tomiyama, Deborah Carr, Ellen M. Granberg, Brenda Major, Eric Robinson, Angelina R. Sutin, and Alexandra Brewis, "How and Why Weight Stigma Drives the Obesity 'Epidemic' and Harms Health," *BMC Medicine* 16, no. 1 (Aug. 15, 2018), https://doi.org/10.1186/s12916-018-1116-5.

14. Kelli E. Friedman et al., "Weight Stigmatization and Ideological Beliefs: Relation to Psychological Functioning in Obese Adults," *Obesity Research* 13, no. 5 (2005): 907–16, https://onlinelibrary.wiley.com/doi/full/10.1038/oby .2005.105.

MYTH 10: "ACCEPTING FAT PEOPLE 'GLORIFIES OBESITY.'"

1. Shyla Watson, "Lizzo Wore an NSFW Outfit to a Basketball Game and It Sparked a Debate About Body Type Double Standards," *BuzzFeed*, Dec. 14, 2019, https://www.buzzfeed.com/shylawatson/lizzo-laker-game-outfit -twitter-debate.

2. "2019-20 Laker Girls," Los Angeles Lakers, Dec. 30, 2020, https:// www.nba.com/lakers/lakergirls/archive/1920.

3. Claire Shaffer, "Lizzo Tells Critics Off After Facing Backlash for Showing Her Thong at a Lakers Game," *Insider*, Dec. 11, 2019, https://www.insider .com/lizzo-thong-critics-response-lakers-game-2019-12.

4. Lindsay Lowe, "Gillette Defends Photo Featuring a Plus-Sized Model in a Bikini." *TODAY.com*, Apr. 10, 2019, https://www.today.com/style/gillette -defends-photo-plus-sized-model-anna-o-brien-t151861.

5. Miley Cyrus, "Mother's Daughter (Official Video)," YouTube, July 2, 2019, https://www.youtube.com/watch?v=7T2RonyJ_Ts.

6. "Piers Clashes with Model Angelina Duplisea on Whether Obesity Is Glorified; Good Morning Britain," *Good Morning Britain*, July 16, 2019, available at YouTube, https://www.youtube.com/watch?v=hxGEJqLEk2c.

MYTH 11: "BODY POSITIVITY IS ABOUT FEELING BETTER ABOUT YOUR-SELF, AS LONG AS YOU'RE HAPPY AND HEALTHY."

1. Judith Shulevitz, "Forgotten Feminisms: Johnnie Tillmon's Battle Against 'The Man,'" *New York Review of Books*, Oct. 28, 2020, https://www .nybooks.com/daily/2018/06/26/forgotten-feminisms-johnnie-tillmons-battle -against-the-man/?lp_txn_id=1329372.

2. Johnnie Tillmon, Laura Merrifield Wilson, and Eleanor J. Bader, "From the Vault: 'Welfare Is a Women's Issue' (Spring 1972)," *Ms.*, Mar. 29, 2021, https://msmagazine.com/2021/03/25/welfare-is-a-womens-issue -ms-magazine-spring-1972.

3. Ann Atwater and Robert Korstad, "Extended Interview with Ann Atwater," School for Conversion, https://www.schoolforconversion.org/extended -interview-with-ann-atwater, accessed Feb. 21, 2022.

4. Charlotte Cooper, "Fat Lib: How Fat Activism Expands the Obesity Debate," *Debating Obesity*, 2011, 164–91, https://doi.org/10.1057/978023 0304239_7.

5. "Curves Have Their Day in Park; 500 at a 'Fat-in' Call for Obesity," *New York Times* June 5, 1967, https://www.nytimes.com/1967/06/05/archives/curves-have-their-day-in-park-500-at-a-fatin-call-for-obesity.html.

6. Charlotte Cooper, *Fat Activism: A Radical Social Movement* (Chicago: University of Chicago Press, 2016).

7. Evette Dionne, "The Fragility of Body Positivity: How a Radical Movement Lost Its Way," *Bitch Media*, Nov. 21, 2017, https://www.bitchmedia.org/article/fragility-body-positivity.

8. Angela Celebre and Ashley Waggoner Denton, "The Good, the Bad, and the Ugly of the Dove Campaign for Real Beauty," *Inquisitive Mind*, https://www.in-mind.org/article/the-good-the-bad-and-the-ugly-of-the-dove-campaign-for-real-beauty, accessed Feb. 21, 2022.

9. Dove, "Dove Real Beauty Sketches: You're More Beautiful Than You Think," YouTube, Apr. 14, 2014, https://www.youtube.com/watch?v=XpaOjMXyJGk.

10. Ian Bogost, "How Dove Ruined Its Body Image," *The Atlantic*, May 9, 2017, https://www.theatlantic.com/technology/archive/2017/05/dove-body-image/525867.

11. Shelley E. Kohan, "Aeo's Aerie Brand, Built on Body Positivity and Inclusion, Is Slowly Edging Out Sexy Supermodel Juggernaut Victoria's Secret," *Forbes*, Dec. 10, 2021, https://www.forbes.com/sites/shelleykohan/2020/06/28/aeos-aerie-brand-built-on-body-positivity-and-inclusion-is-slowly-edging-out-sexy-supermodel-juggernaut-victorias-secret/?sh=728ec7342ba1.

12. Amira Rasool, "Aerie Is Completely Revamping Its Stores to Promote Body Positivity," *Teen Vogue*, Aug. 8, 2018, https://www.teenvogue.com/story/aerie-stores-body-positivity.

13. "Stop Shoulding Yourself," HALO TOP, https://halotop.com/stop-shoulding-yourself, accessed Feb. 22, 2022.

14. Robert Crawford, "Healthism and the Medicalization of Everyday Life," *International Journal of Health Services* 10, no. 3 (1980): 365–88. https://doi.org/10.2190/3h2h-3xjn-3kay-g9ny.

15. Crawford, "Healthism and the Medicalization of Everyday Life."

16. Dionne, "The Fragility of Body Positivity: How a Radical Movement Lost Its Way."

17. Tillmon, Wilson, and Bader, "From the Vault: 'Welfare Is a Women's Issue.'"

18. Shulevitz, "Forgotten Feminisms: Johnnie Tillmon's Battle Against 'The Man.'"

MYTH 12: "WE'RE IN THE MIDDLE OF AN OBESITY EPIDEMIC."

1. Nia S. Mitchell, Victoria A. Catenacci, Holly R. Wyatt, and James O. Hill, "Obesity: Overview of an Epidemic," Psychiatric Clinics of North America, US National Library of Medicine, Dec. 2011, https://www.ncbi.nlm.nih.gov/pmc/articles/PMC3228640.

2. David M. Cutler, Edward L. Glaeser, and Jesse M. Shapiro, "Why Have Americans Become More Obese?" *Journal of Economic Perspectives* 17, no. 3 (2003): 93–118, https://doi.org/10.1257/089533003769204371.

3. Anne McDermott and Elizabeth Cohen, "Who's Fat? New Definition Adopted," CNN, June 17, 1998, http://www.cnn.com/HEALTH/9806/17/weight.guidelines.

4. J. Eric Oliver, *Fat Politics: The Real Story Behind America's Obesity Epidemic* (Toronto: Oxford University Press Canada, 2006).

5. Marina Komaroff, "For Researchers on Obesity: Historical Review of Extra Body Weight Definitions," *Journal of Obesity* 2016 (2016): 1–9, https://doi.org/10.1155/2016/2460285.

6. Oliver, *Fat Politics*.

7. "Satcher: Obesity Reaching Crisis Levels," ABC News, Jan. 6, 2006, https://abcnews.go.com/Health/story?id=117075&page=1.

8. Radley Balko, "The 'War' Against Obesity," Cato Institute, June 16, 2004, https://www.cato.org/commentary/war-against-obesity.

9. Michael Gard, *The End of the Obesity Epidemic* (New York: Routledge, 2011), 87.

10. Theodore K. Kyle, Emily J. Dhurandhar, and David B. Allison, "Regarding Obesity as a Disease: Evolving Policies and Their Implications," Endocrinology and Metabolism Clinics of North America, US National Library of Medicine, Sept. 2016, https://www.ncbi.nlm.nih.gov/pmc/articles/PMC4988332.

11. Andrew Pollack, "A.M.A. Recognizes Obesity as a Disease," *New York Times*, June 18, 2013, https://www.nytimes.com/2013/06/19/business/ama-recognizes-obesity-as-a-disease.html.

12. American Obesity Association, Nov. 2, 2021, https://americanobesity association.org.

13. Oliver, *Fat Politics*, 48.

14. Lauren Medina, Shannon Sabo, and Jonathan Vespa, "Living Longer: Historical and Projected Life Expectancy in the United States, 1960 to 2060," Census.gov, US Census Bureau, Feb. 2020, https://www.census.gov/content/dam/Census/library/publications/2020/demo/p25-1145.pdf.

15. Gard, *The End of the Obesity Epidemic*.

16. Natalie Boero, *Killer Fat: Media, Medicine, and Morals in the American "Obesity Epidemic"* (New Brunswick, NJ: Rutgers University Press, 2013).

17. "Reduce the Proportion of Adults with Obesity—NWS03," Healthy People 2030, https://health.gov/healthypeople/objectives-and-data/browse-objectives/overweight-and-obesity/reduce-proportion-adults-obesity-nws-03, accessed Feb. 8, 2022.

18. Robert J. Davis (with Brad Kolowich Jr.), *Fitter Faster: The Smart Way to Get in Shape in Just Minutes a Day* (New York: Amacom, 2017); Robert J. Davis, *Coffee Is Good for You: From Vitamin C and Organic Foods to Low-Carb and Detox Diets, the Truth about Diet and Nutrition Claims* (New York: Perigee,

2012); Robert J. Davis, *The Healthy Skeptic: Cutting Through the Hype about Your Health* (Berkeley: University of California Press, 2008); and Robert J. Davis, *Supersized Lies: How Myths About Weight Loss Are Keeping Us Fat—and the Truth About What Really Works* (Atlanta: Everwell, 2021); Robert J. Davis, "Why You Shouldn't Exercise to Lose Weight," *Time*, Jan. 12, 2022, https://time.com /6138809/should-you-exercise-to-lose-weight.

19. Gard, *The End of the Obesity Epidemic*.

20. Oliver, *Fat Politics*, 33.

21. "Racism and Obesity Are Inextricably Linked, Says a Harvard Doctor—and Here's How She Thinks That Can Change," *Boston Globe*, Apr. 12, 2021, https://www.boston.com/news/racial-justice/2021/04/12/racism-and -obesity-article-fatima-cody-stanford-daniel-aaron.

22. Tessa Charlesworth and Mahzarin Banaji, "Research: How Americans' Biases Are Changing (or Not) Over Time," *Harvard Business Review*, Sept. 17, 2021, https://hbr.org/2019/08/research-on-many-issues-americans-biases -are-decreasing.

23. Christy Harrison, *Anti-Diet: Reclaim Your Time, Money, Well-Being, and Happiness through Intuitive Eating* (New York: Little, Brown Spark, 2021).

24. "2021 Heart Disease and Stroke Statistics Update Fact Sheet," American Heart Association, https://www.heart.org/-/media/phd-files-2 /science-news/2/2021-heart-and-stroke-stat-update/2021_heart_disease _and_stroke_statistics_update_fact_sheet_at_a_glance.pdf?la=en, accessed Feb. 8, 2022.

25. "Most Parents Don't Believe Their Child's BMI Report Card," *ScienceDaily*, Feb. 14, 2018, https://www.sciencedaily.com/releases/2018/02 /180214093647.htm#:~:text=53%25%20of%20parents%20who%20receive ,Practice%2C%20a%20SAGE%20Publishing%20journal.

26. Katherine Mayer, "An Unjust War: The Case Against the Government's War on Obesity," *Georgetown Law Journal* (June 2004), https://www .proquest.com/openview/4150738197df3b369a81012fa250b3c9/1?cbl=37325 &pq-origsite=gscholar&login=true.

27. Kyle J. Messick and Blanca E. Aranda, "The Role of Moral Reasoning & Personality in Explaining Lyrical Preferences," *PLOS One* 15, no. 1 (Jan. 24, 2020), https://doi.org/10.1371/journal.pone.0228057.

MYTH 13: "FAT PEOPLE DON'T EXPERIENCE DISCRIMINATION."

1. "Elliott-Larsen Civil Rights Act, Act 453 of 1976," Michigan.gov, State of Michigan, https://www.michigan.gov/documents/act_453_elliott_larsen _8772_7.pdf, accessed Mar. 2, 2022.

2. Evelyn Nieves, "New San Francisco Ordinance Decrees That All Sizes Fit," *New York Times*, May 9, 2000, https://www.nytimes.com/2000/05/09/us /new-san-francisco-ordinance-decrees-that-all-sizes-fit.html.

3. Shreya Sabharwal, Karen J. Campoverde Reyes, and Fatima Cody Stanford, "Need for Legal Protection Against Weight Discrimination in the

United States," *Obesity* 28, no. 10 (Oct. 2020): 1784–85, https://doi.org/10 .1002/oby.22974.

4. "Weight Bias: A Policy Brief," UConn Rudd Center for Food Policy and Obesity, University of Connecticut, July 2020, https://uconnruddcenter .org/wp-content/uploads/sites/2909/2020/07/Weight-Bias-Policy-Brief -2017.pdf.

5. Rachel La Corte, "Washington Court: Obesity Covered by Anti-discrimination Law" *Seattle Times*, July 12, 2019, https://www.seattletimes .com/seattle-news/washington-court-obesity-covered-by-antidiscrimination -law.

6. Steven Greenhouse, "Overweight, but Ready to Fight; Obese People Are Taking Their Bias Claims to Court," *New York Times*, Aug. 4, 2003, https://www.nytimes.com/2003/08/04/nyregion/overweight-but-ready-to -fight-obese-people-are-taking-their-bias-claims-to-court.html; Michael D. Malone, "Obesity Alone Is Not a Disability Under the ADA," SHRM, Society for Human Resource Management, July 7, 2021, https://www.shrm.org /resourcesandtools/legal-and-compliance/employment-law/pages/court -report-obesity-ada.aspx; Mark Wallin, "Extreme Obesity Not Necessarily a Disability Under ADA Says Seventh Circuit," Barnes & Thornburg, June 20, 2019, https://btlaw.com/insights/blogs/extreme-obesity-not-necessarily-a -disability-under-ada-says-seventh-circuit; Zachary B. Busey, "Courts Cut the Fat, Clarify When Obesity Is a Disability Under the ADA," Baker Donelson, Apr. 14, 2014, https://www.bakerdonelson.com/Courts-Cut-the-Fat-Clarify -When-Obesity-is-a-Disability-Under-the-ADA.

7. "Current Trends in Combating Weight Discrimination in the Work-place," Fisher Phillips, May 14, 2020, https://www.fisherphillips.com/news -insights/current-trends-in-combating-weight-discrimination-in-the-work place.html.

8. Anjalee Khemlani, "'Borgata Babes' Lose Suit over Weight Bias," *Press of Atlantic City*, July 25, 2013, https://pressofatlanticcity.com/news/local /borgata-babes-lose-suit-over-weight-bias/article_7ff91fbc-f468-11e2-83b3 -001a4bcf887a.html.

9. Roni Caryn Rabin, "Disparities: Obesity Costs Women More, Study Finds," *New York Times*, Sept. 27, 2010, https://www.nytimes.com/2010/09/28 /health/research/28disparities.html.

10. Lesley Kinzel, "New Study Finds That Weight Discrimination in the Workplace Is Just as Horrible and Depressing as Ever," *Time*, Nov. 28, 2014, https://time.com./360603 1/weight-discrimination-workplace.

11. Kinzel, "New Study Finds That Weight Discrimination in the Work-place Is Just as Horrible and Depressing as Ever."

12. Stephen Bevan, "50% Of All Employers Are Less Likely to Hire Obese Candidates," World Economic Forum, Feb. 6, 2019, https://www.we forum.org/agenda/2019/02/half-of-employers-say-they-are-less-inclined-to -recruit-obese-candidates-its-not-ok.

13. Stuart W. Flint, Martin Čadek, Sonia C. Codreanu, Vanja Ivić, Colene Zomer, and Amalia Gomoiu, "Obesity Discrimination in the Recruitment Process: 'You're Not Hired!'" *Frontiers in Psychology* 7 (May 3, 2016), https://doi.org/10.3389/fpsyg.2016.00647.

14. Jennifer Bennett Shinall, "Occupational Characteristics and the Obesity Wage Penalty," *SSRN Electronic Journal*, Jan. 21, 2014, https://doi.org/10.2139/ssrn.2379575.

15. Esther D. Rothblum, Pamela A. Brand, Carol T. Miller, and Helen A. Oetjen, "The Relationship Between Obesity, Employment Discrimination, and Employment-Related Victimization," *Journal of Vocational Behavior* 37, no. 3 (Dec. 1990): 251–66, https://doi.org/10.1016/0001-8791(90)90044-3.

16. Amy Norton, "Weight Discrimination Common, U.S. Survey Finds," Reuters, Apr. 9, 2008, https://www.reuters.com/article/us-weight -discrimination-idUSTON97652720080409.

17. Norton, "Weight Discrimination Common, U.S. Survey Finds."

18. N. A. Schvey, R. M. Puhl, K. A. Levandoski, and K. D. Brownell, "The Influence of a Defendant's Body Weight on Perceptions of Guilt," *International Journal of Obesity* 37, no. 9 (Jan. 8, 2013): 1275–81, https://doi.org /10.1038/ijo.2012.211.

19. Niwako Yamawaki, Christina Riley, Claudia Rasmussen, and Mary Cook, "The Effects of Obesity Myths on Perceptions of Sexual Assault Victims and Perpetrators' Credibility," *Journal of Interpersonal Violence* 33, no. 4 (Dec. 10, 2015): 662–85, https://doi.org/10.1177/0886260515613343.

20. Wesley Lowery, "'I Can't Breathe': Five Years After Eric Garner Died in Struggle with New York Police, Resolution Still Elusive," *Washington Post*, June 14, 2019, https://www.washingtonpost.com/national/i-cant-breathe-five -years-after-eric-garner-died-in-struggle-with-new-york-police-resolution -still-elusive/2019/06/13/23d7fad8-78f5-11e9-bd25-c989555e7766_story .html.

21. Shannon Weber, "Heather Heyer Exposed the Entwined History of White Supremacy and Fat Hatred," *Bitch Media*, Sept. 7, 2017, https://www .bitchmedia.org/article/fat-shaming-heather-heyer-white-supremacy.

22. S. M. Phelan, D. J. Burgess, M. W. Yeazel, W. L. Hellerstedt, J. M. Griffin, and M. Ryn, "Impact of Weight Bias and Stigma on Quality of Care and Outcomes for Patients with Obesity," *Obesity Reviews* 16, no. 4 (Mar. 5, 2015): 319–26, https://doi.org/10.1111/obr.12266.

23. Gail Geller and Paul A. Watkins, "Addressing Medical Students' Negative Bias Toward Patients with Obesity Through Ethics Education," *AMA Journal of Ethics* 20, no. 10 (Oct. 2018), https://doi.org/10.1001/amajethics .2018.948.

24. Yasmin Poustchi, Norma S. Saks, Alicja K. Piasecki, Karissa A. Hahn, and Jeanne M. Ferrante, "Brief Intervention Effective in Reducing Weight Bias in Medical Students," *Family Medicine* 45, no. 5 (May 2015), https://doi .org/https://www.ncbi.nlm.nih.gov/pmc/articles/PMC3791507.

25. Mara Z. Vitolins, Sonia Crandall, David Miller, Eddie Ip, Gail Marion, and John G. Spangler, "Obesity Educational Interventions in U.S. Medical Schools: A Systematic Review and Identified Gaps," *Teaching and Learning in Medicine* 24, no. 3 (July 9, 2012): 267–72, https://doi.org/10.1080/10401334 .2012.692286.

26. David P. Miller, John G. Spangler, Mara Z. Vitolins, Stephen W. Davis, Edward H. Ip, Gail S. Marion, and Sonia J. Crandall, "Are Medical Students Aware of Their Anti-Obesity Bias?" *Academic Medicine* 88, no. 7 (July 2013): 978–82, https://doi.org/10.1097/acm.0b013e318294f817.

27. Janice A. Sabin, Maddalena Marini, and Brian A. Nosek, "Implicit and Explicit Anti-Fat Bias Among a Large Sample of Medical Doctors by BMI, Race/Ethnicity and Gender," *PLOS One* 7, no. 11 (Nov. 7, 2012), https://doi .org/10.1371/journal.pone.0048448.

28. Catriona Harvey-Jenner, "Nail Salon Blasted for Fat-Shaming by Charging More for 'Overweight' Customers," *Cosmopolitan*, Oct. 8, 2017, https://www.cosmopolitan.com/uk/reports/a9155787/fat-shaming-nail-salon -blasted-charging-more-overweight-customers.

29. Shay Arthur, "Woman Says Frayser Salon Posted Sign Charging More for Pedicures If Someone Is Overweight," WREG.com, Mar. 17, 2017, https://wreg.com/news/woman-says-frayser-salon-posted-sign-charging-more -for-pedicures-if-someone-is-overweight.

30. Lisa Stein, "Fat? No Food for You!" *Scientific American*, Feb. 7, 2008, https://www.scientificamerican.com/article/fat-no-food-for-you.

31. "Miss. Considers Restaurant Ban for Obese," CBS News, Feb. 5, 2008, https://www.cbsnews.com/news/miss-considers-restaurant-ban-for-obese.

32. Kim Severson, "For Larger Customers, Eating Out Is Still a Daunting Experience." *New York Times*, Mar. 12, 2019, https://www.nytimes.com/2019 /03/12/dining/larger-customers-restaurants.html.

33. "Peloton Bike Rider Height and Weight Requirements," Peloton Support, https://support.onepeloton.com/hc/en-us/articles/202703749-Peloton -Bike-Rider-Height-And-Weight-Requirements, accessed Mar. 2, 2022.

34. Angela Meadows, "Discrimination Against Fat People Is So Endemic, Most of Us Don't Even Realise It's Happening," *The Conversation*, Oct. 20, 2021, https://theconversation.com/discrimination-against-fat-people-is-so -endemic-most-of-us-dont-even-realise-its-happening-94862.

MYTH 14: "I DON'T LIKE GAINING WEIGHT, BUT I DON'T TREAT FAT PEOPLE DIFFERENTLY."

1. "Average Cost of Gastric Bypass Surgery," Obesity Coverage, https:// www.obesitycoverage.com/insurance-and-costs/how-much/average-laparoscopic -gastric-bypass-prices, accessed Feb. 23, 2022.

2. Michael Brownstein, "Implicit Bias," *Stanford Encyclopedia of Philosophy*, Stanford University, July 31, 2019, https://plato.stanford.edu/entries /implicit-bias.

3. Inge Kersbergen and Eric Robinson, "Blatant Dehumanization of People with Obesity," *Obesity* 27, no. 6 (Apr. 2, 2019): 1005–12. https://doi .org/10.1002/oby.22460.

4. Jean Kim and Josée L. Jarry, "Holding Fat Stereotypes Is Associated with Lower Body Dissatisfaction in Normal Weight Caucasian Women Who Engage in Body Surveillance," *Body Image* 11, no. 4 (2014): 331–36, https:// doi.org/10.1016/j.bodyim.2014.06.002.

5. Judith Rodin, "Cultural and Psychosocial Determinants of Weight Concerns," *Annals of Internal Medicine* 119, no. 7_Part_2 (Oct. 1, 1993): 643, https://doi.org/10.7326/0003-4819-119-7_part_2-199310011-00003.

6. Rachel H. Salk and Renee Engeln-Maddox, "'If You're Fat, Then I'm Humongous!'" *Psychology of Women Quarterly* 35, no. 1 (2011): 18–28, https:// doi.org/10.1177/0361684310384107.

7. Salk and Engeln-Maddox, "'If You're Fat, Then I'm Humongous!'"

8. Salk and Engeln-Maddox, "'If You're Fat, Then I'm Humongous!'"

9. Stacey Tantleff-Dunn, Rachel D. Barnes, and Jessica Gokee Larose, "It's Not Just a 'Woman Thing:' The Current State of Normative Discontent," *Eating Disorders* 19, no. 5 (2011): 392–402, https://doi.org/10.1080 /10640266.2011.609088.

10. Cristen Conger, "How Accurate Is Our Mental Image of Ourselves?" HowStuffWorks Science, June 30, 2020, https://science.howstuffworks.com /life/inside-the-mind/human-brain/mental-image.htm.

11. Diann M. Ackar, Ann Kearney-Cooke, and Carol B. Peterson, "Effect of Body Image and Self-Image on Women's Sexual Behaviors," *International Journal of Eating Disorders* 28, no. 4 (2000): 422–29. https://doi.org/10.1002 /1098-108x(200012)28:4<422::aid-eat10>3.0.co;2-1.

12. Jan Hoffman, "'Fat Talk' Compels but Carries a Cost," *New York Times*, May 27, 2013, https://well.blogs.nytimes.com/2013/05/27/fat-talk -compels-but-carries-a-cost.

13. Anja Hilbert, "Weight Stigma Reduction and Genetic Determinism," *PLOS One* 11, no. 9 (Sept. 15, 2016), https://doi.org/10.1371/journal.pone .0162993.

14. Lauren Breithaupt, Paige Trojanowski, and Sarah Fischer, "Implicit and Explicit Anti-Fat Attitude Change Following Brief Cognitive Dissonance Intervention for Weight Stigma," *Obesity* 28, no. 10 (2020): 1853–59, https:// doi.org/10.1002/oby.22909.

MYTH 15: "FAT PEOPLE SHOULDN'T CALL THEMSELVES FAT."

1. "Body Dysmorphic Disorder," Mayo Clinic, Mayo Foundation for Medical Education and Research, Oct. 29, 2019, https://www.mayoclinic.org /diseases-conditions/body-dysmorphic-disorder/symptoms-causes/syc-20353938.

2. "Tyra Banks' Fierce Reaction to Those Who Called Her Fat," *Daily Mail Online*, https://www.dailymail.co.uk/video/femail/video-1080263/Tyra-Banks -discusses-weight-2007-talk-show.html, accessed Feb. 8, 2022; Natasha Jokic,

"Jessica Simpson Opened Up About Being Body-Shamed by the World in 2009," *BuzzFeed News*, Mar. 26, 2021, https://www.buzzfeednews.com/article /natashajokic1/jessica-simpson-body-shaming-2009-open-book-memoir.

MYTH 16: "PEOPLE WHO HAVE NEVER BEEN FAT HAVE 'INTERNALIZED FATPHOBIA.'"
    1. Laura M. Padilla, "Internalized Oppression and Latinos," *Race, Racism and the Law*, Aug. 25, 2011, https://racism.org/articles/race/65-defining-racial -groups/latina-o-americans/314-latinoso1a.
    2. Suzanne Pharr, *In the Time of the Right: Reflections on Liberation* (Berkeley, CA: Chardon Press, 1996).
    3. Texas A&M Office for Diversity, Aug. 2021, https://web.archive.org /web/20210808072247/https://diversity.tamu.edu/Home/Glossary.
    4. Denarii Monroe, "3 Reasons to Find a Better Term Than '-Phobia' to Describe Oppression," *Everyday Feminism*, Oct. 7, 2016, https://everyday feminism.com/2016/10/find-a-better-term-than-phobia.
    5. Evette Dionne, "The Fragility of Body Positivity: How a Radical Movement Lost Its Way," *Bitch Media*, Nov. 21, 2017, https://www.bitch media.org/article/fragility-body-positivity.
    6. Dionne, "The Fragility of Body Positivity."
    7. James Lindsay, "Internalized Dominance," *New Discourses*, Dec. 15, 2020, https://newdiscourses.com/tftw-internalized-dominance.
    8. Canadian Race Relations Foundation, "Internalized Dominance," Glossary, Nov. 1, 2019, https://www.crrf-fcrr.ca/en/resources/glossary-a -terms-en-gb-1/item/22845-internalized-dominance.

MYTH 17: "NO ONE IS ATTRACTED TO FAT PEOPLE."
    1. Daisy Murray, "People Have Been Sharing Their Stories of Dating Whilst 'Plus-Size' and Their Accounts Will Make You Cry," *ELLE*, Feb. 16, 2018, https://www.elle.com/uk/life-and-culture/culture/news/a40368/dating -whilst-plus-size.
    2. Murray, "People Have Been Sharing Their Stories of Dating Whilst 'Plus-Size' and Their Accounts Will Make You Cry."
    3. Murray, "People Have Been Sharing Their Stories of Dating Whilst 'Plus-Size' and Their Accounts Will Make You Cry."
    4. "Thinner (1996)—Trailer," YouTube, Feb. 28, 2019, https://www .youtube.com/watch?v=p97ds4ZR7zM.
    5. "The Nutty Professor Official Trailer #1—Eddie Murphy Movie (1996)," YouTube, Jan. 9, 2012, https://www.youtube.com/watch?v=o3wJ-jzZqBw.
    6. Alexa Junge, "The One with the Prom Video," *Friends*, NBC, Feb. 1, 1996.
    7. Pamela C. Regan, "Sexual Outcasts: The Perceived Impact of Body Weight and Gender on Sexuality," *Journal of Applied Social Psychology* 26, no. 20 (1996): 1803–15, https://doi.org/10.1111/j.1559-1816.1996.tb00099.x.
    8. Regan, "Sexual Outcasts."

9. E. Robinson and P. Christiansen, "Visual Exposure to Obesity: Experimental Effects on Attraction Toward Overweight Men and Mate Choice in Females," *International Journal of Obesity* 39, no. 9 (May 6, 2015): 1390–94, https://doi.org/10.1038/ijo.2015.87.

10. Ogi Ogas and Sai Gaddam, *A Billion Wicked Thoughts: What the Internet Tells Us About Sexual Relationships* (New York: Dutton, 2011), 33.

11. Ogas and Gaddam, *A Billion Wicked Thoughts*, 136.

12. Charlotte Zoller, "If Your Date Thinks You're Too Fat, Please Dump Them," *Teen Vogue*, Sept. 29, 2020, https://www.teenvogue.com/story/dating -while-fat.

13. Gabrielle Olya, "#Fatsidestories: People Use Hashtag to Share How It Feels to Be Overweight," *People*, Aug. 12, 2016, https://people.com/health /fatsidestories-people-use-hashtag-to-share-how-it-feels-to-be-overweight.

14. sweaterpunk (@Vicious_Circe), "my ex: 'you always gain weight when you're depressed and i'm just not attracted to you when you're unhappy' #FatSideStories," Twitter, Aug. 9, 2016, 4:47 p.m., https://twitter.com/Vicious _Circe/status/763114589487640578.

15. @CrankyAunty, "Date told me 'Let's go for a walk, you don't need dessert'. I didn't before but now I think I'll have two >:(," Twitter, Aug. 9, 2016, https://twitter.com/CrankyAunty/status/763121125542854657.

16. Buttigieg Buttijury Butticutioner (@ValarMorDollars), "Learning that men showing basic decency isn't=showing romantic interest. Realizing how rarely you're treated this way #FatSideStories," Twitter, Aug. 9, 2016, 6:07 p.m., https://twitter.com/ValarMorDollars/status/763134535592587264.

17. Caleb Luna, "Treating My Friends like Lovers: The Politics of Desirability," *The Body Is Not an Apology*, Mar. 17, 2018, https://thebodyisnotan apology.com/magazine/how-to-be-fat-caleb-luna-sub.

MYTH 18: "FAT PEOPLE SHOULD PAY FOR A SECOND AIRPLANE SEAT."

1. Aidan Jones, "Film Director Kevin Smith Thrown Off Southwest Airlines Plane for Being 'Too Big,'" *The Guardian*, Feb. 14, 2010, https://www.theguardian .com/film/2010/feb/15/overweight-filmmaker-banned-southwest-airlines.

2. Jones, "Film Director Kevin Smith Thrown Off Southwest Airlines Plane for Being 'Too Big.'"

3. Allison Klein, "American Airlines Passenger: 'The Cops Were Called on Me for Flying While Fat & Black,'" *Washington Post*, Apr. 30, 2018, https:// www.washingtonpost.com/news/dr-gridlock/wp/2018/04/30/american -airlines-passenger-the-cops-were-called-on-me-for-flying-while-fat-black.

4. Scott Mayerowitz, "Too Fat to Fly: Did This Man Need Three Seats?" ABC News, Dec. 4, 2009, https://abcnews.go.com/Travel/BusinessTraveler /obese-passengers-fat-fat-fly-american-airlines/story?id=9249954.

5. "Customer of Size," Southwest Airlines, https://www.southwest.com /html/customer-service/extra-seat/index-pol.html, accessed Mar. 2, 2022.

6. "Customers of Size—Seating Guidelines," Alaska Airlines, https://www
.alaskaair.com/content/travel-info/policies/seating-customers-of-size, accessed
Mar. 2, 2022.

7. "Customers Requiring Extra Seating," United Airlines, https://www
.united.com/ual/en/us/fly/travel/special-needs/extra-seating.html, accessed
Mar. 2, 2022.

8. "Can I Purchase an Extra Seat for Myself or Something I'm Transport-
ing?" Spirit Airlines Support, https://customersupport.spirit.com/en-us
/category/article/KA-01248, accessed Mar. 2, 2022.

9. "Additional Assistance at the Airport," Delta Air Lines, https://www
.delta.com/us/en/accessible-travel-services/additional-assistance, accessed
Mar. 2, 2022.

10. "Special Assistance—Travel Information," American Airlines, https://
www.aa.com/i18n/travel-info/special-assistance/special-assistance.jsp, accessed
Mar. 2, 2022; "Booking Extra Seats," JetBlue, https://www.jetblue.com/flying
-with-us/booking-extra-seats, accessed Mar. 2, 2022.

11. "'One-Person, One-Fare' on Canadian Airlines," NBCNews.com,
Jan. 10, 2008, https://www.nbcnews.com/id/wbna22599803.

12. Stephanie Sarkis, "Airlines' Seat Pitch Gets Shorter and Passengers
Reach Their Limits," *Forbes*, Feb. 25, 2020, https://www.forbes.com/sites
/stephaniesarkis/2020/02/24/airlines-seat-pitch-gets-shorter-and-passengers
-reach-their-limits/?sh=5e562af7441a.

13. Scott McCartney, "You're Not Getting Bigger, the Airplane Bathroom
Is Getting Smaller," *Wall Street Journal*, Aug. 29, 2018, https://www.wsj.com
/articles/youre-not-getting-bigger-the-airplane-bathroom-is-getting-smaller
-1535553108.

14. "H.R. 1467—115th Congress (2017-2018): SEAT Act of 2017 . . ."
Congress.gov. United States Congress, Mar. 9, 2017, https://www.congress
.gov/bill/115th-congress/house-bill/1467.

MYTH 19: "SKINNY SHAMING IS JUST AS BAD AS FAT SHAMING."

1. Tessa E. S. Charlesworth and Mahzarin R. Banaji, "Research: How
Americans' Biases Are Changing (or Not) Over Time," *Harvard Business
Review*, Aug. 2, 2019, https://hbr.org/2019/08/research-on-many-issues
-americans-biases-are-decreasing.

2. Jim Walsh, "Borgata Babe Servers Can Take Weight-Gain Lawsuit to
Jury," *Courier-Post*, May 21, 2019, https://www.courierpostonline.com/story
/news/2019/05/20/borgata-babes-weight-gain-gender-bias-lawsuit
/3742371002.

3. Ashifa Kassam, "Canada Judge Says Sexual Assault Victim May Have
Been 'Flattered' by the Incident," *The Guardian*, Oct. 27, 2017, https://www
.theguardian.com/world/2017/oct/27/canada-judge-says-sexual-assault-victim
-may-have-been-flattered-by-the-incident.

4. Lindsay Dodgson, "People Who Are Overweight Get Paid Less, According to a New Study," *Insider*, Nov. 1, 2018, https://www.insider.com /overweight-people-earn-less-money-study-shows-2018-11.

5. Dodgson, Lindsay Dodgson, "People Who Are Overweight Get Paid Less, According to a New Study."

6. Ronald Alsop, "Fat People Earn Less and Have a Harder Time Finding Work," BBC Worklife, Dec. 1, 2016, https://www.bbc.com/worklife/article /20161130-fat-people-earn-less-and-have-a-harder-time-finding-work.

7. Melissa A. Fabello, "Skinny Shaming Is Not the Same as Fat Phobia," *SELF*, Jan. 1, 2017, https://www.self.com/story/skinny-shaming-is-not-the -same-as-fat-phobia.

8. Tribune News Service, "Skinny, Fat or Anything in Between—Just Don't Comment on It, Experts Say," *South China Morning Post*, June 10, 2021, https://www.scmp.com/lifestyle/health-wellness/article/3136744/skinny-or -fat-shaming-hurts-either-way-only-one-leads?module=perpetual_scroll _0&pgtype=article&campaign=3136744.

MYTH 20: "ANTI-FATNESS IS THE LAST SOCIALLY ACCEPTABLE FORM OF DISCRIMINATION."

1. Francisco Chairez, "The Year I Spent in Joe Arpaio's Tent Jail Was Hell. He Should Never Walk Free," *Washington Post*, Oct. 28, 2021, https:// www.washingtonpost.com/news/posteverything/wp/2017/08/26/the-year-i -spent-in-joe-arpaios-tent-jail-was-hell-he-should-never-walk-free.

2. Erin Blakemore, "How the GI Bill's Promise Was Denied to a Million Black World War II Veterans," History.com, June 21, 2019, https://www .history.com/news/gi-bill-black-wwii-veterans-benefits.

3. Emily Badger, "The Dramatic Racial Bias of Subprime Lending During the Housing Boom," *Bloomberg CityLab*, Aug. 16, 2013, https://www .bloomberg.com/news/articles/2013-08-16/the-dramatic-racial-bias-of -subprime-lending-during-the-housing-boom.

4. Jason M. Nagata, Kyle T. Ganson, Omar M. Sajjad, Samuel E. Benabou, and Kirsten Bibbins-Domingo, "Prevalence of Perceived Racism and Discrimination Among US Children Aged 10 and 11 Years," *JAMA Pediatrics* 175, no. 8 (May 17, 2021): 861, https://doi.org/10.1001/jamapediatrics .2021.1022.

5. Rachel Layne, "The Hidden Cost of Disability Discrimination," CBS News, CBS Interactive, Oct. 16, 2017, https://www.cbsnews.com/news/the -hidden-cost-of-disability-discrimination.

6. Substantial Gainful Activity, Social Security Administration, https:// www.ssa.gov/oact/cola/sga.html, accessed Feb. 20, 2022.

7. Jordan Gwendolyn Davis, "Op-Ed: Why, No Matter What, I Still Can't Marry My Girlfriend," *The Advocate*, June 29, 2015, https://www .advocate.com/commentary/2015/06/29/op-ed-why-no-matter-what-i-still -cant-marry-my-girlfriend.

8. "Disability Impacts All of Us," CDC, Sept. 16, 2020, https://www.cdc
.gov/ncbddd/disabilityandhealth/infographic-disability-impacts-all.html
.girlfriend.
9. Esther Yoon-Ji Kang, "Study Shows Islamophobia Is Growing in the
U.S. Some Say It's Rising in Chicago, Too," NPR, May 3, 2019, https://www
.npr.org/local/309/2019/05/03/720057760/study-shows-islamophobia-is
-growing-in-the-u-s-some-say-it-s-rising-in-chicago-too.
10. "Vulnerable to Hate: A Survey of Bias-Motivated Violence Against
People Experiencing Homelessness in 2016-2017," National Coalition for the
Homeless, https://www.nationalhomeless.org/wp-content/uploads/2018/12
/hate-crimes-2016-17-final_for-web.pdf, accessed Feb. 20, 2022.
11. Kimberly G. White, Eli Moore, Tamisha Walker, and Stephen
Menendian, "Ending Legal Bias Against Formerly Incarcerated People,"
Othering & Belonging Institute, University of California, Berkeley, Sept. 10,
2019, https://belonging.berkeley.edu/ending-legal-bias-against-formerly
-incarcerated-people.
12. "Disability Impacts All of Us," CDC.